The Life Of Sir Thomas More

Cresacre More

Nabu Public Domain Reprints:

You are holding a reproduction of an original work published before 1923 that is in the public domain in the United States of America, and possibly other countries. You may freely copy and distribute this work as no entity (individual or corporate) has a copyright on the body of the work. This book may contain prior copyright references, and library stamps (as most of these works were scanned from library copies). These have been scanned and retained as part of the historical artifact.

This book may have occasional imperfections such as missing or blurred pages, poor pictures, errant marks, etc. that were either part of the original artifact, or were introduced by the scanning process. We believe this work is culturally important, and despite the imperfections, have elected to bring it back into print as part of our continuing commitment to the preservation of printed works worldwide. We appreciate your understanding of the imperfections in the preservation process, and hope you enjoy this valuable book.

Thomas More

Engraved by E. Scriven from a drawing by Holbein.
in his Majesty's Collection.

London William Pickering. 1818.

THE
Life of Sir Thomas More,

BY HIS GREAT-GRANDSON,

CRESACRE MORE.

WITH

A BIOGRAPHICAL PREFACE, NOTES, AND OTHER ILLUSTRATIONS,

BY THE

REV. JOSEPH HUNTER, F.S.A.

LONDON:

WILLIAM PICKERING, CHANCERY LANE.

MDCCCXXVIII.

Thomas White, Printer,
Crane-Court.

At Thomæ Mori mortem deplorant et ii quorum instituto pro viribus adversabatur: tantus erat hominis in omnes candor, tanta comitas, tantaque benignitas. Quem ille vel mediocriter eruditum ab se dimisit indonatum? Aut quis fuit tam alienus, de quo non studuerit bene mereri? Multi non favent nisi suis, Galli Gallis, Germani Germanis, Scoti Scotis: at ille in Hybernos, in Germanos, in Gallos, in Scythas et Indos amico fuit animo. Hæc naturæ benignitas sic Morum omnium animis penitus infixit, ut non secus ac parentem aut fratrem plorent extinctum. Ipse vidi multorum lachrymas qui nec viderant Morum, nec ullo officio ab eo fuerant affecti: ac mihi quoque dum hæc scribo, nolenti ac repugnanti lachrymæ prosiliunt.

Epistola fidelis de morte Thomæ Mori.

CONTENTS.

	Page
Life of Sir Thomas More	1—344

APPENDICIA.

I. The Epistle Dedicatory, of the first Edition, to Queen Henrietta-Maria	347
II. The Preface to the second Edition	351
III. Verses on a Portrait of Sir Thomas More	359
IV. Copy of Inscriptions on the Painting of the More Family at Burford Priory, the Seat of —— Lenthall, Esq.	361
V. Dedication of the Utopia to Cresacre More	365
VI. Anthony Wood's Account of the More family	367
VII. Extract from Pace, " De fructu qui ex doctrina percipitur"	369
VIII. Letter of Lady More to Cromwell	372
IX. Chronological Abstract of the Life of Sir Thomas More	374

PREFACE.

I. Character of Sir Thomas More.
II. Lives of him, particularly the one here published.
III. "Who wrote More's Life of Sir Thomas More?" answered.
IV. Account of the male posterity of Sir Thomas More.
V. Conjectures respecting the wrong appropriation of this Life.

I.

AMONG the many eminent men who have done honour to the English nation, there are a few whose names are

Familiar in our mouths as household words,

and towards whom a respect is felt which partakes of the nature of a personal attachment.

They are not perhaps the greatest men of our country, or those whose actions and characters have had the most extensive and most lasting influence on the state of society. Even Sir Thomas More, who is one of them, may not attain to the first three. Yet it is evident that there must be some considerable merit where this feeling exists; and in respect of Sir Thomas More, though a writer of high and deserved reputation has lately spoken of him as " that too-highly extolled man," yet it must be allowed by every one, that in him met many great and glorious qualities.

It is not, however, the grander features of his character and history which occasion so many pleasurable associations to be connected with his name, as circumstances of a lighter or adventitious character. We see him in the midst of his family, as that happy group are transmitted in the living and speaking picture, by the great artist of the age; we are delighted with his ingenious political romance; we repeat sayings of his, in which is apparent that agreeable turn of humour by which he was distinguished; and we read the story of his life, told in a lively and popular manner, by two members of his own family, Roper his son-in-law, and More his great grandson.

It is these circumstances which have maintained towards him what we may call a national attachment. But whatever defects there may have been in his character, and whatever mistakes in his public conduct, there must ever remain much that will command the approbation not only of the popular voice, but of those who judge wisely concerning the beauties and defects of human character. On an impartial estimate it might even be found that there is less in More to disturb the feeling of settled admiration, than in the character of, perhaps, any man who has been deeply engaged, as he was, in the great affairs of society in dubious times. But when compared with the time-serving people by whom he was surrounded, the encomium of Burnet is not, perhaps, too high-wrought, when he calls More " the glory of his age." In the profession to which he was educated, we see him making his way along a path crowded with competitors, to the very highest honour. As a diplomatist, he showed great skill. As a member of the council of this empire, he contributed to raise its glory, and to give England a weight unknown before in the politics of Europe. He made his theological knowledge bear with effect upon the controversies which then disturbed the nations. He found time also to cultivate the fields of polite and elegant literature. He was no mean scholar, and to him more than to any individual of the time, is it to be attributed that England was enabled to share so early in the reviving literature of Europe. What can be desired more for a great and venerable name? But whatever he was he became by the most honourable means. All was the result of genius and industry. There was nothing of finesse, nothing of the supple arts by which some men rise. When at the bar he interpreted more rigidly than others do the rule to defend only the right. As a judge, he was ever incorrupt, impartial, and averse to the procrastination of judgment. As a representative of the Commons, he was jealous of his country's rights,—independent, fearless. In his high stations he was above the love of lucre. He scrupled to receive some of the usual profits of his offices. At his death he left little to his family, or rather to those who stepped in between his children and their rights. All his moral qualities were bound together by a strong sense of religious obligation. From his youth up he was one that feared the Lord; and by the providence of God he was called to give the last strong proof of his desire to submit in every thing to his will, by bending his head to the axe rather than do that which his conscience disapproved.

Whether he were right in maintaining that there was a power on earth which, in spirituals, was above the king and parliament, is a question of argument, evidence and intellect, not of morals; or whether it was, as he supposed it to be, his duty to maintain the unity of the great Christian corporation, then about to be broken. But when he had come to a determination on these great questions, it then became a point of morals what his conduct should be. And who shall say that he acted wrongly in following his convictions? He did not put forward his opinions ostentatiously, when they opposed those of the sovereign. He wished for retirement and repose. Nor were the opinions hastily adopted, or maintained merely with a blind obstinacy. They were the deliberate convictions of a cool and understanding mind; and they were held in opposition to the strongest temporal inducements. Can we wonder that those who thought with him, regarded him as " England's honour, faith's zealous champion, and Christ's constant martyr." And those who do not agree with him must allow, that whatever honour belongs to the man who is content to suffer death, rather than yield a point of religious faith or practice, that honour belongs to More.

It is urged by the writer who has ventured to speak of him as " this too-highly extolled man," that he was a persecutor. Alas! this is the evil extreme to which a high sense of religious obligation is always tending. More lived at a time when, rather than at any other period, zeal for the church, or against it, would be likely to avail itself of unhallowed weapons. Some of the facts, however, to which the writer appeals, in proof of his charge, may be questioned, may be doubted, in the form in which they stand in his work. Would that the stain could be entirely removed from the character of More, and far from me to seek to palliate the wrong! But if the memory of More is to be loaded with infamy on this account, candour will ask the question, who in those days had learned to respect the religious scruples of another? And, who had taught men to draw that fine line between the needful defences of a national church, and the persecution of those that dissent from it?

The occasional coarseness which appears in his controversial writings admits of the same sort of apology. It was the allowed and admitted practice of the disputants of the age.

It may be regretted that Sir Thomas More did not sympathise with the efforts which the human mind was then making to free itself from spiritual bondage. Still looking upon him in his public character, seeing his integrity, his self-command, his piety, his knowledge, his wisdom, and his eloquence, rather than seek to reduce the feeling of affectionate veneration with which his countrymen, from age to age, have dwelt upon his memory, I would say, with one of his illustrious contemporaries, " Interfecistis, interfecistis, hominem omnium Anglorum optimum!"

Many of the distinguished persons who appear in our annals have only a public life by which they are known. More may be contemplated by us as he appeared when retired from the affairs of state he sunk into the bosom of his family. By the light afforded us in his correspondence, the memoirs of his life, and the representation of the family circle, by the hand of Holbein, scarcely less particular and distinct, we enter his domestic retirement, and find there every thing to win our esteem and engage our love. Severe to himself, he was indulgent to others. The natural cheerfulness of his spirits, his sweetness of temper, his affability, and that not unbecoming humour which never forsook him, made him the delight of his whole family, and his house one continued scene of harmony and peace. We look upon the picture which the great artist of the age has left, and long to become members of a family in which it is apparent that all the domestic virtues and graces were in perfect vigour. Three more beautiful examples of female excellence than his daughters, England, rich in female excellence, has not yet produced. His house was not the abode only of affection and domestic union. His retirement was into the bosom of a family that was highly accomplished. The severer studies of that house were blended with the cultivation of music, painting, and poetry.* Like his friend Erasmus, who is represented by Albert Durer, with a vase of flowers upon the table at which he is writing, More was a lover of flowers, and of other beautiful or singular productions of nature. His house at Chelsey was a little museum of natural history. Adjoining to it was a garden, with a terrace and alcove, from whence there was a view of the course of the Thames, with the city of London in the distance. No illustrious foreigner visited England without seeking an introduction to More. None departed without admiration of his wisdom, his eloquence, and of the generous hospitality of his house. There was no eminent person of his own country whose name we do not find associated with that of More; and the most eminent for learning, virtues, and accomplishments, he numbered amongst his friends.

II.

We know much concerning him. Many of his own letters are extant. In the correspondence

---

* In that curious tract of Richard Pace, which is full of notices of his literary contemporaries, " De fructu qui ex doctrinâ percipitur" Basil, 1517, it is incidentally mentioned, that More learned to play upon the flute with his wife: " Sicut Morus meus didicit pulsare tibias cum conjuge." p. 35.

of Erasmus he and his family are often mentioned. The notices of him by his learned contemporaries are innumerable. His own writings form two large volumes. His son-in-law, Roper, who lived in the same house with him for sixteen years, has left a memoir on his life and domestic habits which is full of curious and the most authentic information. Stapleton, an able writer, prepared a more elaborate tribute to his memory by interweaving with the simple narrative of Roper, passages from his correspondence, the letters of his friends, and the writings of his contemporaries. In the reigns of Elizabeth and James several persons appear to have employed themselves in translating Stapleton's work into English, introducing at the same time any new facts, or such reflections as the circumstances of the narrative suggested, to their minds. Several of these are in the Bodleian and Lambeth libraries. One is printed by Dr. Wordsworth in his Ecclesiastical Biography.

Another is the Life of Sir Thomas More which is now for the third time committed to the press. It is evident that Roper and Stapleton are the two authorities on which the writer of the following Life chiefly relied: but it is also evident that the writer has introduced no inconsiderable portion of new matter, and that he has given to the work all the air of an original composition. Proceeding as it does from a member of the family of More, who lived at a time when there were still traditions preserved respecting him, it claims to stand as an original authority. Mr. Cayley speaks of this work and the Life by Roper as the safest guides for the biographers of More,* and it has been usually quoted as an original authority by all who have undertaken to write on the character and actions of this illustrious man.

Respecting its literary merits different opinions have been expressed. Anthony Wood pronounces it to be 'incomparably well-written.' Grateful for the new facts which he found in it, he has, perhaps, pronounced too favourable an opinion. Jortin declares this decision to be worthy only such a writer as Wood. That the feebleness of the translations and the general style of the composition might not satisfy one of so pure a taste as Jortin, is what might be expected: yet there is a sincerity, earnestness and occasional depth of feeling which may atone for defects of style, and in some places the language may be said to rise into eloquence. Jortin adds that the author was 'a very fanatic.' That he was deeply impressed with the peculiarities of the catholic system is every where apparent, and also that he did not rise above some of the

* Memoirs of Sir Thomas More, p. 7.

puerile superstitions of the time. But the tone of the work is rather *subdued* than *violent*. The memory of his great ancestor was associated in his mind with the religious feeling. He thought himself honoured above all earthly dignities in being the descendant of such a man, the inheritor of his name, the partaker in his dying benediction. He alludes to some mysterious intercourse which he imagined to have passed between them: *Secretum meum mihi!* But this may, and in fact does, add a charm to his work, which those may feel who are placed at the farthest distance from the point of faith at which he stood. These pages are Parentalia of a grateful descendant at the tomb of an ancestor who deserved them.

In the two editions of this work which have appeared, justice has not been done to the author. The first was hastily and carelessly prepared at some foreign press. There are several errors which are at once apparent. There are many more, and some of them of considerable importance, which discover themselves to one acquainted with another text. In one instance an entire line has been omitted. In the second edition there is a superstitious adherence to the text of the first. The most apparent faults of the press are repeated: we have *worrhie* for *worthie,* and *dearh* for *death,* and the text is carefully set to right in the notes. This in a work like the present, which cannot be looked upon as a monument of the state of our language, is useless scrupulosity. In the present edition, I have corrected at once what were obviously the typographical errors of a printer but imperfectly acquainted with our language. I have done more. I have ventured upon reducing the orthography of the whole work to the standard of our own times, following in this, what has been done for Cavendish and other writers of the age of More.*

The critical reader will also find that the text of the printed copies has been abandoned in some instances for another. Wherever this is done it is on the authority of a manuscript of the work which must have been written during the life of the author. This valuable manuscript was communicated to me in the most obliging manner by Mr. S. W. Singer, to whom the public is indebted for so many reprints of our earlier writers, so many valuable illustrations of them, and so much new and curious information in the literature, the history, and the arts of England. The readings of this manuscript, when they have been adopted, are

* It is proper to add that two or three immaterial passages are omitted in this edition. The most zealous assertors of the integrity of our old writers will not regret them.

so decidedly superior to those of the printed copies, that not a doubt can remain that they are the genuine readings of the author. Yet in some instances when there was a difference between the two, it seemed that the text of the printed copies was to be preferred. The text of this edition is therefore to be taken as the result of the comparison of the printed text with this manuscript.*

The two former editions were printed, the first about 1631, the second in 1726. Another century has now passed: and the two former editions are rarely to be seen. The second edition is far from being of frequent occurrence. The first has always been among the *libri rariores*. Fuller, who lived when it first appeared, says, that it is 'rare to be had,' and in the amiable spirit of his character remarks, that it is more fairly and impartially written than one would expect from so near a relation. Anthony Wood found it difficult to obtain a copy; and Fiddes, who when he had finished his Life of Wolsey

* The manuscript is a small quarto of 202 leaves. It contains the prologue, the verses on the portrait, and an acrostical poem which is not in the printed copy. No name of any author is mentioned, nor is there any title page. The critical reader of the following Life will find some passages in which he will be persuaded, as I am, that we have not the genuine text of the author; but I did not feel myself at liberty to give what is probably the true reading when there was no sanction for doing so either from the printed copies or the manuscript.

began something upon that of More, was unable to procure it.

III.

Besides the injustice which has been done to this author by the very careless manner in which his work was conducted through the press, he has suffered a more serious injury. He who made this offering to the memory of his great ancestor, so creditable to his filial piety and his literary talents, has now for two centuries been deprived of the credit and honour which ought to belong to him. All later writers on the life of More have ascribed this work to a Thomas More, who was a distinguished member of the catholic priesthood in the reign of James I., and he by whose exertions it principally was that the pope was induced to consecrate a bishop for the English catholics. Anthony Wood and Dod, the catholic historian, have interwoven a few of the notices of himself which the author has dispersed through this work, with genuine facts in the life of this Thomas More, and presented the combination as the true account of this writer. In the title-page of the second edition, the work is said to be by Thomas More, who is there, however, converted into an " esquire ;" but it is evident from the preface that the same person is intended. Even the original editor, who produced the work within six or seven years of the death of this Thomas More, ascribed it to him, though indicating his name in the title-page only by the initial letters M. T. M. The whole current of later writers on More's Life is in favor of his right to this work; and no suspicion has, I believe, gathered in any mind that this Thomas More was not the writer. I shall, however, now ask the question,

WHO WROTE MORE'S LIFE OF SIR THOMAS MORE?

Some years ago, when the attention of the editor was first directed upon the fortunes which had attended the posterity of Sir Thomas More, a suspicion arose that there was some error in the account given of them in the Athenæ. It appeared to him confused, disrupt, intricate, and improbable. A hasty comparison of it with the copy of the first edition of this work in the Bodleian, confirmed the suspicion; but having soon after become possessed of that edition, I was convinced that Wood had fallen into a great error, and had misled the many who follow where a writer so generally accurate as he is has led the way.

But, though I was convinced that the work could not possibly belong to the person to whom Wood had ascribed it, I did not discern with equal clearness to what other member of a numerous family it ought to be attributed. To some member of the family of More it indisputably belonged, for the writer speaks throughout of his 'ancestor,' and indeed describes himself as the son of Thomas, son of John only son of the chancellor. But having occasion not long ago to consult one of those records

> Where to be born and die
> Of rich and poor makes all the history,

a date was discovered, coinciding with a fact which the author relates concerning himself, by which the whole mystery was dissipated, and the true author stood confessed in clear day before me. Thus it is that those who are content to toil in even the humblest of the original authorities of our public history are sometimes rewarded.

Anthony Wood's notice of Thomas More, which is the received account of the presumed author, follows.

"Thomas More, born anew and baptized on that day of the year (6th July) on which Sir Thomas suffered death. This Thomas having the estate come to him, married and had several children; but being a most zealous Catholic, and constantly affected to the French nation and crown, did at his own cost and charge, with unwearied industry, assemble all the English persons of note that were then in and about

Rome to supplicate his Holiness for a dispatch of a contract between the King of England and Henrietta-Maria of France, an. 1624-5, which being done, the said Thomas, who was the mouth or speaker for the said English persons, died xi April, (according to the account followed at Rome,) an. 1625, aged 59, and was buried in the middle almost of the church of St. Lewis in Rome, leaving behind him the life of his great grandfather, Sir Thomas More, incomparably well-written, published (at London, I think*) in 4to. about 1627,† and dedicated to Henrietta-Maria before-mentioned. Over the said Thomas More's grave, was soon after laid a monumental

* A glance at the work would satisfy those who are conversant with early typographical execution, that it was printed abroad; and no more need to be said upon it had not Wood expressed this opinion, and were not the fact of its being printed abroad of some consequence in the solution of certain difficulties in its history. For confirmation of this point, see the accented a at p. 14; the apostrophized e at p. 48 and 187; and the word Noe in the ornamented N at p. 286; beside several odd and French blunders in orthography and the division of syllables. It was probably printed either at Paris or Louvaine. No date of place or time, or name of publisher, appears in the title-page.

† This has been since hastily adopted by all who have had occasion to mention this work, as the date of the first impression. But it could not have been printed till several years later than 1627, since the original editor, in his dedication to the queen, speaks of her " hopeful issue."

stone at the charge of the English clergy at Rome, and an epitaph engraven thereon.

D. O. M. S.
Thomæ Moro, Dioc. Ebor. Anglo,
Magni illius Thomæ Mori
Angliæ Cancellarii et Martyris
pronepoti atque hæredi:
Viro probitate et pietate insigni:
qui raro admodum apud Britannos exemplo
in fratrem natu minorem
amplum transcripsit patrimonium
et Presbyter Romæ factus.
Inde jussu sedis Apostolicæ in patriam profectus,
plusculos annos
strenuam fidei propagandæ navavit operam.
Postea
Cleri Anglicani negotia
septem annos Romæ et quinque in Hispania
P. P. Paulo V. et Gregorio XV.
summa cum integritate et industria
suisque sumptibus procuravit.
Tandem
de subrogando Anglis Episcopo
ad Urbanum VIII. missus
negotio feliciter confecto
laborum mercedem recepturus
ex hâc vita migravit
XI. Apr. M.DC.XX.V. æt. suæ LIX.
Clerus Anglicanus Mœstus P." *

* Wood's copy of this inscription, which he received from an unknown hand, is in some places corrupted. It is here

To the memory of Thomas More, an Englishman of the diocese of York, great grandson and heir to the great Thomas More, Chancellor of England and Martyr: a man remarkable for probity and piety; who, by a sacrifice, rare indeed in England, transferred his ample patrimony to a younger brother, and became a priest at Rome. From whence he was sent for some years by order of the Apostolic see into his own country, where he laboured strenuously in propagating the faith. Afterwards he was the agent for the English clergy seven years at Rome and five in Spain, while Paul V. and Gregory XV. were Popes. This office he filled with great integrity and industry, and supported it at his own expence. At length having been sent to Pope Urban VIII. on a mission respecting the appointment of a bishop for England, and having happily accomplished the business, he went to receive the reward of his labours on the 11th of April, 1625, in the 59th year of his age. The English Clergy, lamenting his death, placed this to his memory.

Wood's notice of him is for the most part compiled from an account which the original editor

given from the Appendix to John of Glastonbury, p. 655, where Hearne has printed it, and without reserve described it as the monumental inscription of Thomas More, author of the life of his great grandfather.

has given of the supposed author, in a dedication to Queen Henrietta Maria prefixed to the first edition.

"The author of this treatise, eldest son by descent, and heir by nature of the family of that worthy martyr, whose life is described in it: had he lived himself to have set it forth to the view of Christian eyes, would not have thought upon any other patron and protector to dedicate it unto, than your most excellent majesty. For he was most constantly affected always to the French nation and crown, next after the dutiful obedience which he ought to his own natural lord and sovereign. And this his affection did he manifest in all occasions, but especially in the treaty of the happy marriage of your highness, with the king our sovereign lord and master; assembling at his own costs and charges, with unwearied industry all the English persons of note and esteem, that then were in and about Rome, and with them all (as the mouth of them all) supplicating to his Holiness for the dispatch of this most hopeful and happy contract, yielding such reasons for the effecting thereof, as highly pleased the chief pastor of the church under Christ our Saviour. The same affection did he testify sufficiently in the last period of his life, leaving his body to be buried in the French church at Rome, where with great content of the French nobility it lieth interred."

This notice and the epitaph are evidently the two sources from whence Wood drew his account of Thomas More, and he has inwoven from the work itself only the two additional circumstances of his baptism on the day on which Sir Thomas More suffered death, and of his having been married and having children before he became a priest.

A little more attention to what the author has discovered concerning himself in the work, would have shown that what he relates of himself is wholly irreconcilable with the supposition, that the author is the person indicated in the epitaph and by the original editor of the work.

I. It is manifest that the work was written after the year 1615; for Sir George More is spoken of as lieutenant of the Tower, and in that year he first entered on his office. Now in 1615, and long before, Thomas More was a priest. There are two passages in the life which seem to show that it was not the work of a priest, but a layman; and in the prologue, the writer distinctly speaks of himself as a " worldling," in contradistinction to others of his family who had betaken themselves to a religious life.

II. It is evident from the epitaph that

Thomas More took upon himself the office of the priesthood early in life, so as to render very improbable the supposition that he had married and become the father of a family before he became a priest. There is, moreover, not the slightest evidence that he was ever married.

III. The editor of this work says, that Thomas More was " the eldest son by descent, and the heir by nature of the family of that worthy martyr whose life is described:" and in the epitaph we are told that he was the " pronepos et heres" of Sir Thomas More. This is as opposite as possible to what the writer declares concerning himself, that he was " the youngest of thirteen children of his father, the last and meanest of five sons."

IV. Of Thomas More, we learn from the epitaph, that having inherited the family estate, he disposed of it to a younger brother, having embraced a religious life:

> Qui raro admodum apud Britannos exemplo
> in fratrem natu minorem
> amplum transcripsit patrimonium
> et Presbyter Romæ factus.

In exact correspondency with this, but in fatal correspondency as respects the claim of Thomas More to this work, we read in the author's prologue; " I was the youngest of thirteen children of my father, the last and meanest of five sons, four of which lived to man's estate, and yet it hath been God's holy pleasure to bestow this inheritance upon me." And he proceeds, " which though perhaps I have no cause to boast of, because it may be a punishment unto me for my faults, if I use it not well, and a burthen that may well weigh me down full deep; yet will the world conjecture it to be a great blessing of God, and so I ought to acknowledge it; and, although I know myself unfittest and unworthiest of all the four to manage the estate, yet *they either loathed the world before the world fawned on them,* living in voluntary contempt thereof, and died, happy souls, in that they chose to be accounted abject in the sight of men, or else they utterly cast off all care of earthly trash *by professing a strait and religious life,* for fear lest the dangerous perils of worldly wealth might ruin their souls, and the number of snares which hang in every corner of the world might entrap them to the endangering of their eternal salvation, and left me, poor soul, to sink or swim, as I can, by wading out of those dangerous whirlpools, among which we worldlings are engulphed."

This appears complete as respects the claim of Thomas More; but the comparison of this passage with the epitaph throws a strong light upon the real author. If we can discover to whom Thomas More, the priest, transferred the family inheritance, or in default of this, who possessed the inheritance at the time when this work was composed, and then find that such notices of himself, as the author has thrown out in the progress of his work, meet in the possessor of the family estates, it can no longer be doubted that we have found the person to whom we owe this work.

It has already been shown that it was composed after 1615: it was, however, finished before 1620, for in that year Edward More, the writer's uncle, died, who is spoken of as alive.

During that interval the estates of the More family were possessed by him whose name is placed in the title page of this edition; CRESACRE MORE, of More Place, alias Gobions, in the county of Herts, and of Barnborough, in Yorkshire.

For proof of this I may content myself with a general reference to the pedigrees of the family, and to the historians of the county of Herts. They all show, at that period, a Cresacre More the possessor of the estates of the family. It may be added, that in 1624, when Bernard Alsop published his edition of Robinson's translation of the Utopia, he dedicated it to Cresacre

More, and speaks of his possessing the " land" of his ancestors.

And in this Cresacre More meet all the circumstances which the writer has disclosed concerning himself. He was the son of Thomas, son of John, son of the Chancellor. He was married, and the father of children. He was the youngest of thirteen children, five of whom were sons. This, however, requires some proof. Thomas More, son of John, resided at Barnborough, on the lands of his mother's inheritance, the estates in Hertfordshire being cruelly kept from the family during the whole reign of Elizabeth. The earliest entries in the parish register of Barnborough are in 1557, and from that time we have a series of baptisms of the children of Thomas More, in the following order:

1557 John	1566 Thomas
1562 Jane	1567 Henry
1563 Magdalene	1568 Grace
1564 Catherine	1572 Cresacre:

and from that time there are no more entries of the children of that prolific bed. Here, however, are only eight. But there were others born before the useful practice of registering baptisms began at Barnborough. Of these we know of three, from an entry of his children then born, made by the father at the visitation of Yorkshire in 1563. Eleven of the thirteen are thus accounted for, and it may reasonably be presumed that there might be two others between Grace and Cresacre, whose names do not appear in the register.

But the author has mentioned one circumstance of a very critical nature. When he says that "some one may ask, why he of all the family, being the youngest and the meanest, should undertake to write concerning so famous a person?" he replies, "Let this suffice, that as Doctor Stapleton was moved to take pains in setting forth the actions of Sir Thomas More, because he was born in the very same month and year wherein he suffered his glorious martyrdom, so was I born anew and regenerated by the holy sacrament of baptism on the very same day, though many years after, on which Sir Thomas More entered heaven triumphant, to wit, on the sixth day of July." In the register of Barnborough is this entry,

"1572. Cresacrus More, filius Thomæ More ar. fuit baptizatus sexto die Julii."

IV.

Of Thomas and of Cresacre More, the presumed and the real author of this work, little is known. And while presenting that little to the public, I shall at the same time take notice of some other members of the family of More, who have gained a literary celebrity, and give in fact some account of the male posterity of Sir Thomas More, freed from the errors and misconceptions with which the published accounts generally are infected, owing to the wrong appropriation of this work.

Besides his three accomplished daughters, Margaret Roper, Elizabeth Dauncy, and Cecilia Heron, Sir Thomas More had one son, who was named John, after his grandfather, Sir John More, the judge. The date of his birth is fixed to the year 1510, by an inscription on the painting of the More family, now at Burford Priory, the seat of —— Lenthall, Esq.[*] for it is there said that he married in 1529, being then " ætatis 19." Too much has perhaps been said of the want of capacity in this son. Jortin describes him as one of the " heroûm filii," and compares his life to that of an antediluvian patriarch, of whom nothing is recorded but that he was born,

[*] The inscriptions upon this painting are the best authority for many dates of occurrences in the More family. I have been enabled, through the kindness of a friend, to present them to the reader in the Appendix to this work. The defect in the transcript must be excused; but the inscriptions are in better preservation than would be supposed by the readers of Wood, who says, A. O. i. 35, that they are " now scarce legible." This was said in 1692.

married, and died. Wood speaks of him as "little better than an idiot." Some have seen, or thought they saw, indications of weakness in the portrait left by Holbein. Rawlinson describes the figure as " librum tenens, legensque, sed vultu tristi mitique, demisso ne dicam stultulo."* That he was not what might have been expected from the son of such a father, and the brother of such accomplished ladies, is not improbable. Nature is often seen giving in one generation great weakness and great strength, or denying to a second generation what she had bestowed on the foregoing. But still I cannot but think he has been underrated. In a letter to his children, given in this work, full of affection and kindness, Sir Thomas More speaks of the purity of the Latin phrase in which his children had addressed him; but he commends the letter of his son more than those of his daughters. He had written elegantly and sported pleasantly, returning jest for jest, but not forgetful of the respect owing to a father. His proficiency in the Greek tongue is celebrated by Grinæus, one of his father's friends, who dedicated to him an edition of the works of Plato.†
Erasmus inscribed to him his account of the

* See his letter to Hearne in the preface to Hearne's edition of Roper's Life.
† Basil, 1534, folio.

works of Aristotle. He had a character marked with sufficient strength to venture the denial of the king's supremacy, after the execution of his father. He lay, on this account, some time in the Tower, under sentence of death.

During the happier period of the life of Sir Thomas More, John More and his wife formed part of the family in his house at Chelsey, where he lived with all his children about him. We see them, and seem to live with them, in the painting which the great artist of the age has left of them. The piece is full of mind, and of a sweet-toned morality. What a crime in Henry to have broken up the union of such a family as this!* When the darker times came on they

* The painting here meant is that at Nostell Priory, the seat of Charles Winn, Esq. in Yorkshire. This is the painting which was formerly in the House of the Ropers, Well Hall, in Eltham. In 1729 Sir Rowland Winn, Bart. great grand-father of the present Mr. Winn, married one of the three daughters and co-heirs of Edward Henshaw, Esq. by Elizabeth Roper, his wife, heiress to the Ropers. He purchased the shares of the other co-heirs in this picture, and carried it into Yorkshire. This is the picture described by Lewis, and is indisputably, in all its parts, by the hand of Holbein, possessing the beauties and the defects of that master. The persons represented in it are—

    1. Sir Thomas More, aged 50.
    2. Alice More, his wife, aged 57.
    3. Sir John More, aged 76.
    4. John More, aged 19.

were compelled to separate; each went to his own home, save Margaret, who remained the comfort and peculiar delight of her father. It is doubtful whether John More retired into Yorkshire, where he had a good estate of his wife's inheritance, or continued about London. But when the king had shown a determination to destroy as well as ruin his unbending counsellor, we find John More lingering upon the steps of his honoured father, and casting himself at his feet, as he walked through the streets of London after sentence, the headsman going before, holding the axe with the edge towards

   5. Anne More, wife of John, aged 18.
   6. Margaret Roper, aged 22.
   7. Elizabeth Dauncy, aged 21.
   8. Cecilia Heron, aged 20.
   9. Margaret Clement.
   10. Henry Pattison.
   11. John Harris, aged 27.
   12. An anonymous in an inner room.

One like this is at Barnborough Hall, the seat of the Mores.

Mr. Lenthall's picture has Sir John, Sir Thomas, and John More, with four other male, and four female figures, besides another female, who appears as a portrait in a square frame. Some of these are supposed not to have been members of Sir Thomas More's household, but descendants of his son John. This is implied by the inscriptions, and by the shields of arms, More quartering Cresacre. It probably came from More Place, when the Mores abandoned their estates in Hertfordshire and returned into the North.

him. Sir Thomas raised him from the ground, blessed and kissed him. This was a little before a scene still more affecting; for when Sir Thomas arrived at the Tower Wharf, he found his daughter Margaret there awaiting his arrival, and the moment the sad procession appeared in sight she rushed through the guard, who with bills and halberds encompassed him around, and openly in the sight of all embraced him, took him about the neck and kissed him, unable to pronounce more than " Oh, my father! Oh, my father!" It is circumstances such as these, related by his own family, which endear to us the memory of Sir Thomas More. In a farewell letter, written just before his execution, he remembers his son, " Commend me, when you can, to my son John; his towardly carriage towards me pleased me very much. God bless him and his good wife, and their children, Thomas and Augustine, and all that they shall have."

Of John More, from the time of his release from the Tower, till his death in 1547, nothing is known. He probably retired to Yorkshire, and lived upon the estates of his wife, for the property of Sir Thomas More was confiscated, and his lands settled on the Princess Elizabeth, afterwards queen, who kept possession of them till her death. The principal estate, and the seat of her family was at Barnborough, in the south of Yorkshire, a pleasant village on the high grounds north of the Dearne, consisting of the church, hall, parsonage house, and a few cottages, looking down on the plains of Maisbeli, the supposed scene of the great battle between Hengist and Ambrosius.

Not far from Barnborough is the castle of Coningsborough, the ancient seat of the Earls of Warren. A moiety of Barnborough was held of that castle. Another moiety was held of the castle of Tickhill, a few miles further distant. The two great houses of Newmarch and Fitzwilliam held Barnborough. Both subinfeuded; and the tenants of the Fitzwilliams' moiety was the family of Cresacre.

The Cresacres may be traced at Barnborough to the earliest period to which the records of private families usually ascend; and the estate descended in regular succession from father to son till the death of Edward Cresacre in 1512, who left Ann Cresacre, his only daughter and heir, then aged one year, whom afterwards John More took to wife.

The marriages of the Cresacres had been with the principal families of the vicinity. Their pedigree is adorned with the names of Hastings, Wortley, Mounteney, and Wasteney. Their arms, three rampant lions, appear in the church of Barnborough, and their crest a cat-amountain, with which, in the traditions of the villagers, a romantic story is connected of an encounter between a Cresacre and a wild cat from a neighbouring wood, which ended in the death of both the combatants at the door of the church.

The church contains evidence of the attachment which Cresacre More manifests in this work for the puerile observances of the Catholic system having existed in the earlier Cresacres. A stone, which covers the remains of one of them, has a cross of Calvary wrought upon it, formed by the union of nine strings of beads, three forming the head, three the shaft, and three the feet. But there is a very elaborate monument, with the effigies cut in oak, of one of them, all curiously inscribed with texts of Scripture, and passages from the ancient rituals of the church. To the honours, the estates, and to the deep feeling of religion which characterized this family the Mores succeeded.

The connection was brought about by accident. Sir Thomas proceeded upon the old feudal plan, and *bought* a wife for his son. But the author of the Life before us informs us that his grand-mother was bought in a mistake, " upon error for another body's lands lying in the same town, as was afterwards proved." The intention was, I presume, that John More should have married one of the four co-heirs of Sir John Dynham, in whom the other moiety of Barnborough was vested.

Thus in the days of the court of wards and liveries were matrimonial alliances formed. It is added, however, by her grandson, that while her inheritance formed the only livelihood for the son and grandson of the Chancellor, that she proved a good wife and careful mother. The education of the children of John More devolved upon her, and to her the family may have owed the recovery of the family estates in Hertfordshire. They were granted to her by Queen Mary in the first year of her reign, subject however to the lease of them to the Princess Elizabeth for life.*

After the death of John More she married George West, a gentleman of the neighbourhood, of equal rank with herself, nephew of Sir William West, a favourite of King Henry VIII. They were married on the 13th of June, 1559, and in the same year the only daughter of John

* See History of Hertfordshire, by Mr. Clutterbuck, vol. i. p. 451, who has added some useful particulars respecting the Mores' estates to what was to be found respecting them in the works of his predecessors.

More became the wife of John West,* a son of George by a former marriage. This double marriage of West and More, of which no notice is taken in any of the published accounts of the family, appears in the visitation of Yorkshire of 1563, and in the parish register of Barnborough. These Wests were implicated in the feud between the Wests and the Darcies, which is the subject of a contemporary historical ballad, in which Lewis West, one of the family, lost his life. The "Symboleography" of William West long continued to be the best book of legal precedents. George West appears, after the marriage, to have removed from Aughton, the family seat, to Barnborough, where he was buried on the 12th of June, 1572, a few days before the birth of Cresacre More.

Ann Cresacre, again a widow, conveyed Barnborough and her other estates to her eldest son, Thomas More. A brass-plate, formerly affixed to the stone which covered her remains in the church of Barnborough, is now at the hall,

* The issue of this marriage was three children, Godfrey, Anne, and Jane. Godfrey married Catherine Revel, daughter of Thomas Revel, and had a daughter, Anne, who married Godfrey Bradshaw. The marriage of Thomas Revel and Anne West, widow, appears in the register of a parish near the residence of the Wests, which, there is reason to think, is a second marriage of Anne More, grand-daughter to the Chancellor.

from which we learn that she died on the second of December, 1577, in the sixty-sixth year of her age.

John More and Ann Cresacre had five sons. Their names were Thomas, Augustine, Edward, a second Thomas and Bartholomew. Only the two first were born before the death of Sir Thomas. The names of all of them appear in the Visitation; and we have some account of each in this work of Cresacre More's, who was son to the elder Thomas.

I. Thomas, the eldest son, was born in the house at Chelsey, on the eighth of August, 1531. When Sir Thomas More saw the cloud that was gathering over him, he settled the estates in Hertfordshire on this grandson, then a child of two years old. As this settlement was made before any statute concerning the oath of supremacy had passed, and consequently before any treason could be committed under it, the family thought it hard that this provident conveyance should be frustrated; especially as one like it was respected, made only two days before in favour of the Ropers.

This Thomas More, grandson and next heir to the Chancellor, appears to have been no common character; but he lived in a reign when the religious principles he professed must necessarily have excluded him from all public employments, and when they would subject him to obloquy and active persecution. The writer of the following life of Sir Thomas, who was his son, had an intention of preparing a memoir of his life. " My father, only right heir of his father and grandfather, was a lively pattern unto us of his constant faith, his worthy and upright dealings, his true Catholic simplicity, of whom I have purpose to discourse unto my children more at large, that they may know in what hard times he lived, and how manfully he sustained the combat which his father and grandfather had left unto him as their best inheritance." It is to be regretted if this intention was never embodied in the act.

He married in 1553, Mary Scrope, a niece of Henry Lord Scrope, of Bolton. The grandmother was a daughter of the third Percy, Earl of Northumberland. She was thus related to the succeeding Earls of Northumberland and to the Earl of Arundel, and others of the chief of the nobility. He resided at Barnborough during the whole reign of Elizabeth, and there his numerous children were born. In the parish register he is uniformly described as an esquire; and we find by the names of the sponsors at the baptism of his children, that he lived in respect and amity with the principal families in the neighbourhood.* Most, if not all these sponsors, were professors of the reformed religion; but there were, besides the Mores, several families in that part of the kingdom who adhered to the old profession, and especially one very active family, the Mortons of Bawtry, who were supposed to have had more to do with the movements against Queen Elizabeth than it would have been safe for them to have acknowledged. I have not found the name of Thomas More connected with any of the efforts of the Catholic party in that reign, though the " sea-maid," at whose " music " so many of the chief of the Catholic party of the north, like " stars "

> Shot madly from their spheres,

was lamenting her captivity in the castle of Sheffield, but a few miles distant from Barn-

---

* I add the names, as showing who in those times were the principal friends of the family of a great but obnoxious man.

Francis Frobisher, Esq.	Ursula Wray, Gent.
—— Wentworth.	Thomas Reresby, Esq.
Richard Brown, Gent.	Thomas Wombwell, Gent.
Beatrice Brown.	Dorothy Killam, Gent.
Claricia Scrope.	Henry Maleverer, Gent.
William Hawley, Gent.	Thomas Normavile, Gent.
Elizabeth Hammond, Gent.	Benedicta Mountford, Gent.
Frances Holmes, Gent.	Nicholas Denman.
James Washington, Esq.	Grace Rokeby.
Catherine Vicars, alias Cartwright.	

borough; and the Earl of Northumberland, his relation by marriage, was at the head of one formidable insurrection in her favour. Yet he was an object of suspicion. During the severe administration of the Earl of Huntingdon, Lord President of the north, he was committed to prison on the charge of recusancy. This fact we learn from the heralds' list of the gentry of Yorkshire, made previously to the Visitation of 1584.

He was seventy years of age at the death of Queen Elizabeth. That event restored to him the estates of his family in the south, and he seems to have then abandoned Barnborough. His will, which was proved in 1606, abounds in indications of a mind deeply embued with the religious feeling. He leaves benefactions to the parishes of Barnborough and Chelsey. The prominent feature in the character of the later Mores and of the Cresacres appears in his earnest injunction on his successors to continue the payment of three shillings to the poor of Barnborough, on Saint Cuthbert's day for ever, pursuant to the directions left by his ancestor, Percival Cresacre, on pain of his curse and malediction:

He was the father of Thomas and Cresacre More; but before we take notice of his children, it may be proper to speak of the younger sons of John More and Ann Cresacre.

II. Augustine.—We learn from the life that he continued in the profession of the Catholic faith, and died unmarried.

III. Edward.—The first-born after the death of Sir Thomas, and " so enjoyed not so directly his blessing as his elder brothers Thomas and Augustine did." To this, Cresacre attributes it that he and his two younger brothers " degenerated from that religion and those manners which Sir Thomas More had left, as it were, a happy depositum unto his children and family." And he continues—" as for my uncle Edward who is yet alive, although he were endowed with excellent gifts of nature, as a ready wit, tongue at will, and his pen glib ;* yet God knows he hath drowned all his talents in self-conceit in no worthy qualities, and besides burieth himself alive in obscurity in forsaking God, and his mean and base behaviour." I find him mentioned in the will of a Protestant clergyman in the neigh-

---

* Can this be the Edward More mentioned by Ritson as the author of " A lytle and bryefe treatyse, called The Defence of Women, and especially of Englyshe Women, made agaynst The Schol-hows of Women." Printed by John Kynge 1560, quarto. The author dates from Hambledon, the seat of John Scrope, whose daughter Thomas More married. The date of the work is 1557, when this Edward More was twenty-one.

bourhood, 1580, "To Mr. Edward More, of Barnborough, the dagger which my Lord Darcy gave me." He had a daughter who is mentioned in the will of her uncle. His burial is registered at Barnborough, May 2, 1620, being probably the last surviving grandchild of Sir Thomas More.

IV. Thomas More, the second son of that name. The respect of the family to the memory of their martyred ancestor could not be satisfied with only one child of that name. But this Thomas departed from the faith of his ancestors. "He lived and died a professed minister," by which is meant a minister of the reformed church. Cresacre says of him further, that "for all that he was very poor, bringing up his children, whereof the eldest son is still living, in no commendable profession." Three sons of his are mentioned in the will of the elder Thomas. Their names were Cyprian, Thomas, and Constantine. For any descendants of their's I have inquired in vain.

V. Bartholomew. He also conformed to the Protestant system, but he died early. "Mine uncle Bartholomew," says Cresacre, "died young of the plague, in London, and therefore might have, by the grace of God, excuse and remorse at his end."

Of the thirteen children, the offspring of

Thomas More and Mary Scrope, eight were daughters, most of whom were married to gentlemen of the midland counties. Of the five sons, one died young. We learn from the inscription on the Burford picture that four were alive in 1593. The anonymous life, published by Dr. Wordsworth, informs us that in 1599 only three were living. The few particulars follow which can now be recovered respecting the four who attained to man's estate. Among them is the supposed and the real author of the work before us.

I. John. He was the first-born son, for he is distinctly described as the " son and heir" of his father, in the register of his baptism, 1557. On the Burford picture he is said to be aged 36, 1593. There is thus an exact correspondency between the above date on the picture and the time of the birth of John More. In the pedigree of More, in the Ashmole MS., F. 7., he is said to have died without issue in the lifetime of his father. His name does not appear in his father's will; and it is evident that by his death the number of the sons was reduced to three in 1599.

II. Thomas More, the presumed author of this work was baptized at Barnborough, January 13, 1565. When his elder brother was dead, without issue, he became strictly the head of the family, the " pronepos et heres" of Sir

Thomas More, as he is described in his epitaph. But he had devoted himself, before his brother's death, to a religious life, and had taken upon himself the office and character of a priest. The date of his entrance into the church is fixed by a passage in the Life of Magdalene, Lady Montacute, by Richard Smith, afterwards Bishop of Chalcedon. Smith wrote in 1609, and he says of this Thomas More, that he had then laboured in the conversion of his countrymen, not less than twenty years. He took orders in the English college at Rome, and proceeded immediately to England, at the express command of the Pope. He was received into the household of Lady Montacute, a zealous catholic, daughter of the Lord Dacre who made that free remark to Henry, that he might hereafter absolve himself from his own sins. This lady, of whom Smith has left an exceedingly curious account, lived unmolested in the open enjoyment of the rites of her church, through the whole reign of Elizabeth. She had a house in London, and another at Battel, in Sussex. More was one of three priests entertained in her house, and Smith was another. She died in 1608, when More appears to have returned to Rome to assist Dr. Smith in his character of agent for the English clergy. We are informed, by Dodd, that when Smith was recalled, More received credentials to act wholly, sent him by the arch-priest, Mr. Birket, dated October 27, 1609. He was confirmed in the office by a common letter from the clergy, signed May 1, 1614; and by another from the arch-priest, Dr. Harrison, dated April 23, 1617. We are told in the epitaph that he was seven years at Rome and five in Spain, acting on behalf of the English clergy; and that he was afterwards employed in a mission to Pope Urban VIII. of great delicacy and importance. The object of this mission was to engage the Pope to consecrate a bishop for the English nation. He succeeded, and not long after, his friend Dr. Smith appeared in Lancashire with the ensigns of episcopal authority. It was during that mission, or soon after he had attained his object, that he was engaged in soliciting the Pope to favour the union of King Charles I. with Henrietta-Maria of France, a union which raised for a time the spirits and the hopes of the friends to the old profession in England. The negociations were not concluded when he died, on April 11, 1625. He was interred in the church of St. Lewis, at Rome. The inscription on his tomb has been already given, written it is probable by his friend the Bishop of Chalcedon. Dodd has passed this censure upon him, "He left several schemes unfinished, which he had laid for the benefit of the clergy, but were obstructed by the warmness of his temper, a disposition very disagreeable to the Italians."

The fact that he relinquished the inheritance which had descended to him is noticed by Dr. Smith in 1609; who, after describing him as great-grandson and heir to Sir Thomas More, says, that preferring to possess rather the virtue than the wealth of his ancestor, he transferred his ample patrimony to a younger brother, and devoted himself to the cultivation of literature and virtue.

III. Henry More, baptized March 15, 1567, and aged 26, 1593. He must have been one of those brothers of Cresacre More who betook themselves to a religious life, but I have not been able to recover any particulars of his life and character.

The name of Henry More must not, however, be dismissed without a further notice. In the whole range of the historical literature of the English Catholics, there is no more curious work than the "Historia Provinciæ Anglicanæ Societatis Jesu;" or as it is called in a second title, "Historia Missionis Anglicanæ Societatis Jesu, ab anno salutis, 1580, ad 1619." It was printed at St. Omer's in 1660. The author was Henry More, a priest of that society; and Dodd says that he was "great-grandson of

Sir Thomas More, and brother to Thomas More, a noted person among the clergy."* Dodd refers to Alegambe, p. 176, as his authority. But Alegambe does not say that the author of the history of the mission was great-grandson of Sir Thomas More, but only that he was of his family; and when he describes him as brother of a Thomas More, he does not mean the Thomas More of whom we have just been speaking, but another person of the name. Alegambe further says, that this Henry More was of the county of Essex. He tells us that he studied in Spain, was admitted into the society of Jesuits in 1607, and was living, and in England, when the memoirs of celebrated members of that order were collected. Alegambe then mentions the two works translated by him as in Dodd; and says nothing of the History of the Mission, which, however, as it was posthumous, Dodd is doubtless right in adding to the catalogue of his writings.

That the Thomas More mentioned by Alegambe as being brother to this Henry, was not the Thomas More the supposed author of the life of Sir Thomas More, is evident from Alegambe's own notice of him; where we find that he was of the county of Cambridge, and that he

* Church History, vol. iii. p. 120.

died in 1623, at the age of 36; so that he was born after, and died before the person with whom Dodd has confounded him.

IV. Cresacre More. The name of this person may hereafter find a place in the collections of our literary biography. At present he is absent from all; not excepting Dodd's, which is a large catalogue of Catholic writers. While his elder brethren betook themselves to a religious life, he continued a layman. On the Burford picture and in his father's will he is called Christopher Cresacre More. It was not unusual for the Catholics of those times to assume other names than those given at baptism. He took the estates of the family, both in Yorkshire and Hertfordshire, by the gift of his brother and the will of his father, who made him his sole heir. The estates must have been considerable, but there were many sisters to be portioned.

He resided at More-Place, or Gobions, in Hertfordshire. It is in the parish of North Mimms. In that parish Henry Peacham was born, who tells us that there "Merrie John Heywood wrote his Epigrammes, and also Sir Thomas More his Utopia."* To its literary honours may now be added that there in all

* The Complete Gentleman, p. 95.

probability Cresacre More composed the account of the life of his great grandfather.

North Mimms, I am sorry to add, has not been careful to preserve the memory of her distinguished inhabitants. On enquiry lately made by a friend residing near that place, it was discovered that there were no memorials of the Mores in the church, and that all the early registers are lost.

From Chauncy we learn that Cresacre More married a daughter of Thomas Gage, Esq. of Firle, and that she died on July 15, 1618;* also that Cresacre was living in 1638. He might survive that date some years, as no will or administration of his is to be found before 1640.

The spirit of religious devoteeism which appears in his work would probably give a colouring to his whole life and character; and the retirement of a man who had persuaded himself that he had communication with the spirit of his martyred and sainted ancestor, would probably partake of monastic seclusion; and this may account for the little that is now to be collected concerning him. He had one son and two daughters. The daughters entered fully

---

* Vincent (MSS. in the College of Arms, vol. iii. f. 370) says, 1610.

into the spirit of the family. Helen More, of whom there is a portrait by Lochon, was one of them; she was born in the house of her grandfather at Layton on March 25, 1606; she changed her baptismal name for the name of Gertrude, and became a Benedictine nun in the English congregation of our Ladies of Comfort at Cambray; she died in early life in 1633, and many years after her death there appeared a volume of her " Spiritual Exercises." This work is dedicated to the other daughter of Cresacre More, whose name was Bridget; who, like her sister, devoted herself to a religious life, and became prioress of the English Benedictine nuns of our Lady of Hope in Paris. Dodd has a valuable notice of this lady. She had lived with her sister at Cambray, from whence she removed to Paris, in 1652, and was the first prioress of the English Monastery of Benedictines; she died on October 11, 1692, at the age of 83.*

As we recede from the illustrious person, who is the glory of this race, the interest becomes weaker. Cresacre More left one son; who bore the family name of Thomas, and married a daughter of Sir Basil Brooke. In the civil wars he adhered to the king, and suffered

* Dodd, vol. iii. p. 497.

much in his estate on account of his loyalty. His son and heir, Basil More, sold the property in Hertfordshire, and Barnborough became once more the retreat of this family. Basil More lived till the year 1702. In his time it is probable that much of the present house at Barnborough was built, of which a wood-cut is here given.

Basil More had a numerous progeny, of whom another Christopher Cresacre More was the second but eldest surviving son. Christopher Cresacre More had a daughter married to Charles Waterton, Esq. of Walton, from whom is descended the distinguished traveller and naturalist of that name; and a son Thomas More, of Barnborough, Esq. who died on the 28th of August, 1739. By Catherine, his wife, daughter of Peter Gifford, Esq. of White Ladies he had his son and heir, Thomas More, the last male of the family. This Thomas More embraced a religious life, and was the Principal of the English Jesuits at the dissolution of the order. He did what his relation and namesake had done two centuries before; voluntarily divesting himself of the family estates, settling them on his sisters, and going to reside abroad. He returned to England, and died at Bath on the 20th of May, 1795, when it is supposed that the whole male progeny of Sir Thomas More became extinct.

One of his sisters was a nun professed; another was twice married; her first husband was Peter Metcalfe, Esq. and her second Robert Dalton, of Thurnham, Esq. There was issue of both marriages. Thomas Peter Metcalfe, the only son of the first marriage, by Theresa Throckmorton, his wife, had one daughter, now the wife of Charles Eyston, Esq. and one son, Thomas Peter Metcalfe, who by royal sign manual, dated June 24, 1797, took the name, arms, and crest of More, and is the present owner of Barnborough.*

* See for this descent, D. 7. 14. f. 332 in the College of Arms.

V.

It having now been shown,

I. That Thomas More could not have been the author of this work, although in the Epistle Dedicatory of the first Edition published while the true author was alive, it is ascribed to him: and

II. That it was the work of his younger brother, Cresacre More, it becomes a curious part of our enquiry, how it happened that so misleading an account of the author should accompany the first Edition, especially since there must at that time have been many persons who would instantly perceive that there were pointed contradictions between the account of the author, which the editor had given, and notices of himself in the work from his own pen.

But here I am sorry to say, we are left entirely to conjecture and probability. The simplest hypothesis on which the fact can be explained appears to be this: That the manuscript was found amongst the papers of Thomas More, when he died at Rome, in 1625; that it was hastily concluded to be his own work; and the Epistle Dedicatory prefixed to it without much consideration, or by some person ignorant of the fact that it would be contradicted by the work itself.

Another conjecture may, however, be made.

As the name of the author is indicated in the title page only by the initial letters M. T. M. so to the dedication the initials M.C.M.E. are subscribed. As the former is evidently Magister Thomas More, so may these be read Magister Cresacre More Eboracensis, especially as on a close inspection the letter E appears a size taller than the other letters. And nothing is more probable than that Cresacre More might not be unwilling to recal to the mind of the queen what Thomas More, his brother, had done to further her union with the king, and the merit generally of his family in respect of a cause to which all of Medicis blood were so devotedly attached. He might also by an allowable fraud in which he himself was the sufferer, not be indisposed to give to his brother the credit of having produced this memoir of their common ancestor, and consent to its publication in his name from a foreign press. The manuscript we may suppose was abroad; had been written some years; Cresacre's recollections of its contents were but imperfect; the printer was in haste; and Cresacre's intentions that its contents should conform to the tenor of the dedication, frustrated by some negligence of his agent. When the work appears, the inconsistency is perceived, and he endeavours to suppress it: whence its rarity.

This more complex hypothesis has the advantage of taking up the initial letters subscribed to the Epistle Dedicatory, and also of accounting for such a dedication at all being prefixed to it, which would hardly have been found there, had the publication been absolutely surreptitious, and no member of the family of More hoping to be in any way benefited by it.

It is remarkable, and the coincidence is probably not accidental, that Roper's life of Sir Thomas More made its appearance from a foreign press soon after the king's marriage with Henrietta-Maria. Both brought out, it is possible, by the better prospects which at the beginning of the reign of Charles I. began to dawn upon the Catholics. It is curious, indeed, to observe how the parties interested in the reputation of Sir Thomas More seem to have availed themselves of every possible opportunity for exalting his character, and bringing it to bear upon the state of religious feeling and opinion in England. For in the reign of Queen Mary, and nearly in the same year, 1556, Roper wrote the life of More; an anonymous life, now in the Lambeth library, was composed; Ellis Heywood wrote his "Il Moro," dedicated to Cardinal Pole; and the great folio of the works of More was published. In 1588, when the conversion of England was expected through the

Spanish Armada, the "De Tribus Thomis," of Stapleton, appeared. In 1599, when there was a prospect of a disputed succession, the anonymous life was composed, which Dr. Wordsworth has published; and soon after Charles I. had taken a Catholic for his queen, the lives by Roper and by Cresacre More issued from the press.

Perhaps the present edition may be the means of bringing to light some new fact which may bear upon this enquiry; and this curious literary question may not be left to hypothesis and conjecture. Other facts concerning the work are, it is believed, now firmly established, and the public will no longer read as the work of a priest that which belongs to a layman, or attribute sentiments to a long residence abroad which were the natural growth of our own soil. We read a work with the greater pleasure when we know something of the habits, character, feeling, and prejudices of its author. There is also a beauty in truth that she should be desired; and be the truth established of what insignificance it may, the removal of error is the eradication of a prolific weed, which for aught we know may overrun and infect the whole garden.

Some books of considerable rarity in our early literature are quoted in this volume. I should not do justice to the sense I entertain of obligation and respect, if I did not add that I have been indebted for the opportunity of consulting them at leisure to my valued friend, Benjamin Heywood Bright, Esq. to whom others engaged in similar pursuits owe the like obligations.

CORRIGENDA.

P. 157, l. 20, for 'sister's,' read 'sisters'.—p. 190, l. 12, for 'Manners,' read 'Manners'.—p. 299, l. 7, for 'spake of it a sermon,' read 'spake of it in a sermon.'—p. 369, l. 14, for 'verbal,' read 'verba.'

THE LIFE
OF SIR THOMAS MORE.

THE PROLOGUE.

AS I have much and often thought of the rare and admirable virtues both of nature and grace, which did shine most perspicuously in the blessed life and glorious death of that worthy champion of Christ's church, Sir Thomas More, so also have I often had an earnest desire, especially for the spiritual behoof of myself and my children (who are as small brooks derived by natural propagation from that spacious sea of rare perfections; or like tender twigs drawing sap from the fruitful root of his noble excellencies) to give them a taste, according to my poor ability, of some few of his most heroical virtues; yet professing myself utterly unable to set down his life in writing, as he deserveth.

For if that Apelles, the principal painter that ever lived, was thought only fit to draw with his pencil the portraiture of Alexander the Great; or if Lysippus, the most curious engraver, was the only man which was suffered to carve in brass the beauteous feature of the same so worthy a personage; for fear lest that some unskilful workman might rather blemish his favour than any ways grace it; what courage can I have to undertake a work of so great difficulty as this, who know myself a very puny in comparison of so many famous men, that have undergone this business already, finding in the very beginning of this mine enterprise, my small capacity overwhelmed with the plenty and copiousness of this subject? And if I should boast my wit and skill to be equal with learned Stapleton's, who at large and with great diligence and dexterity hath set forth the life of this great servant of God in his book, intitled, "The Three Thomases," I should vanish away in mine own pride, knowing myself right well most unworthy to be compared unto him; or if I should challenge unto myself more certainty of the matter related than my great uncle Mr. William Roper could have, every one might judge me both vain and arrogant, of whose sincerity none that ever knew him or heard of him can doubt, I being the third in descent from Sir Thomas, and he his own son-in-law, with whom he had familiarly conversed the space of sixteen years together, as he himself confesseth. Yet for all this, I have now at last ventured to discourse a little of the life and death of this glorious martyr (for so without envy I hope I may call him), "non ut electus ex multis, sed quasi relictus ex omnibus," not as one that may be thought fit to set his life forth with good grace, but as he, who only upon a natural affection to his ancestor, trusting chiefly of God's aid, and this saint's holy prayers, is emboldened to say somewhat thereof; this being one property of affection, to suppose that whosoever hath spoken, or whatsoever hath been said of him whom we love, all that we think nothing, if we ourselves have not said somewhat in his praise; although, alas! we are often the unfittest men for that purpose, we being not able to utter what we conceive, because our passion taketh away much of our conceit; and therefore we utter for the most part either broken words or unperfect' sentences, more intelligible to him that searcheth the secrets of men's hearts, than to others that hear them spoken, or read them in our writings.

But one may ask me, why I should challenge more affection to this man than any other of my kin, of whom few or none have endeavoured to write any thing hitherto; I answer, that though I have had more cause perhaps than any man else to love him, and honour him, which is best known to myself, and not fit to be related unto all men; "secretum meum mihi;" yet will I not ascribe to myself so great a privilege of loving him best, I being the youngest and meanest of all my family; let this suffice him, that is a curious searcher of this my deed, that as Doctor Stapleton was moved to take pains in setting forth the actions of Sir Thomas More, because he was born in the very same month and year, wherein he suffered his glorious martyrdom; so was I born anew and regenerated by the holy sacrament of baptism on the very same day, though many years after, on which Sir Thomas More entered heaven triumphant, to wit, on the sixth day of July. And therefore have I had some special confidence of his particular furtherance and blessing. For how, I pray you, could I ever have hoped to have lived as heir of Sir Thomas's family, and to enjoy at this time some part of his inheritance, all which, by his attainder, he had lost utterly from himself and his children, if his prayers had not, as it were, begged it at God's hands? Besides, I was the youngest of thirteen children of my father's, the last and meanest of five sons, four of which lived to men's estate; and yet it hath been God's holy pleasure to bestow this inheritance upon me; which, though perhaps I have no cause to boast of it, because it may be a punishment for my unworthiness, and a burden which may weigh me down full deep, yet will the world conjecture it to be a great blessing of God, and so I ought to acknowledge it. And although I know myself the unfittest and unworthiest of all the four to manage this estate, yet they either loathed the world, before the world fawned on them, living in voluntary contempt thereof, and died happy souls, in that they chose to be accounted abject in the sight of men; or else they utterly cast off all care of earthly trash, by professing a straight and religious life, for fear lest the dangerous perils of worldly wealth might gall their souls, and the number of snares which hang in every corner of this world, might entrap them to the endangering of their eternal salvation, and left me, poor soul, to sink or swim as I can, by wading out of those dangerous whirlpools amongst which we worldlings are engulphed; the multitude of which eminent perils do force me to cry first and chiefly to Christ Jesus, saying, with his apostle, " Lord, save me, for I am in danger of drowning;" and then also to crave the especial assistance of Sir Thomas More's prayers, by whose intercession I hope to waft this my poor bark unto her assured haven of heaven, though shaken and crushed with wind and weather.

But none of us must think that his assistance is all; we must put our own helping hands thereto:

> Nam genus et proavos, et quæ non fecimus ipsi
> Vix ea nostra voco:

his merits are not our warrant, yea rather his examples have laid a greater load on the backs of his posterity, in that we are bound to imitate his actions more than any other, or else more harm will fall upon us, because we have not followed the footsteps of our worthy forefather, according as Moses commanded the Israelites, saying in his canticle, "Interroga patrem tuum, et annunciabit tibi; majores tuos, et dicent tibi;" which the apostle also counselleth all Christians in these words, "Quorum videntes conversationem, imitamini fidem." But should I therefore wish I had not been his grandchild, because I have incurred a greater bond, and shall run into greater infamy by forsaking my duty? No, God forbid; yea rather this will I boldly affirm, not upon vain glory, but upon the confidence I have of this singular man's blessing; if God would have given me choice, before he created me of nothing, whether I would be the son of some famous emperor, magnificent king, noble duke, courageous lord, or his whose I was, I would most willingly have chosen to be the same I am, to God's eternal glory be it spoken.

Wherefore relying upon the assistance of this most excellent saint, I will endeavour briefly to set down for mine own instruction, and my children's, the life and death of Sir Thomas More; who was as a bright star of our country in the tempestuous storms of persecution, in which we sail to our heavenly city; on whom God heaped a number of most singular endowments; as, abundance of wit, profound wisdom, happy discretion, perfect justice, exceeding temperance, sweet affability, and all excellencies of nature and morality, besides supernatural and theological gifts; as, charity in a high degree, both towards God and his neighbour; a faith most constant, which would not be daunted with any threats or disgraces that his prince or his counsellors could thunder out against him, nay not with death itself; a magnanimity not to be overcome either by fear of any losses, or hopes of any dignities; religion, and such devotion as scarcely could be looked for in any of a lay profession; which perfections began to shine in his infancy, and continued in the progress of his actions, and did not end, but increased by his most glorious death, which was an entrance into a most happy kingdom, wherein he both can and will have compassion, and help us in these our miseries; because he was raised by God to be one of the first famous warriors in this our long persecution. Wherefore he may worthily be set before our eyes, as a perfect pattern and lively example to be imitated by us; for he had more to lose than most men in the land, being second to none but to the chiefest, either in worldly dignity or his prince's favour; and yet did he willingly forego all, yea life itself, rather than to wrong his conscience, in consenting to any thing against the law of God and justice, as by this ensuing discourse will particularly appear.

CHAPTER I.

SIR THOMAS MORE was the only son of Sir John More, knight, one of the justices of the King's-bench; a singular man for many rare perfections which his son setteth down in his own epitaph, extant amongst his Latin works, terming his father a man "civil," that is to say, courteous and affable to all men: "sweet and pleasant in conversation," that is, full of merry conceits and witty jests: "innocent and harmless," to wit, neither desirous of revenge nor maligning any for his own private gain: "meek and gentle," that is to say, of an humble carriage in his office and dignity: "mercyful and pitiful," that is, bountiful to the poor and full of compassion towards all distressed persons: "just and uncorrupted," which are the aptest titles which can be given to a judge, as if he would say, that he was neither moved with friendship, stirred up with hope of gain, nor wrested with any threats from performing his duty, and that he shut up always his left eye to all affection of friendship, and from all bribery.* Camden also reporteth of him, for proof of his pleasantness of wit, that he would compare the multitude of women which are to be chosen for wives unto a bag full of snakes having among them but one eel; now if a man should put his hand into this bag, he may chance to light on the eel, but it is a hundred to one he shall be stung with a snake.† Many such witty similitudes would he use in private discourses and in public auditory.

By these his perfections of wit and grace one might guess that his child was likely to prove singular, having so good a father. But he far surpassed in all these and many more excellencies; so that our family hath been much more dignified by this son than he any way drew worth and dignity from his ancestors; the consideration whereof hath caused many men to think and say, that Sir Thomas More was of mean parentage, and the first of his house; yea, some have not stuck to write, " by birth no gentleman," grounding their error upon those words which he setteth down in his epitaph, " Thomas

---

* The words of the Epitaph which are here commented on are these: " Homo civilis, suavis, innocens, mitis, misericors, æquus et integer."

† See Remains, p. 251. Camden however had the anecdote from the writings of Sir Thomas More. He does not say from which, and it is not worth searching for.

More, born of no noble family, but of an honest stock;" which is true as we here in England take nobility and noble; for none under a baron, unless he be of the privy council, doth challenge it, and in this sense he meant it. But as the Latin word "nobilis"* is taken in other countries for gentry, it was otherwise: for Judge More bore arms from his birth, having his coat quartered,†

---

* The word "nobilis" does not however in fact occur in the epitaph. The expression is, " familiâ non celebri sed honestâ natus." Sir John is, as far as is known, the first of his family. The only attempt at carrying up the pedigree above him is in that valuable volume of the Ashmole Library, F. 7, where we have the descent and alliances of many persons connected with our literature. But the attempt is very unsuccessful. It only shows the name of his grandmother, who was Joan, daughter of John Leicester. She married —— More, and had —— More, father to Sir John. This pedigree shows two brothers of Sir John, named Richard and Christopher, who are not noticed in the printed accounts of the family. It might be in reference to reflections cast on Sir Thomas More's descent, that Richard Croke, in the dedication of his translation of a grammatical work of Theodorus in 1516, having occasion to mention Sir Thomas More, describes him as " vir et moribus et literis et *natalibus* generosissimus."

† More does not write as if he were acquainted with the technical language of armoury. What he means is, that Sir John More used to quarter the arms of some other family with his own; which showed, that he not only inherited arms from his paternal ancestors, but that he was descended also from the heiress of some other family entitled to the distinction of coat-

which doth argue that he came to his inheritance by descent; and therefore, although by reason of King Henry's seizure of all our evidences, we cannot certainly tell who were Sir John's ancestors, yet must they needs be gentlemen, and as I have heard, either came out of the Mores of Ireland, or they came out of us. And as for Sir Thomas More, he was, as I have said, a knight's eldest son, and sole heir to a judge of this realm.

But whatsoever the family was or is, if virtue can ennoble any, sure it hath by these two excellent men been made no ways contemptible. Yet if we, as God forbid we should, degenerate from their footsteps, we may cause it soon to be base and of small reckoning, vice being the chief stain that tainteth even the noblest families.

The name of Sir Thomas' mother was Handcombe, of Holliwell in Bedfordshire; yet Doctor Stapleton had not heard so much, who saith, that her name is unknown;[*] by reason of which words some have taken great exceptions, as though she had been some base woman, though he doth in the same place tell this reason thereof,

---

armour. The arms quartered with those of More on the monument at Chelsey are, three bezants on a chevron between three unicorns' heads.

[*] Stapleton's words seem to imply, that Sir Thomas did not himself know the name of his mother: "Matris nomen nescitur, quippe quæ adhuc infante Thoma Moro mortua est."

"because she died soon after she had brought forth this child;" but to have been a woman of more than ordinary virtue, that, which Doctor Clement reporteth from Sir Thomas' own mouth of a vision which she had the next night after her marriage, seemeth, in my judgment, forcibly to argue: in which she saw in her sleep, as it were engraven in her wedding ring, the number and favour of all her children she was to have, whereof the face of one was so dark and obscure, that she could not well discern it; and indeed afterwards, she suffered of one of her children an untimely delivery. But the face of one of her other, she beheld shining most gloriously, whereby no doubt Sir Thomas's fame and sanctity were fore-showed and presignified.

She brought forth before him to Sir John two daughters; one called Jane, afterwards married to a noble gentleman called Richard Stafforton; and Elizabeth, wife to the worthy gentleman Mr. John Rastall, Judge Rastall's father. Sir John, after his first wife's death, married successively two others; Mrs. Bowes, widow, before called Barton, and Alice, one of the Mores of Surry, great aunt unto Sir William More, whose son now living, is Sir George More, lieutenant of the Tower of London, a man no way inferior to his noble ancestors.* This lady outlived her

* The printed copies omit the name of the second wife.

son-in-law, Sir Thomas, dwelling upon her jointure in Hertfordshire, at a capital messuage called then More Place, now Gobions, in the parish of North Mimms; but being a little before her death thrust out of all by King Henry's fury, she died at Northall, a mile from thence, and there lieth buried.

Sir Thomas was born at London, in Milk Street, where the judge his father, for the most part dwelt, in the year of our Lord 1480,* in the twentieth year of the reign of Edward the Fourth. Shortly after his birth God would show by another sign, how dear this babe was unto him:

After speaking of Sir George More, this clause is added, " if his religion were answerable to their's;" and " *no way* inferior," is changed to " *little* inferior."

* This is the date usually given as that of More's birth, on the authority of this work; neither Roper nor Stapleton having mentioned it. More has here followed the inscription on the painting of the More family at Burford. We may observe, that if Lewis has given the inscriptions correctly from the Well Hall picture, or if those inscriptions were themselves correct, Sir Thomas More's birth should be carried back to 1476, for he was " aged 50" when Anne Cresacre was " aged 15," and her birth is fixed by very decisive evidence to 1511. As there is a correspondency between the two paintings in the ages of the other parties, we should probably rather follow the Burford picture in the age of Anne Cresacre, who is there said to be " 18" when Sir Thomas was " 50," and Sir John " 76." Pitz says, that Sir Thomas was in his 52nd year at the time of his death, 1535; which would bring down his birth to about 1484.

For his nurse chancing to ride with him over a water, and her horse stepping aside into a deep place put both her and the child in great jeopardy; whose harms she seeking suddenly to prevent, threw the infant over a hedge into a field near adjoining, and after by God's help escaping safe also, when she came to take him up again, she found him to have no hurt at all, but sweetly smiled upon her, that it might well be said of him "Angelis suis Deus mandavit de te, ne te forte offendas ad lapidem pedem tuum;" and not his foot only but his whole body.

This was no doubt a happy presage of his future holiness, and put his parents in mind that he was that shining child of whom his mother had that former vision. Wherefore the father had the greater care to bring him up in learning as soon as his tender age would permit it. And so he put him to the free school in London called St. Anthony's,* where he had a famous

---

* One of the four Grammar Schools founded in London by King Henry VI. a great patron of good learning, in the twenty-fourth year of his reign. In the time of Sir Thomas More, St. Anthony's was the most famous school in London. " I myself in my youth," saith Stowe, " have yearly seen, on the eve of St. Bartholomew, the apostle, the scholars of divers grammar schools repair unto the church-yard of St. Bartholomew, the Priory in Smithfield, where, upon a bank boarded about, under a tree, some one scholar hath stepped up, and

and learned man, called Nicholas Holt, for his master; under whom, when he had rather greedily devoured than leisurely chewed the grammar rules, he outstripped far, both in towardliness of wit and diligence of endeavour, all his schoolfellows, with whom he was matched. And being born to far greater matters, his father procured him to be placed shortly after in the house of the most worthy prelate that then lived in England, both for wisdom, learning and virtue, whose like the world scarce had, Cardinal Morton, archbishop of Canterbury, and lord high chancellor of England, whose grave counte-

there hath apposed and answered, till he were by some better scholar overcome and put down: and then the over-comer taking the place, did like as the first: and in the end the best apposers and answerers had rewards: which I observed not but it made good schoolmasters and also good scholars diligently against such times to prepare themselves for the obtaining of this garland. I remember there repaired to these exercises, amongst others, the masters and scholars of the free schools of St. Paul's in London, of St. Peter's at Westminster, of St. Thomas Acon's Hospital, and of St. Anthony's Hospital; whereof the last named commonly presented the best scholars and had the prize in those days."—London, p. 75. He mentions among the famous persons who have sprung from this school, Sir Thomas More, Nicholas Heath, archbishop of York and lord chancellor, and Whitgift, archbishop of Canterbury. The school was in Threadneedle Street. It had fallen to decay in the time of Stowe, and come to nothing.—London, p. 186. Of Nicholas Holt, the good schoolmaster, little is known.

nance and carriage was such that he easily allured all men to honour and love him: a man, as Sir Thomas More describes him in his Utopia, of incomparable judgment, a memory more than credible, eloquent in speech, and, which is more to be wished in clergymen, of singular wisdom and virtue; so that the king and the commonwealth relied chiefly on this man's counsel, as he by whose policy king Henry the seventh both got the crown of England from Richard the the usurper, and also most happily procured the two houses of Lancaster and York to be united by marriage.

In this famous man's house this youth learned most diligently abundance of wisdom and virtue; and now he began to show to the world what man he was likely to prove. For the Cardinal often would make trial of his present wit, especially at Christmas merriments, when having plays for recreation, this youth would suddenly step up amongst the players, and never studying before upon the matter, make often a part upon his own invention, which was so witty and so full of jests, that he alone made more sport and laughter than all the players besides; for which his towardliness the Cardinal much delighted in him, and would often say of him unto divers of the nobility who at sundry times dined with him, that that boy there waiting on him, whosoever should live to see it, would prove a marvellous rare man.

But when this reverend prelate saw that he could not profit so much in his house as he desired, where there were many distractions of public affairs, having great care of his bringing up, he sent him to the University, and placed him in Canterbury College at Oxford, now called Christ Church, where in two years' space that he remained there, he profited exceedingly in rhetoric, logic and philosophy, and showed evidently, what wonders wit and diligence can perform, when joined, as seldom they are, in one painful student. There his whole mind was set on his book; for in his allowance, his father kept him very short, suffering him scarcely to have so much money in his own custody as would pay for the mending of his apparel, even no more than necessity required; and for his expenses he would expect of him a particular account; which course of his father he would often speak of and praise, when he came to riper years; affirming that by this means he was curbed from all vice and withdrawn from many idle expenses, either of gaming or other naughty company, so that he knew neither play nor other riot, wherein most young men in these our lamentable days plunge themselves too timely, to the utter overthrow as well of learning as all future virtue.

This strictness of his father increased in him also great reverence after unto him again, in so much that in all his life after he was so dutiful unto him, that he never offended nor contradicted him in any the least word or action, still showing towards him admirable deeds of humility, even in that time when in the eye of the world, he far surpassed his father in dignity, which may be seen by [his] asking him blessing every day duly, even after he was lord chancellor of England. And when he and his father met publickly at Lincoln's Inn, or other where, he would still offer him the place of precedence, though the Judge, by reason of his son's office, did still refuse it: such was the piety and submissive mind of this humble man. Such again was the provident care of the father towards his son, that one can hardly guess which of the two were more worthy—the father of such a son, or the son of such a father: yet I judge the father more happy that enjoyed such an admirable son, and wish that my children may imitate in this kind their virtuous ancestor.

CHAPTER II.

WHEN this towardly youth was come to the age of eighteen years, he began to show to the world his ripeness of wit; for he wrote many witty and goodly epigrams, which are to be seen in the beginning of his English works. He composed also many pretty and elegant verses of the vanity of this life, and the inconstancy thereof, which his father caused to be set up with pictures and pageants, which are also in the beginning of his great English volume.* He translated for his exercise one of Lucian's Orations out of Greek into Latin, which he called his first fruits of the Greek tongue; and thereto he added another oration of his own to answer that of Lucian's; for as he defended him who had slain a tyrant, he opposeth another with such forcible arguments that this seemeth not to

* Those to whom the Works of More is a book not easily accessible, may find these verses in the Appendix to Mr. Singer's Edition of Roper's Life of More. No. XXI.

give place to Lucian's, either in invention or eloquence. Now as concerning his divers Latin epigrams, which he either translated out of Greek into Latin, or else composed of his own, many famous authors that then lived do make mention of them with great praise. For Beatus Rhenanus in his epistle to Bilibaldus Pickheimerus writeth thus; "Thomas More is marvelous in every place, for he compoundeth most elegantly, and translateth most happily. How sweetly doth his verses flow from him. How nothing in them seemeth constrained. How easy are all things there that he speaketh of. Nothing is hard, nothing rugged, nothing obscure. He is pure, he is witty, he is elegant. Besides he doth so temper all things with mirth, that I never read a merrier man. I could think that the Muses have heaped on him alone, all their pleasant conceits and witty merriments. Moreover his quips are not biting, but full of pleasantness and very proper; yea rather any thing than stinging; for he jesteth, but without mordacity; he scoffeth, yet without contumely." The like judgment of his epigrams doth that famous poet, Leodegarius a Quercu, public reader of Humanity in Paris, give, and that not so much by his words as by his deeds: for he, having gathered of the epigrams of divers singular famous men a collection, he hath set out more epigrams of Sir Thomas More's than of any other writer. Yet because rareness of any excellent quality is still envied by some man or other, one Brictius, a German, wrote a book against these epigrams of Sir Thomas More, which he calleth Anti-Morus, but with such commendation that, Erasmus earnestly besought Sir Thomas that he would not overwhelm his friend Brictius with such an answer as his rashness deserved: adding this of his foolish book Anti-Morus—" I hear what learned men speak of Brictius now after he hath written his Anti-Morus, which as I hear them not willingly of him, so would I not willingly hear them so spoken of you. Wherefore seeing, I perceive, how hard a matter it is to temper an answer to so spiteful a book, but that you must give scope unto your passions, therefore I deem it best for you to despise and condemn utterly the whole matter. Yet this I could not, most excellent More, counsel you to do, if there were any thing in that malicious Anti-Morus which did truly blemish your fame, so that it were necessary for you to wipe it away," &c. Which friendly counsel Sir Thomas in some sort followed: for although he had answered Brictius fully in a little treatise, which already he had published, before this letter from Erasmus came to his hands, yet upon the receipt thereof, he endeavoured by all the means he could, to get all the copies again into his hands, and then suppress the book, so that it is now very hardly to be found, though some have seen it of late. And Sir Thomas sent Erasmus a letter to this effect, that although Brictius by his malicious book had endeavoured so much to disgrace him, that he wanted no will but skill and power to overthrow his name utterly, yet this should prevail more with him, that Brictius was friend to Erasmus than that he was his own enemy. Which kind of answer showeth expressly how easy he was to forgive injuries, especially such as touched him so near in his reputation: following herein the counsel of Christ himself in the Gospel of St. Matthew, who saith, "Love your enemies, and do good to them that hate you: that you may be the true imitators of God, who causeth the sun to shine as well upon the wicked as on the just." But can we think so heroical an act in so young years, for he was not now of the full age of twenty years, as Rhenanus writing to Bilibaldus testifieth, could proceed from one who had not been practised before in the school of Christ, and in the earnest search of perfection. Surely no; for this young man had, even from his infancy, laboured with all might and main to enrich himself with all virtues; knowing that learning without virtue is to set precious stones in rotten wood, and, as the wise man saith, as a gold ring in a hog's snout.*

When he was about eighteen or twenty years old . . . . . . he began to wear a sharp shirt of hair next the skin, which he never left off wholly, no, not when he was lord chancellor of England. Which my grandmother on a time in the heat of

---

* Mr. Cayley has given a satisfactory account of the affairs between More and Brictius. "Brictius had written a poem in 1513, entitled Chordigera, describing an action of that year between the English ship Regent, and the French ship La Cordeliere. As he had given a false account of the engagement, and insulted and calumniated the English, More wrote several epigrams in derision of the poem. Brictius piqued at the affront, revenged himself by an elegy, which he entitled, Anti-Morus, in which he severely censured all the faults which he thought he had found in the poems of More: but the piece was not published till 1520, and then at Paris, "in compliance with the wishes of the author's friends." Erasmus in a very good letter to Brictius, civilly though freely, insinuated to him, that he was a very child compared to More, and launched out as usual in praise of his English friend. More at first despised the poem, and wrote to Erasmus that, to prove to the world the contempt in which he held it, he had a design of re-printing it himself. He however afterward wrote an answer to it; which was no sooner published, than he received a letter from Erasmus, wisely exhorting him to pass the matter in silent contempt, for that alone was the conduct which the attack deserved. Sir Thomas soon saw his error, and following his friend's advice, he immediately recalled the publication, so that very few copies of it escaped into the world."—Cayley's Memoirs of Sir Thomas More, p. 79.

summer espying, laughed at, not being much sensible of spiritual exercises, being carried away in her youth with the bravery of the world, and not knowing " quæ sunt spiritus," what is the true wisdom of a Christian man. He added also to his austerity a whip every Friday and high fasting days, thinking that such cheer was the best alms that he could bestow upon himself . . . . . . He used also much fasting and watching, lying often upon the bare ground, or upon some bench, laying some log under his head; allotting himself but four or five hours in a night at the most, for his sleep, imagining with the holy saints of Christ's church, that his body was to be used as an ass, with strokes and hard fare, lest provender might prick it, and so bring his soul, like a head-strong jade, to the bottomless pit of hell . . . . . . He had enured himself with straitness, that he might the better enter in at the narrow gate of heaven, which is not got with ease, " sed violenti rapiunt illud," that is, they that are boisterous against themselves snatch it away by force.

For this cause he lived four years amongst the Carthusians, dwelling near the Charter-House, frequenting daily their spiritual exercises, but without any vow. He had an earnest mind also to be a Franciscan friar, that he might serve God in a state of perfection. But finding that at that time religious men* had somewhat degenerated from their ancient strictness and fervour of spirit, he altered his mind. He had also, after that, together with his faithful companion Lillie, a purpose to be a priest; yet God had allotted him for another state, not to live solitary, but that he might be a pattern to remind married men how they should carefully bring up their children; how dearly they should love their wives, how they should employ their endeavours wholly for the good of their country, yet excellently perform the virtues of religious men, as piety, charity, humility, obedience, yea, conjugal chastity.

He heard mass every day before he undertook any worldly business; which custom he kept so religiously, that being on a time sent for to the king whilst he was hearing mass, he would not once stir, though he were twice or thrice sent for, until it was wholly finished, answering them that urged him to run quickly, that he thought fit to perform his duty first to a better man than the king was; imitating therein the famous act of St. Ludgar, first bishop of Munster, who being sent for to Charles the Great, whilst he was singing in the quire the canonical hours, he would not once stir till all were ended. And

---

* The printed copies add, "in England."

being asked by the emperor, why he neglected to come when he was sent for unto him, answered, " I have always thought your command is by me to be obeyed, as I doubted not but God is to be preferred: therefore, I have been careful to finish that which I was about, not for the contempt of your imperial majesty, but for your safety and the duty which I owe unto God;" with which answer the emperor no whit displeased, but delighted, answered him with thanks, saying, that he had now found him such a one as he had ever formerly thought him to be. Neither was King Henry at that time any way angry with Sir Thomas, but rather highly pleased for this his neglect. He used every day to say our Lady's matins, the seven psalms and litanies, and many times the gradual psalms with " Beati immaculati in via," and divers other private prayers, which he himself composed. He selected also many sentences of the psalms, imitating therein St. Jerome's Psalter; which are extant in the latter end of his English works.

When he determined to marry, he propounded to himself for a pattern in life a singular layman, John Picus, Earl of Mirandula, who was a man most famous for virtue, and most eminent for learning. His life he translated and set out, as also many of his most worthy letters, and his Twelve Precepts of Good

Life, which are extant in the beginning of his English works. For this end he also wrote a treatise both learned, spiritual, and devout, of the Four last Things of Man. He left it imperfect, being called by his father to other studies. He frequented many sermons, especially of those men who were most excellent for good life, and spiritual direction, such as Doctor Colet, the most famous Dean of Paul's; who, as Erasmus writeth, was wont every day to preach at Paul's; besides many other sermons which he made at the court, or elsewhere, expounding in them the Pater Noster, the Apostles' Creed, the Ten Commandments, the Seven Sacraments, or some other matter of necessary instructions, which he never left off until he had perfected the whole; that thereby every one might learn what they should believe, what to follow, and what to shun; and the means how every Christian might come to perfection in their sundry states of life: and his life did not disagree with his doctrine, for he exercised himself in all works of charity, and mortification of the flesh. He erected and founded the goodly free school of Paul's, dedicating it to the little boy Jesus, as he was found disputing with the doctors, at twelve years old; of which famous act, Sir Thomas writing unto him, compareth it by a fit antithesis to the horse of Troy, out of which the

Grecians issued to surprise that city: " in like manner," saith he, " out of this your school many had come that have subverted and overthrown all ignorance and rudeness." But fearing lest all these his devout exercises might not be so meritorious if he followed only his own will, for a young man is in great danger of himself to want discretion, the mother of all virtues; therefore he chose this worthy dean for his ghostly father, for he was accounted one of the cunningest physicians for the soul that could be found, and a safe guide of perfection in the dangerous passage of youth, that by his experience he might the more easily overcome the devil, the world, and his own flesh, by following his wholesome lessons; neither to overthrow his own body, nor do harm to his soul; to whom he was as obedient in all spiritual affairs, as he was to his father in all dutiful obligation, whereby he arrived to proper obedience, one of the chiefest helps that a spiritual man can have to heaven. And because every man may see what affection he bore unto this man, his ghostly physician, I set down here a most excellent letter of Sir Thomas More's to Doctor Colet, which beginneth thus:—

" As I was lately walking in Cheapside, and busying myself about other men's causes, I met by chance your servant, at whose first encounter I was marvellously rejoiced, both because he hath been always dear unto me, and also especially for that I thought he was not come to London without yourself. But when I had learned of him that you were not returned, nor minded to return of a long space, it cannot be expressed how my great joy was turned into extreme sorrow and sadness: for what could happen more troublesome unto me than to be deprived of your most grateful and moral conversation, whose wholesome counsels I was wont to enjoy, with whose delightful familiarity I was accustomed to be recreated, by whose weighty sermons I have been often stirred up to devotion, by whose life and example I have been much amended in mine own, finally in whose very face and countenance I have settled my trust and confidence of my progress in virtue. Wherefore as I found myself greatly strengthened whilst I found and enjoyed those helps, so do I see myself weakened and brought almost to nothing, being deprived of them so long. For having heretofore by following your footsteps, almost escaped out of the pit of hell, so now, like another Eurydice, but in a contrary manner, for she was left there, because Orpheus looked back upon her, but I fall again by a certain fatal necessity in that dangerous downfall, for that you cast not your eye upon me. And what I pray is there in this city that doth move any man to live well, and not rather by a thousand subtleties and devices swallow him up in wickedness, who would endeavour to climb up to the hard hill of virtue. Whither soever any one cometh, what can he find but the feigned love, and the honey poison of venomous flattery; in one place cruel hatred, and in another suits and quarrels most pestiferous and hateful.

"Whither soever we cast our eyes what can we see but victualling-houses, fishmongers, butchers, cooks, pudding-makers, fishermen, and fowlers, who minister matter to our bellies, and set forward the service of the world and the flesh. Yea, the houses themselves, I know not how, bereave us of a great part of our sight of heaven, neither do they suffer us to look freely towards it, so that our horizontal circle is wholly cut short by the height of continued buildings. For which cause I pardon you the more easily that you do delight to remain still in the country where you are, for you find there a company of plain souls void of all craft wherewith citizens do most abound. Wheresoever you look, the earth yieldeth you a pleasant prospect, the temperature of the air refresheth you, and the very bounds of the heavens do delight you. You find nothing there but bounteous gifts of nature, and saint-like tokens of innocency. Yet I would not have you so carried away with those contentments, that you should be stayed from hastening hither; for if the discommodity of the city do pester you, yet your parish of Stepney, of which you should have great care, may afford you like delight to these which you now enjoy, from whence you may quickly return to London as into your inn, where you may find great matter of merit. In the country men are most commonly innocent, or at least not loaden with great offence, and therefore any physician may administer physic unto them; but as for citizens, both because they are a multitude, and also for their inveterate customs in sinning, none can help them but he that is very skilful. There come into the pulpit at Paul's divers men that promise to cure the diseases of others, but their lives do so jar with their sayings, that when they have preached a goodly process, they rather provoke to anger than assuage any sore; for they cannot persuade men that they are fit to cure others, when themselves (God wot) are most sick and crazy, which causeth them that have ulcered sores not to endure to be touched or lanced by such ignorant physicians. But if such a one be accounted by learned men most fit to cure, in whom the sick man hath greatest hope, who doubteth then that you alone are the fittest to cure their maladies, whom every one is willing to touch their imposthumes, and in whom what confidence every one hath, both you have heretofore sufficiently tried, and now the desire that every one hath of your speedy return may manifest the cause more evidently. Return, therefore, my dear Colet, at least for Stepney's sake, which mourneth your absence no less than a child doth for his mother; or else for London's sake, in respect it is your native country, whereof you can have no less regard than of your own parents. Finally, although this be the least motive, return for my sake, who have wholly dedicated myself to your direction, and do most earnestly desire your return. In the mean while I pass my time with Grocine, Linacre, and Lilly[*]; the first, as you know, the

---

[*] Happy is the man who has three such friends. The age did not present, at least in England, three more learned, more useful, or better men than Grocine, Linacre, and Lilly. Grocine was many years older than More. He was the divinity reader at Oxford, and the first who taught Greek literature in that university. Linacre was the famous physician of that name, and had been More's tutor in Greek, at Oxford; and Lilly, who was nearer More's own age, was distinguished by his attainments in Greek literature, and his accuracy as a grammarian. He has been mentioned before in this life. When More intended to take upon himself the office of the priesthood, Lilly, it appears, entertained the same design. With this agrees what Wood relates of him, that soon after he left Oxford, he undertook a journey to Jerusalem for reli-

director of my life in your absence; the second, the master of my studies; the third, my most dear companion. Farewell, and see you love me as you have done hitherto.

"London, 21 October."

By this letter it may clearly be seen how he gave himself, even from his youth, to the true rules of devotion, that thereby he sought to profit as well in holiness as in learning; for if Christ hath pronounced them happy that hunger and thirst after justice, surely in this letter he showed a great earnestness to aspire to perfection[*]; and his example may move all his to follow his footsteps herein, that their chief and principal endeavour in their youth be to seek

gion's sake. On his return he stayed some time in the Isle of Rhodes, studying the Greek and Latin tongues. At Rome he attended the lectures in grammar and rhetoric of Sulpitius and Sabinus; and on his return home, opened a school in London, where he taught grammar, poetry, and rhetoric. When Colet had founded his school at St. Paul's, he named Lilly the first master. Such a choice of intimate friends is highly honourable to More, who was then young; and not less honourable is it to him that he was thought worthy of their friendship.

[*] This word, "perfection," which occurs so often, is used in a Catholic sense of it, founded on the saying of our Lord, "If thou wilt be perfect, go and sell that thou hast and give to the poor." In the mendicant orders this state of perfection was supposed to be exhibited.

out a skilful physician of the soul, who both can and will guide us in the path of Catholic doctrine and duty, and when we have found him, to follow his counsel precisely, and make the secrets of our hearts known unto him.

This dutifulness of the ghostly child to so rare a father made Colet also admire this young man's towardliness, so that this doctor would profess to many, and at sundry times say that there was but one wit in England, and that was young Thomas More, although many flourishing youths at that time lived in England which were of hopeful expectation. And no doubt God did further him with particular grace and towardliness, because he was so extraordinarily devout, so that I do imagine it may be said of Sir Thomas which Saint Thomas Aquinas witnesseth of himself, that he learned more by prayer and spiritual exercises, than ever he could do by any study; for what study soever Sir Thomas applied himself unto, he grew in short time most famous therein.

And, first, how great a poet he was accounted even in his youth, we have already partly rehearsed. Then what declamations he made, full of all rhetorical eloquence, to the amazement of all his auditory, many have witnessed who heard them and have read them. How pure a Latin style he attained unto, his singular epistles, yet extant, to divers personages do evidently show; so that one would imagine he had spent all his life time in humanity only. And although his towardliness to eloquence seemed far to disagree with the serious studies of the common law of this land, so that few could suppose that such a wit would have had the patience to have taken a law-book in hand, yet such was his obedience to his father, that at his command he studied busily the law.

He used to eat at his meals but of one dish, which was most commonly powdered beef, or some salt meat (although his table was always furnished with much variety), and what meat he first tasted, on the same would he for that time make his whole refection upon. In his youth he abstained wholly from wine. In his latter years he would taste thereof, but first it must be well allayed with water, as Erasmus to Huttenus witnesseth. He had no care what apparel he wore, insomuch that being once told by his secretary, Mr. Harris*, that his shoes were

---

* John Harris, a favourite servant, who has the honour to be introduced into Holbein's painting of the family. He lies buried at Neumarck, in Germany, in the same church with his son-in-law, John Fowler, a native of Bristol, who settled as a printer at Antwerp and Louvaine. Fowler published an edition of " The Dialogue of Comfort," Antwerp, 1573, 8vo. with a portrait of Sir Thomas More, very well executed.

all torn, he bade him tell his man that looked to him thereof to buy him new, whom for this cause he called his tutor, for he bought all his apparel at his own discretion, Sir Thomas never busying his head about such base matters, chusing rather to be in all things at the discretion of others than at his own guiding, that he might in all his actions exercise the true virtues of a Christian man, obedience and humility. Yea, although he were more wise and dexterous in discerning all truth from falsehood and virtue from cloked vice, yet would he for the most part in his greatest affairs and studies ask his man Harris his advice and counsel, and if he thought the contrary better, he would willingly submit himself to his opinion, for Harris was a man of great judgment, a trusty servant, and of an excellent deep understanding.

These were his foundations on which he laid his future building: which by how much the more it was to be raised to splendour and beauty by so much he laid his ground-work of humility the lower: and whatsoever hardness he used secretly, still kept he in outward semblance a singular alacrity, being merry in all company and full of jests, chiefly eschewing the vice of singularity. Yea he was very cunning in dissembling his virtues so that few came to know what holy exercises he practised, even as in his writings he often feigned matters cunningly to have heard them of others which he himself invented, as in the preface of his Utopia he artificially discourseth as though Raphael Hithlodius had told that whole story unto him, " commento perjucundo,' as Paulus Jovius doth testify. So he feigned as if an Englishman called Rosseus had pleasantly confuted Luther's book, as he discoursed with his host in Italy, who afterwards published all their communication in print, by which means Luther could never learn who he was that answered him, after his own furious fashion, which angered him sore. Lastly, his three books of Comfort in Tribulation, a work most excellent and divine, he invented to have been spoken by two Hungarian kinsmen, about the Turk's persecution; but thereby he most lively represented the terrible storms of cruelty which King Henry the Eighth and heresy would raise in our poor distressed country.

CHAPTER III.

SIR Thomas having determined, by the advice and direction of his ghostly father, to be a married man, there was at that time a pleasant conceited gentleman, of an ancient family in Essex, one Mr. John Colt, of New Hall, from whom Sir Henry Colt that now liveth is lineally descended, that invited him unto his house, being much delighted in his company, proffering unto him the choice of any of his daughters, who were young gentlewomen of very good carriage, good complexions, and very religiously inclined; whose honest and sweet conversation, and virtuous education, enticed Sir Thomas not a little; and although his affection most served him to the second, for that he thought her the fairest and best favoured, yet when he thought with himself that it would be a grief and some blemish to the eldest to have the younger sister preferred before her, he out of a kind of compassion, settled his fancy upon the eldest, and soon after married her with all her friends' good liking*.

Now when he began to be clogged with wife and family, children also began to grow fast upon him, for his wife (whose name was Jane) as long as she lived, which was but some six years, brought unto him almost every year a child, for whose maintenance he applied himself busily to the practice of the law; and because he would have his wife near unto his father, he placed her in Buckler's Bury. By her he had one son, called John More, my own grandfather, who was his youngest child, and three daughters; his eldest Margaret, a woman of singular wit and wisdom, rare piety, and more than extraordinary learning, who was married to William Roper, of Eltham, in the county of Kent, esq., whose grandchild, now living, is Sir William Roper. The second, Elizabeth, was afterwards matched with Sir John Dancey's son and heir. The third, called Cecily, was married to Giles Heron, of Shacklewell, in the county of

* The Baronetage speaks of five daughters of the Colts, who all married: Jane to Sir Thomas More, Alice to Edmund Buggs, esq., Mary to William Kemp, of Finchingfield, esq., whose daughter married George Cavendish, gentleman usher to Cardinal Wolsey, Bridget to Lawrence Foster, esq. and ——— to ——— Copledike.

Middlesex, esq. His son, my grandfather, married Anne Cresacre, sole daughter and heir of Edward Cresacre, of Baronborough, in the county of York, esq., whom Sir Thomas bought of the king, being his ward, upon error for another body's land, lying in the same town, as was afterwards proved. My great grandmother, having brought forth these four children, died soon after; and within two or three years he Sir married one Mrs. Alice Middleton, a widow, in London, by whom he had no children. This he did, because she might have care of his children, that were very young, from whom of necessity he must be very often absent. She was of good years, of no good favour nor complexion, nor very rich; by disposition very near and worldly. I have heard it reported, he wooed her for a friend of his, not once thinking to have her himself; but she wittily answering him, that he might speed if he would speak in his own behalf, telling his friend what she had said, with his good liking he married her; and did that perhaps which otherwise he would never have thought to have done. And indeed her favour, as I think, could not have bewitched or scarce ever moved any man to love her; but yet she proved a kind and careful mother-in-law to his children, as he was always a most loving father, not only to his own, but to her daughter, who was married after to Mr. Allington, and mother to Sir Giles*. He brought up together with his own children, as one of them, Margaret Giggs, after wife to Doctor Clement, a famous physician, who proved also very famous for her many excellent parts, as learning, virtue, and wisdom. All these he bred most carefully to learning, and many godly exercises; often exhorting them to take virtue for their meat, and play for their sauce; getting good means to maintain them by his practice in the law, which he first studied in an inn of chancery, called New Inn, where he profited exceedingly; and from thence went to Lincoln's Inn, of which house his father then was, where he allotted him small allowance for the reasons before alleged; and, as it seemed, his great patron, the good cardinal was now dead.

But he so applied that study whereto he betook himself (being apt to any), that in short

* This is inconsistent with what is found concerning the Allingtons, in the peerages. A Sir Giles Allington, who was with Henry VIII. at the siege of Bulloigne, married to his second wife, Alice, daughter of John Middleton, sister and heiress of Thomas Middleton, and widow of Thomas Erlington, esquires. She had three sons, William, Richard, and Philip; but no Giles. Sir Giles, who appears to be the person intended by Mr. More, was a grandson of Sir Giles, who married Alice Middleton, but by a former wife. Such at least is the account in the peerages.

time he was made and accounted a worthy outer barrister; yea, still proceeding with most notable fame, he became a double reader*, to which few but rare and singular lawyers do ever attain. Every one began to admire him both for a man of judgment, uprightness, and other most excellent parts, as ready delivery, boldness in a just cause, and diligence in his client's case, and no great taker of money, unless he had thoroughly deserved; for which causes every man strived to have him of their counsel in all suits. The city of London chose him within a while judge of the Sheriff's Court†, some say recorder of

* Stapleton, in his Life of More, thus explains what is meant here by a double reader. " Juri municipali seu legum Britannicarum studio operam dedit, in eoque tantos progressus fecit, ut tum in hoc jure bis legerit, vacationum tempore, quod à festo S. Joan. Baptistæ usque ad S. Michaelem excurrit. Est autem hoc legendi munus valde apud nostros splendidum, quod non nisi senioribus defertur, et non nisi à peritissimis exercetur, reliquis minus idoneis magnam quandam pecuniæ taxam lecturæ loco solventibus." P. 168.

† Roper says one of the under sheriffs. The anonymous life published by Dr. Wordsworth, " Under Sheriff of London." Hoddesden says, " one of the under sheriffs of London; some say recorder;" but Hoddesden's is so poor a compilation that it has no independent authority. Stapleton writes thus: " There are in London three public officers, a mayor, and two sheriffs; but because for the most part the persons holding those offices are unskilful in the law, est unus perpe-

London, which I think not. Yea, there was not at that time any cause of importance in any of the king's courts of this realm, but he was of counsel for one of the parties, still chusing the justest side, and therefore he continually went away victorious. By all which means he got yearly, as he told his son Roper, without any grudge of conscience, to the value of four hundred pounds, which was a large gain in those days, when lawyers sped not so well as now they do; neither were they then so plentiful. But his fame exceeded all others, wherefore he was chosen twice agent for the Still-yard merchants*, which business he dispatched with singular dexterity.

King Henry the Seventh now reigning, was a prince of singular virtues, as wisdom and reli-

---

tuus (ut in jure vocatur) syndicus civitatis, qui pro istis shyrevis jus dicit, judicisque urbani officio fungitur." P. 169. Pitz states the matter thus: " electus est primum populi Londinensis orator, deinde syndicus urbis." P. 718.

* The merchants of the Steel-yard were foreign merchants, chiefly of Germany, who enjoyed certain privileges in London, by charters from our kings. They were the great importers of corn. See Stowe's " London," p. 234. The writer of the anonymous Life says, that he was twice sent abroad on the business of these merchants. Roper that he was engaged by the merchants of London to go abroad on their business.

gion, if that covetousness, the root of all mischief, had not seized upon him towards his latter days, which caused him to lay upon his subjects many impositions, and to raise sore exactions, by the instigation of two caterpillars of the commonwealth, Empson and Dudley, who in the beginning of King Henry the Eighth's reign were rewarded according to their deserts for their wicked counsel, to teach other men by their deaths, how injustice and rapine is punished by God. This king, I say, had called together a parliament, wherein he demanded three-fifteenths for the marriage of his eldest daughter, the Lady Margaret's grace, who then should be, as she was indeed shortly after, bestowed upon the King of Scots. It chanced that Sir Thomas was then one of the burgesses, for many had now taken notice of his great sufficiency. When the consent of the lower house was demanded to these impositions, most of the rest, either holding their peace, or not daring to gainsay them, though they seemed unwilling, Sir Thomas, making a grave speech, pronounced such urgent arguments why these exactions were not to be granted, that hereupon all the king's demands were crossed, and his request denied; so that Mr. Tyler, one of the king's privy chamber, went presently from the house, and told his majesty that a beardless boy had disappointed him of all his expectations.* Whereupon the king conceived great indignation against him, and could no way be satisfied until he had in some sort revenged it. But forasmuch as he, having yet but little, could not lose much, he devised a causeless quarrel against Sir John More, his most innocent father, and clapped him up in the Tower of London, keeping him there prisoner until he had forced him, against all justice, to pay one hundred pounds, as a fine for a causeless offence. Many also counselled Sir Thomas More to ask the king's mercy, that his father might be released, amongst whom was Doctor Fox, then Bishop of Winchester, one of the king's privy council, who pretended great love towards him, purposing indeed to get the king thereby a better means to revenge his displeasure. But when Sir Thomas had asked the bishop's chaplain, Doctor Whitford, a very holy and grave man, afterwards a father of Sion, he that translated the "Following of Christ" into English, what he were best to do, he requested him for the passion of God not to follow his lord's advice; saying moreover, that the bishop would not stick to agree to the death of his own

* This was probably in 1502, when the treaty for the marriage was settled. She was not delivered up to the King of Scots till August or September, 1503.

father, if it was to serve the king's affection; for which cause he returned no more to my Lord of Winchester, but determined to have gone over sea, thinking he could not live in England without great danger, standing now in the king's displeasure, and therefore he studied the French tongue at home, sometime recreating his tired spirits on the viol; where he also perfected himself in most of the liberal sciences, as music, arithmetic, geometry, astronomy, and grew to be a perfect historian; his chief help in all his labours being his happy memory, of which he modestly speaketh thus: " I would I were as wise and as learned 'ut memoria non usquequaque destituor,' as that my memory doth not altogether fail me."

But King Henry dying shortly after, and his son, King Henry the Eighth, striving at the beginning of his reign to win the applause of his people, cast Empson and Dudley into prison, and attainted them of high treason, for giving pernicious counsel to his father their prince, and when they were going to execution Sir Thomas asked Dudley, whether he had not done better than they; to whom with a sorrowful heart he answered, " Oh, Mr. More, God was your good friend, that you did not ask the king's forgiveness as many would have had you done: for if you had, perhaps you should have been in the like case with us now." So that to shun present dangers by offending God, or our country, is not always the safest way even for our bodily good, the contrary turning oftentimes to our great fame, glory and profit.

Those great parts of nature and diligence which every one noted in Sir Thomas, coming to the young king's ear, who was at that time greedy to entertain all rare men into his service, he caused Cardinal Wolsey, then Lord Chancellor, to move him to come to the court: and albeit the cardinal travailed earnestly with him to effect it, alleging how dear his service must needs be to his majesty, who could not with his honour allow him less than he should lose thereby to recompense him fully, yet loath to change his estate, which was certain, made such means to the king by the cardinal, as that his majesty was at that time satisfied to forbear him.

Yet did the king use him in divers embassages: sending him into France to challenge certain debts which the king of England demanded to be due unto him, that had been there unjustly kept back; in which charge he satisfied both the kings fully of his wise demeanour and sufficiency. After this he was also sent embassador into Flanders, to confirm a league betwixt England and Burgundy, which he happily finishing, the king offered him at his return a yearly pension, which Sir Thomas refused, as he writeth to Erasmus in these words:

"When I returned from my embassage of Flanders, the king's majesty would have granted me a yearly pension; which surely, if I should respect honour or profit, was not to be contemned by me, yet have I as yet refused it, and I think I shall still refuse it, because either I should forsake my present means which I have in the city, which I esteem more than a better, or else I should keep it with some grudge of the citizens, between whom and his highness if there should happen any controversies (which may sometime chance) they may suspect me as not trusty and sincere unto them, because I am obliged to the king with an annual stipend."

About this time he composed the famous book, his Utopia, in Latin, so much praised and extolled by all the learned men of the age, about the year of our Lord 1516, being six and thirty years of age. This was of all nations so much applauded that very shortly after it was translated both into French, Italian, Dutch, and English. The judgments of divers learned men concerning which work I think good to set down here in English, as Doctor Stapleton reciteth them in his Three Thomases. And first Budæus, a singular man, sayeth thus of it in an epistle to Lupsetus, " We owe to Thomas More the discovery of Utopia, for he hath divulged to the world in this our age a pattern of a happy life and perfect rule of good behaviour. This age and our posterity shall have this history as a seminary of most wholesome doctrine and precepts, from whence they may transport and accommodate every one to their own cities and kingdoms, these excellent ordinances and decrees."

John Paludanus to Peter Giles speaketh thus thereof, " You may see in Utopia, as in a looking-glass, whatsoever belongeth to a perfect common-wealth. England truly hath many excellent learned men, for what may we conjecture of the rest, if More has performed so much; first, being but a young man, and then distracted with many public and domestic businesses; last of all, professing any thing rather than learning."

Peter Giles also, to Jerome Buslidian, speaketh thus, and giveth it this praise: " So many miracles meet here together, that I am in doubt which most to admire, his most happy memory, which could set down so many divers sayings verbatim, having but heard them once, and his wisdom for marking and setting down all the fountains from whence either the happiness or mischief of any common-wealth do arise: or else his elegant style, that hath comprised, with such pure Latin and such rigour of speech, so many and sundry matters, and especially he that is so much distracted with public and domestical affairs."

Buslidian, a great counsellor of Charles the emperor, in a letter to Sir Thomas sayeth thus: "In the happy description of the Utopian common-wealth there is nothing missing which might shew most excellent learning together with most perspicuous and absolute knowledge of all human things: for you excel many in sundry sciences, and in them are so skilful that you affirm every matter in writing as though you tried it by experience, and you write most eloquently whatsoever you affirm; a marvellous and rare happiness, and the more rare by how much few can attain thereunto." And further in the said letter he affirmeth, that this Utopian commonwealth far exceedeth the Lacedemonian, Athenian, or even the Roman; in that it is rather framed to provide for upright and able magistrates than in decreeing laws and statutes; by whose prototypon, that is the pattern of their honesty, the example of their manners and behaviour, and the portraiture of their justice, the whole state and true government of every perfect common-wealth may be framed.

Paulus Jovius in his book of the praises of learned men, speaketh thus: " More's fame will always last in his Utopia, for he therein hath described a kingdom very well governed with most wholesome laws, and much flourishing with rich peace, shewing how he loathed the corrupt manners of this wicked age, and that he might shew by a pleasant fiction the right path to a blessed and most happy life!

Finally, Hutten, Vives, Graphius, and Lasius affirm that Sir Thomas had an incomparable wit, greater than a man's, and "pene divinum."

About this time he also wrote for his exercise the history of King Richard the Third, both in Latin and English, which is so well penned that if our Chronicles of England were half so well set out, they would entice all Englishmen to read them over often.

These his works set out at that time when he was most employed in other men's affairs, shew how diligent and industrious he was; for thus he writeth in his Utopia: "Whilst I daily either plead other men's causes, or hear them sometimes as an arbitrator, otherwhiles as a Judge; whilst this man I visit for friendship, another for business: whilst I busy myself abroad about other men's matters all the whole day, I leave no time for myself, that is for study, for when I come home I must discourse with my wife, chat with my children, and speak with my servants. And seeing it must needs be done, I number them amongst my affairs and needful they are, unless one will be a stranger in his own house, for we must endeavour to be affable and pleasant unto those whom either nature chance or choice hath made our companions: but with such measure it must be done that we do not mar them with affability, or make them of servants our masters by too much gentle entreaty and favour. Whilst these things are a-doing, a day a month a year passeth, when then can I find time to write: for I have not yet spoken of meat or sleep, which things only, bereave most men of half their lives. As for me, I get only that spare time which I steal from my meat or sleep, which because it is but small, I proceed slowly: yet it being somewhat, now at the length I have prevailed, and have sent unto thee, Peter, my Utopia."

Besides all these, to show the more his excellent parts of ready utterance, pleasant conceits, and sharpness of wit, even to the admiration of all men, he read a lecture in St. Laurence's church at Lothbury, where Sir John More, his father lieth buried, out of St. Augustine's books De Civitate Dei, not so much discussing the points of divinity, as the precepts of moral philosophy and history, wherewith these books are replenished. And he did this with such an excellent grace, that whereas before all the flower of English youths went to hear famous Grocinus, who was lately come out of Italy to teach Greek in the public university, under whom, as also that famous grammarian Thomas Linacre, Sir Thomas himself had profited greatly, of whom he had Aristotle's work interpreted into Greek, now all England almost left this lecture and flocked to hear Sir Thomas More.

CHAPTER IV.

IT fortuned shortly afterwards that a ship of the pope's arrived at Southampton, which the king claimed as a forfeiture; yet the pope's legate so wrought with the king, that being seized on, he obtained to have the matter pleaded by learned counsel: for the pope's side, as their principal man, was chosen Sir Thomas More; and a day of hearing being appointed before the lord chancellor and other the chief judges in the Star-Chamber, Sir Thomas argued so learnedly and so forcibly in defence of the pope's part, that the aforesaid forfeiture was restored, and he by all the audience so highly commended for his admirable, upright demeanour, that for no entreaty would the king forbear any longer to use him. Whereupon he brought him perforce to the court and made him one of his privy council, as Sir Thomas testifieth himself, in a letter to that worthy prelate, John Fisher, bishop of Rochester:

"I have come to the court extremely against my will, as every body knoweth, and as the king often twitteth me in sport for it. And hereto do I hang so unseemly as a man not using to ride doth sit unhandsomely in his saddle. But our prince, whose special and extraordinary favour I cannot claim, is so affable and courteous unto all men, that every man who hath some little hope may find somewhat whereby he may imagine that he loveth him dearly, even as the citizens' wives of London do, who imagine that our Lady's picture near the Tower doth smile upon them as they pray before it. But I am not so happy that I can perceive such fortunate signs of love, and of a more abject spirit than I can persuade myself that I have it. Yet the king's majesty is so virtuous and learned, and so industrious in both, that by how much the more I see his highness increase in those kingly ornaments, by so much the less troublesome this courtier's life seemeth unto me."

And indeed King Henry's court for the first twenty years, was a seat of many excellent wits; a palace of rare virtues, according as Erasmus witnesseth thereof in an epistle to one Henry Gilforde,* a gentleman of an ancient family, thus:—

* This was Sir Henry Guilford, K. G. There is a good account of him in Wotton's Baronetage, vol. iv. p. 4. His brother Sir Edward was father to Jane Duchess of Northumberland.

"The fragrant odour of the most honourable fame of the court of England, which spreadeth itself over all the world, it having a king singularly endowed with all princely excellencies, a queen most like unto him, and plenty of sincere, learned, grave, and wise personages, hath stirred up the prince of Berghes to put his son Anthony to no other school but that."

Within a while after that the king had created him one of his high counsellors of state, perceiving every day more and more his fidelity, uprightness, dexterity, and wisdom, he dubbed him knight: and after Mr. Weston's death, he made him treasurer of the exchequer, a place of great trust, of which increase of honour Erasmus writeth thus Goclenius:[*]

"When you shall write to More you shall congratulate him for his increase of dignity and good fortune. For being before only of his privy council, now of late by the free gift of his most gracious prince, neither desiring nor seeking it, he hath not only made him a knight but treasurer of the king's exchequer, an office in England both honourable and commodious for the purse."

Yea, King Henry finding still sufficiency

---

[*] "Cochleus" in the printed copies. Stapleton, from whom More derived it, has it Goclenius, which is right.

more and more in Sir Thomas used him with particular affection for the space of twenty years together; during a good part whereof the king's custom was upon holy days, when he had done his own devotions, to send for Sir Thomas into his traverse; and there, sometimes in matters of astronomy, geometry, and divinity, and such other faculties, to sit and confer with him: otherwhiles also, in the clear night, he would have him walk with him on the leads, there to discourse with him of the diversity of the courses, motions, and operations of the stars, as well fixed as the planets. And because he was of a very pleasant disposition it pleased his majesty and the queen, after the council had supped, at supper time commonly to call for him to hear his pleasant jests. But when Sir Thomas perceived his pleasant conceits so much to delight them that he could scarce once in a month get leave to go home to his wife and children, whom he had now placed at Chelsey, three miles from London, by the water's side, and that he could not be two days absent from the court, but he must be sent for again, he much misliking this restraint of his liberty, began therefore to dissemble his mirth, and so by little and little to disuse himself, that he from thence forth at such seasons was no more so ordinarily sent for.

The great opinion which the city of London

had of him, caused the king to send Sir Thomas as a special man to appease the apprentices which were risen up in mutiny against the strangers that dwelt then amongst them upon a May-day: and surely Sir Thomas had quieted them utterly and soon, had not an extraordinary chance hindred it in St. Martin's, as Stowe witnesseth.

The king also used, of a particular love, to come on a sudden to Chelsey, where Sir Thomas now lived, and leaning on his shoulder to talk with him of secret counsel in his garden, yea, and to dine with him upon no inviting; for Sir Thomas used seldom to feast noblemen, but his poor neighbours often, whom he would visit often in their houses, and bestow upon them his large liberality, not groats but crowns of gold; yea, more than according to their wants. He hired a house for many aged people in Chelsey, whom he daily relieved; and it was my aunt Roper's charge to see them want nothing. And when he was a private lawyer he would take no fees of poor folks, widows, nor pupils.*

In the fourteenth year of the reign of King Henry the eighth there was a parliament called,

---

* The whole of this clause, from "For Sir Thomas," &c. is wanting in the printed copies, in this place, but is inserted afterwards in the eighth chapter.

and thereof (which was a strange thing) Sir Thomas was chosen speaker for the lower house, being now one of the privy council, who being very loth to take this charge upon him, made a worthy oration to the king (not now extant), whereby he vehemently laboured to be discharged of the said place of the speakership, whereunto his highness would by no means give his consent.

At the beginning of the parliament he made another oration, very wisely set down by my uncle Roper in his work of Sir Thomas More's Life, thus:—" Since I perceive most redouted sovereign, that it accordeth not to your high pleasure to reform this election and cause it to be changed, but have by the mouth of the most reverend father in God the legate (who was then Cardinal Wolsey), your high chancellor, thereunto given your assent, and have of your benignity determined far above that I may bear, to enable me, and for this office to repute me fit, rather than that you would seem to impute to your commons that they had unmeetly chosen me; I am therefore, and always shall be, ready obediently to conform myself to the accomplishment of your high command." And then he maketh two humble petitions; the one concerning himself, the other the whole assembly: the first, that if he should chance to mistake his message, or for lack of good utterance by mis-rehearsal to pervert their prudent instructions, that his majesty would then pardon his simplicity, and suffer him to repair unto them again for their more substantial advice. His other request was to the king's majesty, that it would please his inestimable goodness, to pardon freely, without doubt of his dreadful displeasure, whatsoever it shall happen any man to say, interpreting every man's words, how unseemly soever they be couched, to proceed of a good zeal towards the profit of the realm and the honour of his royal person.

Cardinal Wolsey at this parliament found himself much grieved at the burgesses, that nothing could be either done or spoken in both the houses, but it was immediately blown abroad in every alehouse. It fortuned after, that when a great subsidy was demanded, and that the cardinal fearing it would not pass the lower house unless he were there present himself, before whose coming it was long debated whether they should admit him with a few of the lords, as the most opinion of the house was, or that they should receive him with his whole train. " Masters," quoth Sir Thomas, " for as much as my lord cardinal lately, ye wot well, laid to our charge the lightness of our tongues for things uttered out of this house, it should not in my mind be amiss to receive him with all his pomp, with his maces, his pillars, his poleaxes, his cross, his hat, and the great seal, to the intent that if he find the like fault with us, we may lay the blame on those which his grace bringeth with him." Upon which words the house wholly agreed, and so he was received accordingly. There the cardinal with a solemn speech by many reasons proved, how necessary it was that the demand there moved should be granted. But he, seeing the company silent contrary to his expectation, shewing no towardliness of inclination thereunto, demanded of them some reasonable answer. But when every one still held their peace, he spake in particular to Mr. Murrey,[*] who making no answer neither, he asked others also, but they all had determined to answer him by their speaker; who spake therefore reverently on his knees, excusing the silence of the house, abashed, as he said at the sight of so noble a personage, who was able to amaze the wisest and best learned in a realm. But by many probable arguments he proved this his manner of coming to be neither expedient, nor agreeable to the ancient liberties of that house. And for himself, in conclusion, he shewed, that except all they

[*] The name is Murrey, both in the MS. and the printed copies; but Roper, from whom More had the fact, calls the person Marney, which is right.

could put their sundry wits into his head, that he alone in so weighty a matter was unmeet to make his grace a sufficient answer. Whereupon the cardinal, displeased with Sir Thomas, that he had not in that parliament satisfied his expectation, suddenly rose in a rage and departed. And afterwards in the gallery of Whitehall he uttered unto him his grief: saying, "I would to God you had been at Rome, Mr. More, when I made you speaker." "Your grace not offended, so would I too, my lord, for then I should have seen the place I long have desired to visit." And when the cardinal walked without any more speech, he began to talk to him of that fair gallery of his, saying, "This gallery of yours, my lord, pleaseth me much better than your other at Hampton Court;" with which digression he wisely broke off the cardinal's displeasant talk, that his grace at that present wist not more what to say unto him. But for a revenge of his displeasure he counselled the king to send him his embassador leiger into Spain, commending to his highness his learning, wisdom, and fitness for that voyage, the difficulty of many matters considered between the Emperor Charles the Fifth and our realm, so as none was so well able to serve his majesty therein; which the king broke to Sir Thomas. But when Sir Thomas had declared to the king how unmeet that journey was for him, the nature of Spain disagreeing with his constitution, that he was unlike to do his sovereign acceptable service there, being that it was probable that he should send him to his grave: yet for all that, he shewed himself ready according as duty bound him, were it with the loss of his life, to fulfil his majesty's pleasure in that behalf. The king most graciously replieth thereunto, " It is not our meaning, Mr. More, to do you any hurt, but to do you good we would be glad; we will therefore employ your service otherwise;" and so would not permit him to go that long journey. For the king in his wisdom perceived that the cardinal began to grow jealous of Sir Thomas's greatness, fearing that which after happened, that he would outstrip him in the king's gracious favour, who still heaped more honour upon Sir Thomas. And although he was never the man that asked the king any request for himself, yet upon the death of Sir Richard Wingfield, who had been chancellor of the duchy of Lancaster, that dignity was bestowed upon Sir Thomas More;* of which his honour Erasmus writing to Goclineus biddeth him to send congratulatory letters for his late honour, saying, that he came unto it " nec ambiens nec expetens, ultroneo favore principis humanissimi:" that is, neither am-

* Sir Richard Wingfield was sent embassador to Spain with the Bishop of London, and died at Toledo, July 22, 1525.

bitiously seeking it, nor once asking it, but by the mere favour of a most gracious prince.

King Henry took such extraordinary love in Sir Thomas's company, that he would sometimes on a sudden come over to his house at Chelsey and be merry with him; whither on a time unlooked for he came and dined with him, and after dinner walked with him for the space of an hour, holding his arm about his neck most lovingly, in the garden. And when his majesty was gone my uncle Roper rejoiced, and told his father how happy he was that the king had shewed him such extraordinary signs of love as he had never seen him do to any other except the cardinal, whom he saw with the king walk once arm in arm. Whereto Sir Thomas answering said, "I thank our Lord God, I find his grace my very good lord indeed, and I believe he doth as singularly favour me as any other subject within this realm; howbeit, son Roper, I may tell thee, I have no cause to be proud thereof, for if my head would win him a castle in France (for then there was war between France and us) it should not fail to go off." By which words he evidently shewed how little he joyed either in the king's favour or his worldly honour; piercing with his singular eye of judgment into King Henry's nature, that what show of friendship soever he made to any, yet he loved none but to serve his own turn, and no longer was any in his favour than he applied himself to his humours. Yet could he not chuse but love Sir Thomas for his singular parts, his profound judgment, his pleasant wit and sincere integrity. For which cause, as the rare and admirable Queen Catherine, King Henry's first wife, would often say, that the king her husband had but one sound counsellor in his kingdom, meaning Sir Thomas More; for the rest she said, that either they spake as the king would have them, or had not such matter of judgment in them: and as for Cardinal Wolsey, who was then the greatest subject in the realm, for his own benefit or end he cared not what counsel he gave to the king. He was of base parentage, and as they say, a butcher's son of Ipswich; yet had he crept up into favour partly by his learning, partly by his nimble wit and lovely carriage, whereby he could insinuate himself into great men's favours. He had also a ready tongue and a bold countenance, and had gotten much spiritual living together, bestowing it upon vanities, as great and sumptuous buildings, costly banquets, and great magnificence: for he was vain glorious above all measure, as may be seen by Sir Thomas's book of Comfort in Tribulation, where he meaneth of him what is spoken of a great prelate in Germany, who when he had made a speech or oration before a great audience, would bluntly ask them that sat at his table with him, how they all liked it; then he that should bring forth a mean commendation of it was utterly shamed: and so telleth of a spiritual man, when he should have commended it least of all, was put to such a non plus that he had nothing to say, but crying, "Oh," and fetching a deep sigh, he cast his eyes into the welkin and wept. Another time, the cardinal had drawn a draft of certain conditions of peace between England and France, and he asked Sir Thomas his counsel therein, beseeching him earnestly that he would tell him if there were any thing therein to be misliked; and he spake this so heartily, saith Sir Thomas, that he believed verily that he was willing to hear it indeed. But when Sir Thomas had dealt really therein, and showed wherein that draft might have been amended, he suddenly rose in a rage, saying, "By the mass, thou art the veriest fool of all the council:" at which Sir Thomas smiling said, "God be thanked the king our master hath but one fool in his council." But we shall have occasion hereafter to speak more of this cardinal.

CHAPTER V.

SIR Thomas for all his honour and favour with his prince, was not puffed up with pride, disdain or arrogancy, but was of such a mild behaviour and excellent temper, that he could never be moved to any passion or anger, as mine uncle Roper witnesseth, who affirmeth that in sixteen years' space and more that he dwelt in his house and was conversant with him always, he could never perceive him so much as once in a fume; yea, Margaret Giggs, who was brought up as a child among Sir Thomas's children, and used by him as one of them, and afterwards married to Doctor Clement, a singular learned woman, would say, that sometimes she would commit a fault for the nonce, to hear Sir Thomas chide her, he did it with such gravity, such moderation, such love, and compassion. His meekness and humility were also perceived in this, that if it had fortuned any learned man to come to him, as there did many daily either from Oxford, Cambridge or elsewhere, some for desire of his acquaintance, (as he had intercourse of letters with all the men of fame in all Christendom); some again for the report of his learning and singular wisdom; some for suits of the universities: if any of them, I say, had entered into argument, wherein few of them were able to dispute long with him, he would urge very forcibly, and if it fortuned that they entered together so far to dispute that he perceived they could not without some inconveniency hold out much further against his arguments, then lest he should discourage them, as he sought not his own glory, he would seem confuted, that the student should not be discomfited, ever shewing himself more desirous to learn than to teach; and so by some witty devise he would courteously break out into some other matter.

Such was also his readiness of wit, that going ever in progress with the king either to Oxford or Cambridge, when they were received with very eloquent orations, he was always the man appointed by his majesty ex tempore to make answer unto them, as he that was promptest and most ready therein. Yea, when the king went into France to meet the French king, Sir Thomas More made a speech of their congratulation; which he also did, when Charles the Fifth landed in

England to see Queen Catherine, his aunt. And whensoever he had occasion, either in England or beyond the sea, to visit any university, he would not only be present at their readings and disputations, but would also learnedly dispute there amongst them himself, to the great admiration of all the auditory, for his skill in all sciences. But when at Bruges, in Flanders, an arrogant fellow had set up a Thesis, that he would answer whatsoever question could be propounded unto him, in any art whatsoever, Sir Thomas made this question to be put up, for him to answer thereto, " An Averia capta in Withernamia sunt irreplegibilia ;" adding, that there was one of the English ambassador's retinue would dispute with him thereof. This Thraso, or braggadocio, not so much as understanding those terms of our common law, knew not what to answer to it; and so he was made a laughing stock to the whole city for his presumptuous bragging.

Now, as he was ungrateful to vain proud men, so was he an entire and special good friend to all the learned men in Christendom; and first he affected especially that famous man, Cuthbert Tunstall, lately Bishop of London, and then of Durham; of whom Sir Thomas speaketh in his epitaph, made by himself whilst he was in good health and state, thus, " Than whom the whole world hath not a man more learned, wise, or better." He speaketh also of him in his Utopia, thus: "The king sent me ambassador into Flanders, as a colleague to that excellent person, Cuthbert Tunstall, whom lately he hath chosen (to the congratulation of all men) his master of the rolls, of whose singular praises I will not speak, not that I fear I should be suspected, because he is so dear a friend unto me, but for that his virtues and learning are greater than I can express, and also more known than that I should need to go about to declare them; except I would seem to set a torch to lighten the sun. In this embassage many things delighted me much; first the long and never interrupted familiarity which I had with Tunstall, than whom as there is none more learned, so also no man more grave in his life and manners, no man more pleasant in his manner of carriage and conversation." He wrote unto him divers letters, which may testify what entire friendship there was between these two excellent men; as this: " Although every letter which I receive from you, most worthy friend, is very grateful unto me, yet that which you wrote last was most welcome, for that besides the other commendations, which the rest of your letters deserve, in respect of their eloquence, and the friendship they profess towards me, these last of yours yield a peculiar grace, for that they contain your peculiar testimony (I would it were as true as it is favourable) of my Commonwealth. I requested my friend Erasmus, that he would explain to you the matter thereof in familiar talk; yet I charged him not to press you to read it, not because I would not have you to read it, for that is my chief desire, but remembering your discreet purpose, not to take in hand the reading of any new work, until you had fully satisfied yourself with the books of ancient authors, which if you measure by the profit you have taken by them, surely you have already accomplished your task; but if by affection, then you will never bring your said purpose to a perfect end. Wherefore I was afraid that seeing the excellent works of other men could not allure you to their reading, you would never be brought to condescend willingly to the reading of my trifles, and surely you would never have done it, but that your love towards me drove you more thereto than the worth of the thing itself. Therefore I yield you exceeding thanks for reading so diligently over my Utopia; I mean, because you have for my sake bestowed so much labour; and no less thanks truly do I give you for that my work hath pleased you; for no less do I attribute this to your love, because I see you rather have testified what your love towards me did suggest, than the authority of a censor. Howsoever the matter is, I cannot express how much I joy that you have cast your whole account in liking my doings; for I almost persuade myself all those things to be true which you speak thereof, knowing you to be most far from all dissembling, and myself more mean than that you should need to flatter me, and more dear to you than that I should expect a mock from you. Wherefore, whether that you have seen the truth unfeignedly, I rejoice heartily in your judgment; or whether your affection to me hath blinded your judgment, I am for all that no less delighted in your love; and truly vehement and extraordinary great must that love be, which could bereave Tunstall of his judgment."

And in another letter he saith, " You deal very courteously with me, in that you give me in your letter such hearty thanks, because I have been careful to defend the causes of your friends, amplifying the small good turn I have done you therein, by your great bounty; but you deal somewhat too fearfully in regard of the love which is between us, if you imagine that you are indebted unto me for any thing I have done, and do not rather challenge it of right to be due unto you, &c. The amber which you sent me, being a precious sepulchre of flies, was for many respects most welcome unto me, for the matter thereof may be compared in colour and brightness to any precious stone, and the form is more excellent, because it representeth the figure of a heart, as it were the hieroglyphic of our love; which I interpret your meaning is, that between us it will never fly away, and yet be always without corruption; because I see the fly (which hath wings like Cupid, the son of Venus, and is as fickle as he,) so shut up here and enclosed in this gluey matter of amber, as it cannot fly away, and so embalmed and preserved therewith as it cannot perish. I am not so much as once troubled that I cannot send you the like gift again; for I know you do not expect any interchange of tokens; and besides, I am willing still to be in your debt; yet this troubleth me somewhat, that my estate and condition is so mean that I am never able to shew myself worthy of all and singular your friendship. Wherefore, though I cannot give testimony myself herein before other men, yet must be satisfied with mine own inward testimony of mind, and your gentle acceptance."

He dedicated one of his books unto him, saying in this wise: " When I considered to which of all my friends I should dedicate these my collections out of many authors, I thought you most fit for the same, in respect of the familiar conversation, which of long time hath been between us, as also in respect of the sincerity of your mind, because you would be always ready to take thankfully whatsoever in this work should seem grateful unto you; and whatsoever should be barren therein, you would make a courteous construction thereof; whatsoever might be unpleasing, you would be willing to pardon.* I would to God I had as much wit and learning, as I am not altogether destitute of memory."

As for Bishop Tunstall he was a learned man, and wrote a singular book of the real presence. And although, during King Henry's reign, he went with the sway of the time (for who almost did otherwise?) to the great grief of Sir Thomas More; yet living to the time of Queen Elizabeth, whose godfather he was, .. in his old age, seeing her take strange courses against the church, he came from Durham, and stoutly admonished her not to change religion, which if

---

* It is observed by the editor of the edition of this Life, published in 1726, that this is not a quotation from More to Tunstall, but from Tunstall to More. It is from the dedication of Tunstall's work, " De Arte Supputandi," which was printed at Paris in 1529. More had it from Stapleton, and appears to have misunderstood his author's meaning. The sentence which follows, " I would to God," &c. is not Tunstall's, but More's; and occurs in the Epistle to Peter Giles, prefixed to the Utopia.

she presumed to do, he threatened her to lose God's blessing and his. She, nothing pleased with his threats, made him be cast into prison, as most of the bishops were, where he made a glorious end of a confessor, and satisfied for his former crime of schism contracted in the time of King Henry's reign.

Sir Thomas More's friendship with the glorious Bishop of Rochester was neither short nor small, but had long continued, and ended not [but] with their famous martyrdoms. See how good Bishop Fisher writeth unto him: " Let, I pray you, our Cambridge men have some hope in you to be favoured by the king's majesty, that our scholars may be stirred up to learning by the countenance of so worthy a prince. We have few friends in the court, which can or will commend our causes to his royal majesty, and amongst all we account you the chief, who have always favoured us greatly, even when you were in a meaner place; and now also shew what you can do, being raised to the honour of knighthood, and in such great favour with our prince, of which we greatly rejoice, and also do congratulate your happiness. Give furtherance to this youth, who is both a good scholar in divinity, and also a sufficient preacher to the people. For he hath hope in your favour, that you can procure him great furtherance, and that my commendations will help him to your favour."

To this Sir Thomas More answereth thus: " This priest, Reverend Father, whom you write to be in possibility of a bishoprick, if he might have some worthy suitor to speak for him to the king, I imagine that I have so prevailed, that his majesty will be no hindrance thereto, &c. If I have any favour with the king, which truly is but little, but whatsoever I have I will employ all I can to the service of your fatherhood and your scholars, to whom I yield perpetual thanks for their dear affections towards me, often testified by their loving letters, and my house shall be open to them as though it were their own. Farewell, worthy and most courteous prelate, and see you love me as you have done."

His love and friendship with young Poole, afterwards cardinal, may be seen by their letters. He maketh mention of him with great praise, in a letter he wrote to his well-beloved daughter, Margaret Roper, in this wise: " I cannot express in writing, nor scarcely can conceive it by thought, how grateful to me your most eloquent letters, dear daughter Margaret, are. Whilst I was reading them, there happened to be with me Reginald Poole, that most noble youth, not so noble by birth as he is singularly learned, and excellently endued with all kind of virtue. To him your letter seemed as a miracle; yea, before he understood how near you were beset with the shortness of time, and the molestation of your weak infirmity, having, notwithstanding, sent me so long a letter, I could scarce make him believe but that you had some help from your master, until I told him seriously that you had not only never a master in your house, but also never another man that needed not your help rather in writing any thing than you needed his." And in another to Doctor Clement, a most famous physician, and one that was brought up in Sir Thomas's own house, he saith thus: " I thank you, my dear Clement, for that I find you so careful of my health, and my children's; so that you prescribe, in your absence, what meats are to be avoided by us. And you, my friend Poole, I render double thanks, both because you have vouchsafed to send us in writing the counsel of so great a physician; and besides have procured the same for us from your mother, a most excellent and noble matron, and worthy of so great a son; so as you do not seem to be more liberal of your counsel than in bestowing upon us the thing itself which you counsel us unto; wherefore I love and praise you, both for your bounty and fidelity."

And of Sir Thomas More's friendship, Cardinal Poole boasteth much after his martyrdom, in his excellent book, " De unitate Ecclesiæ," saying, " If you think that I have given scope to my sorrow, because they were my best beloved friends that were put to death," meaning Sir Thomas More and Bishop Fisher, " I do both acknowledge and profess it to be true, most willingly; that they were both dear unto me above all others. For how can I dissemble this, seeing that I do rejoice more of their love towards me, than if I should boast that I had gotten the dearest familiarity with all the princes of Christendom."

His friendship also with Doctor Lee, afterwards the worthy Archbishop of York, was not small nor feigned, although he had written an excellent book against Erasmus's " Annotations upon the New Testament," Erasmus being then Sir Thomas's entire friend, and, as it were, the one half of his own heart; for Sir Thomas writeth thus unto him: " Good Lee, that you request of me not to suffer my love to be diminished towards you; trust me, good Lee, it shall not; though of myself I incline rather to that part that is oppugned. And as I could wish that this city were freed from your siege, so will I always love you, and be glad that you do so much esteem of my love." He speaketh also of

Lupset,* a singular learned man of that time, in an epistle to Erasmus. "Our friend, Lupset, readeth with great applause, in both tongues, at Oxford, having a great auditory; for he succeedeth my John Clement in that charge." What familiarity there was betwixt him and Doctor Colet, Grocine, Linacre, and Lillie, all singular men, we have spoken of heretofore. William Mountjoy, a man of great learning,† and William Latimer, not Hugh, the heretic, that was burned,‡ but another most famous for virtue and

* Thomas Lupset was born in that part of London in which Sir Thomas More resided. He was educated in Dean Colet's school, under Lillie, and became an eminent scholar. He died at the age of thirty-six.

† By William Mountjoy is meant William Blount Lord Mountjoy, one of the nobility of that age, who devoted himself to literature. There is a poem, in which he is celebrated among the Encomia illustrium virorum of Leland. His acquaintance with Erasmus is there noticed, and in the epistles of that great man his name often appears. Pitz has a brief notice of him as William Mountjoy, p. 857, and, like our author, does not appear to have perceived that Blount was his name, and Mountjoy his title of honour.

‡ In this unfeeling manner can the hand write, when the heart is hardened by religious bigotry. Yet Hugh lives, while William is almost forgotten. He was, however, one of the lights of his age, and one of the restorers of Greek learning. He was the tutor of Pole, and the friend of Erasmus, who says of him that he was, Verè Theologus integritate vitæ conspicuus. He died in 1545.

good letters, were his very great acquaintance; as also John Croke,* that read Greek first at Lipsia in Germany, and was after King Henry's Greek master, to whom he writeth thus: " Whatsoever he was, my Croke, that hath signified unto you that my love is lessened, because you have omitted to write unto me this great while, either he is deceived, or else he seeketh cunningly to deceive you; and although I take great comfort in reading your letters, yet am I not so proud that I should challenge so much interest in you, as though you ought of duty to salute me every day in that manner, nor so wayward nor full of complaints to be offended with you for neglecting a little this your custom of writing. For I were unjust if I should exact from other men letters, whereas I know myself to be a great sluggard in that kind. Wherefore be secure as concerning this; for never hath my love waxed so cold towards you, that it need still to be kindled and heated with the continual blowing of missive epistles; yet shall you do me a great pleasure if you write unto me as often as you have leisure, but I will never persuade you to spend that time in saluting your friends

---

* For John Croke we should read Richard Croke, another student in Greek literature, raised from an inferior condition by Grocine. He is the person satirized by Leland, under the name of Corvus.

which you have allotted for your own study, or the profiting of your scholars. As touching the other part of your excuse, I utterly refuse it; for there is no cause why you should fear my nose as the trunk of an elephant, seeing that your letters may without fear approach in the sight of any man; neither am I so long snouted that I would have any man fear my censuring. As for the place which you require that I should procure you, both Mr. Pace and I, who love you dearly, have put the king in mind thereof."

But now as concerning the familiarity he had with the most famous men of other nations, it may be likewise seen by his letters to them; as to that famous John Cochlee, who was Luther's scourge, he writeth thus: "It cannot be expressed, most worthy sir, how much I hold myself indebted unto you, for certifying me so often of those occurrences, which happen in your country. For Germany now daily bringeth forth more monsters, yea prodigious things, than Afric was wont to do. For what can be more monstrous than the Anabaptists; yet how have those kind of plagues, risen forth and spread for many years together. I for my part seeing these sects daily to grow worse and worse, do expect shortly to hear, that there will arise some who will not stick to preach, that Christ himself is to be denied; neither can there arise so absurd a knave, but he shall have favourers; the madness of the people is so great." In which letter he foretelleth of David George, the Hollander, who called himself Christ, and had divers followers at Basil. So was there in England the like desperate fellow called Hackett, whose disciples were Arden* and Coppinger. At another time he writeth thus unto the same man: "I would have you persuade yourself, dear Cochlie, that I have not received any letter from any of my friends these many years, more grateful than your last were to me; and that for two causes especially; the first, for that I perceive in them your singular love unto me, which though I have sufficiently found heretofore, yet do these shew it most plentifully, and I account it as a great happiness: for to let pass your benefits done me, who would not highly esteem the friendship and favour of such a friend? Secondly because in these letters you certify me of the news of many actions of princes," &c.

Afterwards he had also intire familiarity with Budæus, which was often renewed by letters, and once by personal meeting in France, when the kings of England and France had a parley

* For Arden read Arthington. For an account of Hacket's strange opinions and conduct see Camden, Annales, A.D. 1591. He was executed. A milder government would have disposed of him differently.

together. For Budæus was in great favour with his king, Francis, yea, one of his privy council, as Sir Thomas was to King Henry; all which may be perceived by his letter to Budæus in this manner: "I know not, my good Budæus, whether it were good for us to possess any thing that were dear unto us, except we might still keep it. For I have imagined that I should be a happy man, if I might but once see Budæus, whose beautiful picture the reading of his works had represented unto me. And when God had granted me my wish, it seemed to me that I was more happy than happiness itself; yet after that our business were so urgent, that I could not fulfil my earnest desire to enjoy your sweet conversation often, and that our familiarity scarce begun was broken off within a while, the necessary affairs of our princes calling us from it, so as it is now hard to say, whether we shall ever again see one another, each of us being enforced to wait upon our own prince; by how much the more joyful our meeting was, by so much the more was my sorrow in the parting; which you may lessen somewhat, if that you would please to make me often present by your letters: yet dare I not crave them of you: but my desire to have them is great."

Another friend he had, called Martin Dorpe, a famous reader in Louvaine, and a singular good man, whom by letters fraught with sound arguments he brought to the love of the Greek tongue, being altogether before averted therefrom: thus he speaketh of him in a letter to Erasmus; " I cannot let Martin Dorpius pass unsaluted, whom I respect highly for his excellent learning, and for many other respects; but for this not a little, because he gave you occasion to write your Apology to Brictius' Moria."

He mentioneth also John Lascarus as a dear friend of his, as also Philip Beroalde, in a letter of his to Budæus, in this manner: " Commend me heartily to Lascarus that excellent and most learned man; for I imagine that you would of yourself remember me to Beroaldus, though I should not put you in mind thereof; for you know him to be so dear unto me as such a one ought to be, than whom I have scarcely found a more learned man, or a more pleasant friend."

Jerome Buslidian, who built the college called Trilingue in Louvaine, we have mentioned before, when we spake of his learned Utopia, of whom thus he speaketh in a certain letter of his to Erasmus: " Amongst other things which delighted me much in my Embassage, this is none of the least, that I got acquaintance with Buslidian, who entertained me most courteously according to his great wealth and exceeding good nature, where he shewed me his house built most artificially, and enriched with costly household stuff, replenished with a number of monuments of antiquity, wherein you know I take great delight, finally such an exquisite library, yea his heart and breast, more stored than any library; so that it astonished me greatly."

And presently after, in the same letter, he speaketh of Peter Giles as followeth: " But in all my travels, nothing happened more to my wish than the acquaintance and conversation of Peter Giles of Antwerp, a man so learned, so merry, so modest and so friendly, that let me be baked if I would not purchase this one man's familiarity with the loss of a good part of my estate." And in his Utopia he speaketh thus of him: " Whilst I live here in Antwerp, I am visited often, amongst the rest, by Peter Giles, than whom none is more grateful unto me: he is a native of Antwerp, and a man of good reputation amongst his countrymen, and worthy of the best. For he is such a young man that I know not whether he is more learned, or better qualified with good conditions, for he is a most virtuous man and a great scholar, besides of courteous behaviour towards all men, of such a sincere carriage, love and affection towards his friend, that you can scarce find such another youth to set by him, that may be compared unto him; he is of rare modesty, all flattery is far from him;

plainness with wisdom are seated in him together; moreover so pleasant in talk and so merry without any offence, that he greatly lesseneth by his pleasant discourse the desire I have to see my country, my house, my wife, my children, of whose company I am of myself too anxious, and whom to enjoy I am too desirous. Of Beatus Renanus a very learned man, he writeth in an epistle to Erasmus, thus: "I love Renanus marvellously and am much in his debt for his good preface; whom I would have thanked a good while ago, but that I have been troubled with such a gout of the hand, that is to say, idleness, that by no means I could overcome it."

Cranvilde also, an excellent learned man and one of the Emperor Charles's privy council, was brought to Sir Thomas More's friendship by Erasmus; for which both of them thanked Erasmus exceedingly as appeareth first by Cranvilde's letter to him, which is thus: " I cannot but thank you greatly with these my (though rude) letters, most learned in all sciences, for your singular benefit lately bestowed upon me which I shall always bear in remembrance, and which I esteem so much as that I would not lose it for Crœsus' wealth. You will ask me what benefit that was? truly this, that you have brought me to the acquaintance and sweet conversation of your friend More, but now I will call him mine, whom after your departure I often frequented, because he often sent for me unto him; whose bountiful entertainment at his table I esteem not so much as his learning, his courtesy, and his liberality. Wherefore I account myself deeply indebted unto you, and desire God that I may be able to demonstrate unto you a grateful signification of this good turn done me. In his absence he sent my wife a ring of gold, the posy whereof in English was: 'All things are measured by good-will.' He gave me also, certain old pieces of silver and gold coin; in one whereof was graven Tiberius' picture, in another Augustus'; which I am willing to tell you, because I am somewhat to thank you for all." Whom Erasmus answered thus: "This is that sure, which is vulgarly spoken: I have by the means of one daughter gotten two sons-in-law: you thank me because by my means you have gotten so special a friend, as More is; and he on the other side thanketh me also, for that I have procured his knowledge of Cranvilde. I knew well enough that because your wits and manners were alike, there would easily arise a dear friendship betwixt you; if so were that you did but know each other; but as the having of such friends is precious, so is the true keeping of them as rare." Hear how Sir Thomas writeth to Cranvilde: "I both perceive and acknowledge how much I am in your debt, my dear Cranvilde, because you never cease to do that which is most grateful unto me, in that you certify me still of your affairs and friends. For what can be either more acceptable to Thomas More in his adversity, or more pleasing unto him in his prosperity, than to receive letters from Cranvilde, except one could bring me to the speech of him, a most learned man of all others. But as often as I read your writings, I am enamoured therewith, as if I were conversing with you in presence. Wherefore nothing troubleth me more, than that your letters are no longer; yet have I found a means to remedy that, because I read them over again and again, and I do it leisurely that my sudden reading them may not bereave me of my pleasure. But so much for this. That which you write concerning our friend Vives, who hath made a discourse of wicked women, I agree so well with your opinion, that I think one cannot live without inconveniencies with the very best woman. For if any man be married, he shall not be without care; and in my conceit Metellus Numidicus spoke truly of wives; which I would speak the rather, if many of them through our own faults were not made the worse. But Vives hath gotten so good a wife, that he may not shun only, as much as possible any man, all the troubles of marriage, but also thereby he may receive great contentment; yet now men's minds are so busied with public garboils, whilst the fury of war doth so rage every where, that no man is at leisure to think of his private cares: wherefore if any household troubles have heretofore oppressed any, they are now all obscured by reason of common mischief. But this sufficeth for this matter. I return to yourself, whose courtesies and friendship towards me as often as I think of (which is very often) it shaketh from me all sorrow. I thank you for the book you sent me, and I wish much joy with your new child, not for your own sake only, but for the common-wealth's, whose great benefit it is, that such a parent should increase it with plenty of children. For from you none but excellent children can be born. Farewell, and commend me carefully and heartily to your wife, to whom I pray God send happy health and strength; my wife and children also wish you health, to whom by my report you are as well known and as dear as to myself. Again farewell. London, 10 Aug. 1524." Another letter he wrote unto him in this sort: " I am ashamed, so God help me, my dear Cranvilde, of this your great courtesy towards me, that you do salute me with your letters so often, so lovingly, and so carefully, when as I so seldom do salute you

again, especially seeing you may pretend yea alledge as many troubles of businesses as I can: but such is the sincerity of your affection and such the constancy thereof, as although you are ready to excuse all things in your friends, yet you yourself are always ready to perform every thing, and to go forward without omitting that which might be pardoned in you, But persuade yourself, good Cranvilde, that if there happen any thing at any time, wherin I may really show unto you my love, there, God willing, I will never be wanting. Commend me to my mistress your wife, for I dare not now invert the order begun, and to your whole family, whom mine doth with all their hearts salute. From my house in the country this 10th of June, 1528."
Conradus Goclenius, a Westphalian, was commended by Erasmus unto Sir Thomas More, thus:" I praise your disposition, my dearest More, exceedingly, for that your content is to be rich in faithful and sincere friends, and that you esteem the greatest felicity of this life to be placed therein. Some take great care that they may not be cozened with counterfeit jewels; but you contemning all such trifles, seem to yourself to be rich enough, if you can but get an unfeigned friend. For there is no man taketh delight, either in cards, dice, chess, hunting, or music, so much as you do in discoursing with a

learned and pleasant-conceited companion. And although you are stored with this kind of riches, yet because that I know that a covetous man hath never enough, and that this manner of my dealing hath luckily happened both to you and me divers times heretofore, I deliver to your custody one friend more, whom I would have you accept with your whole heart. His name is Conradus Goclenius, a Westphalian, who hath with great applause and no less fruit, lately taught rhetoric in the college newly erected at Louvaine, called Trilingue. Now, I hope, that as soon as you shall have true experience of him, I shall have thanks of you both; for so I had of Cranvilde, who so wholly possesseth your love, that I almost envy him for it."

But of all strangers Erasmus challenged unto himself his love most especially, which had long continued by mutual letters expressing great affection; and increased so much that he took a journey of purpose into England to see and enjoy his personal acquaintance and more entire familiarity; at which time it is reported how that he, who conducted him in his passage, procured that Sir Thomas More and he should first meet together in London at the Lord Mayor's table, neither of them knowing each other. And in the dinner time, they chanced to fall into argument, Erasmus still endeavouring to defend the worser part; but he was so sharply set upon and opposed by Sir Thomas More, that perceiving that he was now to argue with a readier wit than ever he had before met withal, he broke forth into these words, not without some choler, "Aut tu es Morus aut nullus." Whereto Sir Thomas readily replied, "Aut tu es Erasmus aut diabolus," because at that time he was strangely disguised, and had sought to defend impious positions; for although he was a singular humanist, and one that could utter his mind in a most eloquent phrase, yet had he always a delight to scoff at religious matters, and find fault with all sorts of clergymen. He took a felicity to set out sundry commentaries upon the fathers' works, censuring them at his pleasure, for which cause he is termed "Errans-mus," because he wandereth here and there in other men's harvests; yea, in his writings he is said to have hatched many of those eggs of heresy which the apostate Friar Luther had before laid; not that he is to be accounted an heretic, for he would never be obstinate in any of his opinions, yet would he irreligiously glance at all antiquity, and find many faults with the present state of the church. Whilst he was in England, Sir Thomas More used him most courteously, doing many offices of a dear friend for him, as well by his word as his purse;

whereby he bound Erasmus so straitly unto him, that he ever after spoke and wrote upon all occasions most highly in his praise; but Sir Thomas, in success of time, grew less affectionate unto him, by reason he saw him still fraught with much vanity and unconstancy in respect of religion; as when Tindall objecteth unto Sir Thomas, that his darling Erasmus had translated the word " church" into " congregation," and " priest" into " elder," even as himself had done, Sir Thomas answered thereto, " if my darling Erasmus hath translated those places with the like wicked intent that Tindall hath done, he shall be no more my darling."* Finally, long after having found in Erasmus's works many things necessarily to be amended, he counselled him, as his friend, in some latter book, to imitate the example of Saint Augustine, who did set out a book of retractations, to correct in his writing what he had unadvisedly written in the heat of youth; but he that was far different from Saint Augustine in humility, would never follow his counsel, and therefore he is censured by the church for a busy fellow: many of his books are condemned, and his opinions accounted erroneous, though he always lived a Catholic priest, and hath written most

* The printed copies add, " but the devil's darling."

sharply against all those new gospellers, who then began to appear in the world; and in a letter to John Fabius, Bishop of Vienna, he saith that he hateth these seditious opinions, with the which the world was miserably shaken; neither doth he dissemble, saith he, being so addicted to piety, that if he incline to any part of the balance, he will bend rather to superstition than to impiety; by which speech he seemeth, in doubtful words, to tax the church with superstition, and the new apostolical brethren with impiety.

Now, to conclude this matter of Sir Thomas More's friends, let us hear what Erasmus speaketh of him, in an epistle to Ulderick Hutten: "More seemeth to be made and born for friendship, whereof he is a most sincere follower, and a fast keeper; neither doth he fear to be taxed for that he hath many friends, which thing Hesiodus praiseth nothing: every man may attain to his friendship; he is nothing slow in chusing, most apt in nourishing, and most constant in keeping them; if by chance he falls into one's amity whose vices he cannot amend, he slackeneth the reins of friendship, disjointing it by little and little, rather than dissolving it suddenly. Whom he findeth sincere and constant, agreeing with his own good disposition, he is so delighted with their company and familiarity, that he seemeth to place his chief worldly pleasure in such men's conversation; and although he be very negligent in his own temporal affairs, yet none is more diligent than he in furthering his friends' causes. What need I speak many words? If any were desirous to have a perfect pattern of friendship, none can make it better than More. In his company there is such rare affability, and such sweet behaviour, that no man is of so harsh a nature but that his talk is able to make him merry, no matter so unpleasing, but he with his wit can shake from it all tediousness;" declaring plainly in these words, the most pleasant disposition of Sir Thomas More, whose only merry jests and witty sayings were able to fill a whole volume, if they were all gathered together; some of which Doctor Stapleton hath set down in two several chapters, whereof I shall also mention some hereafter; but the greatest number have never been set down in writing, as daily falling from him in his familiar discourse. All which shew plainly, that he had a quiet conscience, full of alacrity, and a witty conceit, able to please all men that resorted unto him. And who would not be glad of his company, who was by nature most affable, in his prince's favour very high, and stored with worldly blessings, as ample possessions, wealth enough and pomp of the world even to satiety.

He used, when he was in the city of London a justice of peace, to go to the sessions at Newgate, as other justices did; amongst whom it happened that one of the ancient justices of peace was wont to chide the poor men that had their purses cut, for not keeping them more warily, saying that their negligence was cause, that there were so many cutpurses brought thither, which, when Sir Thomas had heard him often speak, at one time especially, the night after he sent for one of the chief cutpurses that was in prison, and promised him that he would stand his good friend, if he would cut that justice's purse, whilst he sat the next day on the bench, and presently make a sign thereof unto him; the fellow gladly promiseth him to do it. The next day, therefore, when they sat again, that thief was called amongst the first, who, being accused of his fact, said that he would excuse himself sufficiently, if he were but permitted, in private, to speak to some one of the bench; he was bid therefore to chuse one whom he would; and he presently chose that grave old man, who then had his pouch at his girdle; and whilst he roundeth him in the ear, he cunningly cuts his purse, and, taking his leave solemnly, goeth down to his place. Sir Thomas knowing by a sign that it was dispatched, taketh presently an occasion to move all the bench to distribute some alms upon a poor needy fellow that was there, beginning himself to do it. When the old man came to open his purse, he sees it cut away, and wondering, said, that he had it when he came to sit there that morning. Sir Thomas replied, in a pleasant manner, " What! will you charge any of us with felony?" He beginning to be angry and ashamed of the matter, Sir Thomas' calls the cutpurse, and wills him to give him his purse again, counselling the good man hereafter not to be so bitter a censurer of innocent men's negligence, when as himself could not keep his purse safe in that open assembly. For these his witty jests, he may well be said to have been neither hateful to the nobility, nor unpleasing to the people. If we read his letters, they show great eloquence, a pure Latin phrase, and a religious mind; for always they express either humility in himself, zeal of God's honour, love to his neighbour, compassion of the afflicted, or a dear affection to his wife and children; so that it may be said, that he had, pectus vere candidum, a very sincere heart; and surely they breathe out matter either of wonderful devotion, or admirable wisdom.

CHAPTER VI.

ALTHOUGH he lived a courtier, and a lay married man, yet when he came home, he would, both in the morning and in the evening, before he went to bed, say in his chapel certain prayers, devoutly upon his knees, with his wife, children, and family, and because he was desirous sometimes to be solitary, and would sequester himself from the world, to recollect himself, and shake off the dust of earthly businesses, which otherwise would easily defile his soul, he built for himself a chapel, a library, and a gallery, called the New Buildings, a good distance from his main house, wherein, as his custom was upon other days, to busy himself in prayer and meditation, whensoever he was at leisure; so usually he would continue there on the Fridays, in memory of Christ's bitter passion, from morning until night, spending the whole day in devotion; so that he became an excellent man in the contemplative life; of all which let us hear what

Erasmus writeth: "More hath built near London, upon the Thames side, to wit, at Chelsey, late my Lord of Lincoln's,* a commodious house, neither mean, nor subject to envy yet magnificent enough; there he converseth affably with his family, his wife, his son, and daughter-in-law, his three daughters and their husbands, with eleven grandchildren. There is not any man living so loving to his children as he; and he loveth his old wife as well as if she were a young maid; and such is the excellency of his temper, that whatsoever happeneth that could not be helped, he loveth it as though nothing could happen more happily. You would say there were in that place Plato's academy; but I do the house injury in comparing it to Plato's academy, wherein there was only disputations of numbers and geometrical figures, and sometimes of moral virtues. I should rather call his house a school, or university of Christian religion; for there is none therein but readeth or studieth the liberal sciences; their special care is piety and virtue; there is no quarrelling, or intemperate words heard; none seen idle; which household discipline that worthy gentleman doth not govern by proud

---

* The printed copies read, "that which my Lord of Lincoln bought of Sir Robert Cecil."

and lofty words, but with all kind and courteous benevolence. Every body performeth his duty, yet is there always alacrity, neither is sober mirth any thing wanting." And again he writeth thus: " His first wife, which was but young, he caused to be instructed in learning, and to be taught all kind of music; she dying after she had brought forth four children, he married, as is aforesaid, a widow, not for lust, but to be a governess to his young family, who, although she were inclining to old age, and of a nature somewhat harsh, and besides very worldly, yet he persuaded her to play upon the lute, viol, and some other instruments, every day performing thereon her task; and so with the like gentleness he ordered his whole family." He suffered none of his servants either to be idle, or to give themselves to any games; but some of them he allotted to look to the garden, assigning to every one his sundry plot; some again he set to sing, some to play on the organs; he suffered none to give themselves to cards or dice. The men abode on the one side of the house, the women on the other, seldom conversing together; he used before bed-time to call them together, and say certain prayers with them, as the " Miserere" psalm, " Ad te, Domine, levavi;" " Deus misereatur nostri;" " Salve Regina;" and " De profundis" for the dead, and some others. He suffered none to be absent from mass on the Sundays, or upon great feasts or holidays. He watched much in the night all the matins time. Upon Good Friday he would call them together in the New Buildings, and read the holy passion unto them; he would now and then interpose some speeches of his own to move them either to compassion, compunction, or such pious affections. Erasmus saith, " That there was a fatal felicity fallen on the servants of that house, that none lived in better estate. After Sir Thomas More's death, none ever was touched with the least aspersion of any evil fame."*

* To the description given by Erasmus of the house of Sir Thomas More at Chelsey, of whose hospitalities he had often partaken, more correctly and more beautifully than is seen in the bald translation of our author, I shall annex another, which appears to have been overlooked by all who have written on the life and manners of More. It occurs in the " Il Moro" of Ellis Heywood, printed at Florence in 1556, and dedicated to Cardinal Pole. I give it from a translation of this rare volume, made by a female pen. " Along the beautiful banks of the Thames there are many delightful villas and chateaus situated in charming spots, in one of which, very near the city of London, dwelt Sir Thomas More. It was a beautiful and commodious residence, and to this place it was his usual practice to retire, when weary of London. At this house, as well on account of its proximity to London, as on account of the admirable character of its owner, men distinguished by their genius and learning, who dwelt in the city, were often accus-

> He used to have one read daily at his table, which, being ended, he would ask of some of them

tomed to meet; where, when alone and at leisure, they would enter into some useful argument or discourse on things pertaining to human nature; and each using in the best manner his intellect and extensive knowledge, their arguments were attended with great profit to each other. And although, when I call to memory so choice a company as this was, I feel inclined to write concerning them, in order to present before the world a true picture of a real and genuine academy; nevertheless, leaving that unto those who, being members of it, have a more perfect knowledge of the subject, I have now only undertaken to give a single discourse." Heywood's work is a dialogue, supposed to take place at Sir Thomas More's; not, as Wood says, in consolation with him, but on the sources of happiness. The six gentlemen, amongst whom the dialogue passes, having dined one day with Sir Thomas More, " retired after dinner into a garden, distant about two stone-throws from the house, and all went together to stand upon a small green eminence, and gaze on the prospect. The place was wonderfully charming, both from the advantages of its site, for from one part almost the whole of the noble city of London was visible; and from another, the beautiful Thames, with green meadows and woody eminences all around: and also for its own beauty, for as it was crowned with an almost perpetual verdure, it had flowering shrubs, and the branches of fruit trees which grew near, interwoven in so beautiful a manner, that it appeared like a living tapestry woven by Nature herself, and much more noble than any other work, inasmuch as it gave entire satisfaction, whereas the copies of beautiful objects leave the mind rather in desire than content." Sir Thomas More's house was situated at the north end of Beau-

how they understood such and such a place, and so there grew a friendly communication, recreating all men that were present with some jest or other. My aunt Roper writing hereof to her father in the Tower saith: "What do you think, my most dear father, doth comfort us at Chelsey in this your absence? surely the remembrance of your manner of life passed amongst us, your holy conversation, your wholesome counsels, your examples of virtue, of which

---

fort Row, in Chelsey, extending westward at the distance of about a hundred yards from the Thames. After More's death it had a succession of illustrious possessors. By Henry it was granted to Sir William Pawlet, afterwards Marquis of Winchester, and lord high treasurer. From his family it successively passed into the hands of Lord Dacre, the great Lord Burghley, the Earl of Salisbury his son, the Earl of Lincoln, Sir Arthur Gorges, the Earl of Middlesex, lord treasurer, Villiers Duke of Buckingham, Sir Bulstrode Whitlock, the second Villiers Duke of Buckingham, the Earl of Bristol, the Duke of Beaufort, and, finally, of Sir Hans Sloane, in 1738, who pulled it down two years afterwards. Lysons' "Environs of London," vol. ii. p. 80. The house of an illustrious man should be regarded with the same feeling as his tomb, and pity it is that the destruction of this mansion, which had been the "domicilium musarum et omnium virtutum et charitatum," and where had been so often the "felix contubernium" of the men who cherished in its growth the then young and thriving plant of western literature should rest on such a name as Sloane.

there is hope that they do not only persevere with you, but that they are by God's grace much more increased."

His children used often to translate out of English into Latin, and out of Latin into English: and Doctor Stapleton testifieth that he hath seen an Apology of Sir Thomas More's to the university of Oxford in defence of learning, turned into Latin by one of his daughters, and translated again into English by another. And to stir up his wife and children to the desire of heavenly things, he would sometimes use these and the like words unto them: "It is now no mastery for you, my joys, to get heaven; for every body giveth you good example, every one storeth your heads with good counsels; you see also virtue rewarded, and vice punished; so that you are carried up thither by the chins; but if you chance to live that time, wherein none will give you good example, nor none any good counsel; when you shall see before your eyes virtue punished and vice rewarded, if then you will stand fast, and stick to God closely, upon pain of my life, though you be but half good, God will allow you for whole good." If his wife or any of his children chanced to be sick or troubled, he would say unto them: "we must not look to go to heaven at our pleasure and on feather beds; that is not the way, for our Lord himself went thither with great pain; and the servant must not look to be in better case than his master." As he would in this sort animate them to bear their troubles patiently, so would he in like manner teach them to withstand the devil and his temptations valiantly, comparing our ghostly enemy to an ape, which if he be not looked unto, he will be busy and bold to do shrewd turns; but if he be espied and checked for them, he will suddenly leap back and adventure no further; so the devil finding a man idle, sluggish, and using no resistance to his suggestions, waxeth hardy, and will not fail still to continue them, until he hath thoroughly brought us to his purpose; but if he find a man with diligence still seeking to withstand and prevent his temptations he waxeth weary, and at last he utterly forsaketh him, being a spirit of so high a pride, that he cannot endure to be mocked; and again so envious that he feareth still least he not only thereby should catch a foul fall, but also minister unto us more matter of merit. When he saw any of his take great pains in dressing themselves to be fine either in wearing that which was uneasy, or in stroking up their hair to make themselves high foreheads, he would tell them that if God gave them not hell, he should do them great injury; for they took more pains to please the world and the devil, than many even virtuous men did to cleanse their souls and please God.

Many such speeches tending to devotion and care of their souls had he every day at dinner and supper, after the reading was done, as is before said, with such heavenly discourses flowing with eloquence, that it might well be said of him, which the Queen of Sheba said of Solomon: " Blessed art thou; and blessed be thy Lord God; and blessed are all they that attend and wait on thee:" for no doubt there was the spirit of God in that family, where every one was busied about somewhat or other; no cards, no dice, no company keeping of the men with the women; but as it were in some religious house, all chaste, all courteous, all devout; their recreation was either music of voices or viols; for which cause he procured his wife, as I have said, to play thereon, to draw her mind from the world to which by her nature she was too much addicted; but so, as Sir Thomas would say of her, that she was often penny-wise and pound-foolish, saving a candle's end, and spoiling a velvet gown. Of her also he meant it, when in his book of Comfort in Tribulation he telleth of one, who would rate her husband because he had no mind to set himself forward in the world, saying unto him: " Tillie vallie, tillie vallie: will you sit and make goslings in the ashes; my mother hath often said unto me, it is better to rule than to be ruled." "Now in truth," answered Sir Thomas, "that is truly said, good wife; for I never found you yet willing to be ruled." And in another place of the same book he calleth this wife of his, a jolly master-woman.

For all his public affairs and household exercises, he never left off to write learned books either of devotion or against heresies, which now began to spread themselves from Germany into Flanders, and from thence into England by many pestiferous pamphlets and books, against which Sir Thomas More laboured with his pen more than any other Englishman whatsoever, in regard of his zeal to God, and the honour of his immaculate spouse the Catholic Church, as appeareth by his four books of Dialogues, a work full of learning and wit, where he argueth most profoundly of the invocation of saints, pilgrimages, relics, and images; he teacheth also substantially, how we may know, which is the true church, and that that church cannot err.

After he had ended this book, there was a lewd fellow set out a pamphlet intituled the Supplication of Beggars; by which under pretence of helping the poor, he goeth about to cast out the clergy and to overthrow all abbies and religious houses, bearing men in hand, that after that the Gospel should be preached, beggars should decrease, thieves and idle people be the fewer, &c. Against whom Sir Thomas wrote a singular book, which he named, A Supplication of the Souls in Purgatory, making them there complain of the most uncharitable dealing of certain upstarts, who would persuade all men to take from them the spiritual alms that have been in all ages bestowed upon these poor souls, who feel greater misery than any beggar in this world; and he proveth most truly, that an ocean of many mischievous events would indeed overwhelm the realm: " Then," saith he, " shall Luther's gospel come in; then shall Tindal's testament be taken up; then shall false heresies be preached; then shall the sacraments be set at naught; then shall fasting and prayer be neglected; then shall holy saints be blasphemed; then shall Almighty God be displeased, then shall he withdraw his grace, and let all run to ruin; then shall all virtue be had in derision, then shall all vice reign and run forth unbridled; then shall youth leave labour and all occupation; then shall folks wax idle and fall to unthriftiness; then shall thieves and beggars increase; then shall unthrifts flock together, and each bear him bold of other; then shall all laws be laughed to scorn; then shall servants set naught by their masters, and unruly people rebel against their governors; then will rise up rifling and robbery, mischief and plain insurrection; whereof what the end will be, or when you shall see it, only God knoweth." And that Luther's new gospel hath taken such effect in many parts of Christendom, the woful experience doth feelingly, to the great grief of all good folks, testify to the world: of all which, and that the land would be peopled to the devouring of one another, he writeth particularly, more like one that had seen what has ensued already, than like one who spoke of things to come.

He wrote also a laboursome book against Tindal refuting particularly every period of his books; a short treatise also against young Father Fryth, in defence of the real presence, which that heretic did gainsay, and for that was after burnt: against Fryer Barnes' Church he wrote also an Apology, and a Defence thereof, under the name of Salem and Byzance; which are all set forth together with that most excellent piece of work, comprised in three books, of Comfort in Tribulation; which subject he handleth so wittily as none hath come near him either in weight of grave sentences, devout considerations, or fit similitudes; seasoning always the troublesomeness of the matter with some merry jests or pleasant tales, as it were sugar, whereby we drink up the more willingly these wholesome drugs, of themselves unsavory to flesh and blood; which kind of writing he hath used in all his works, so that none can ever be weary to read them, though they be never so long.

Wherefore I have thought it not amiss to set down in this place amongst a thousand others, some of the apophthegms, which Doctor Stapleton hath collected in two whole chapters:

Do not think, saith Sir Thomas More, that to be always pleasant, which mad men do laughing; for one may often see a man in Bedlam laugh when he knocks his head against the wall: uttering this to condemn them that esteem all things good or bad, which the common people judge to be.

Again; A sinner, saith he, cannot taste spiritual delights; because all carnal are first to be abandoned.

By an excellent similitude he teacheth us why few do fear death, thus: Even as they which look upon things afar off, see them confusedly, not knowing whether they be men or trees; even so he that promiseth unto himself long life, looketh upon death as a thing afar off, not judging what it is, how terrible, what griefs and dangers it bringeth with it. And that none ought to promise himself long life he proveth thus: Even as two men that are brought out of prison to the gallows, one by a long way about, the other by a direct short path, yet neither knowing which is which until they come to the gallows, neither of these two can promise himself longer life, the one than the other, by reason of the uncertainty of the way; even so a young man cannot promise himself longer life than an old man. Whereby he supposeth that every man that is born is condemned to die for his original sin: the old man hath a direct path; the young man about.*

Against the vanity of worldly honour he speaketh thus: Even as that criminal person, who is to be led to execution shortly should be accounted vain, if he should engrave his coat of arms upon the prison gate; even so are they vain, who endeavour to leave, with great industry, monuments of their dignity in the prison of this world.

By a subtile dilemma he teacheth us, why we are not to think that we can be hurt, by the loss of our superfluous goods, in this manner: he that suffereth any loss of his goods, he would either have bestowed them with praise and liberality, and so God will accept his will instead of the deed itself, or else he would have wasted

---

* This clause from "Whereby he supposeth," &c. is omitted in the printed copies.

them wickedly, and then he hath cause to rejoice, that the matter of sinning is taken away.

To express lively the folly of an old covetous man he writeth thus: A thief that is to die to-morrow stealeth to-day, and being asked, why he did so? he answered, that it was a great pleasure unto him to be master of that money but one night; so an old miser never ceaseth to increase his heap of coin, though he be never so aged.

To express the folly and madness of them that delight wholly in hoarding up wealth, he writeth in the person of the souls in purgatory thus; in his book of the Supplication of the Souls: We that are here in purgatory when we think of our bags of gold, which we hoarded up in our life time, we condemn and laugh at our own folly no otherwise than if a man of good years should find by chance the bag of cherry-stones which he had carefully hid when he was a child.

In his book of Comfort in Tribulation, that men should not be troubled in adversity, he writeth thus: The minds of mortal men are so blind and uncertain, so mutable and unconstant in their desires, that God could not punish men worse, than if he should suffer every thing to happen that every man doth wish for. The

I

fruit of tribulation he describeth thus: All punishment inflicted in hell, is only as a just revenge because it is no place of purging: in purgatory all punishments purge only, because it is no place of merit; but in this life every punishment can both purge sin and procure merit for a just man, because in this life there is place for both.

He saith also, that they which give themselves to pleasure and idleness in this time of pilgrimage, are like to him, who travelling to his own house where there is abundance of all things, would yet be an hostler in an inn by the way, for to get an innkeeper's favour, and so end his life there in a stable.

Speaking of ghostly fathers that seek to please their penitents, he saith: Even as a mother sendeth forth her child to school with fair words and promises that hath slept too long in the morning, and therefore feareth the rod; when he weepeth and blubbereth, she promiseth him all will be well, because it is not so late as he imagineth, or that his master will pardon him for that fault this time, not caring what he endureth when he cometh thither indeed, so she send him merry from home with his bread and butter in his hand: even so many pastors of souls speak pleasing things to their sheep that are rich and delicate, they promise them, when they are dying and fear hell, that all things shall be well with them, telling them, that either they have not offended God so grievously as they fear, or that God being merciful will easily forgive them; nothing careful whether after this life they feel hell or no, so that they make them not sad in this world, and shew themselves grateful unto them here.

Pleasure, saith he, doth not only withdraw wicked men from prayer, but also affliction sometimes; yet this is the difference; that affliction doth sometimes wrest some short prayer from the wickedest man alive; but pleasure calleth away even one that is indifferent good from all prayer.

Against impenitent persons and such as defer the amending of their life till the latter end of their days, he saith thus: A lewd fellow that had spent all his life in wickedness, was wont to brag, that he could be saved, if he spoke but three words at the hour of his death; riding over a bridge that was broken, his horse stumbling, and not being able to keep himself from tumbling into the water, as he saw himself fall headlong into it, casting away the bridle, he said: the devil take all; and so with his three words he perished in the river.

He that is lightened with a true vision, differeth from him that hath an illusion; even as a man awake differeth from him that dreameth.

Even as he that passeth over a narrow bridge by reason of his fear often falleth, especially if others say unto him, you fall; which otherwise he would safely pass over: even so he that is fearful by nature and full of pusillanimity often falleth into desperation, the devil crying unto him, thou art damned, thou art damned; which he would never hearken to nor be in any danger, if he should take unto him a good heart, and by wholesome counsel fear nothing the devil's outcry.

The prosperity of this world is like the shortest winter's day; and we are lifted up in it as an arrow shot up on high, where a hot breath doth delight us, but from thence we fall suddenly to the earth, and there we stick fast, either bemired with the dirt of infamy, or starving with cold, being pluckt out of our feathers.

Again he saith: As it is a hard thing to touch pitch and not to be defiled therewith; a dry stick to be put into the fire and not to burn; to nourish a snake in our bosom and not to be stung with it; so a most hard thing it is to be rich and honoured in this world and not to be struck with the dart of pride and vain glory.

Let there be two beggars, saith he, who have

long timed begged together; one of whom some rich man hath entertained in his house, put him in silk, given him money in his purse, but with this condition as he tells him, that within a short space he will thrust him out of his doors and take all that away from him again: if he in the meanwhile, being thus gallant, should chance to meet with his fellow-beggar, would he be so foolish as for all this not to acknowledge him for his companion? or would he for these few days' happiness hold himself better than he? Applying this to every man's case, who cometh naked into this world, and is to return naked again.

He compareth covetousness to a fire, which by how much the more wood there is laid on it to burn, so much apter is it to burn more still.

That there are many in this life, that buy hell with more toil than heaven might be won with, by half.

He foresaw heresy in England, as appeareth by this witty comparison: Like as before a great storm the sea swelleth, and hath unwonted motions without any wind stirring; so may we see here many of our Englishmen, which a few years ago could not endure to hear the name of an heretic, schismatic, Lutheran, or sacramentary, now to be very well contented both to suffer them and to praise them somewhat, yea, to learn by little and little as much as they can be suffered, to find fault, and to tax willingly the church, the clergy, the ceremonies, yea, and sacraments too.

Also he hath this argument: If he be called stout that hath fortitude, he hot who hath heat, wise that hath wisdom; yet he who hath riches cannot be said presently to be good; therefore riches cannot be numbered amongst good things. Twenty, yea a hundred bare heads standing by a noble man do not defend his head from cold so much as his own hat doth alone, which yet he is enforced to put off in the presence of his prince.

That is the worst affection of the mind which doth delight us in that thing, which cannot be gotten but by offending God. He that doth get or keep worldly wealth by offending God, let him fully persuade himself, that those things will never do him good; for either God will quickly take away evil gotten goods, or will suffer them to be kept for a greater mischief.

Even as he that knoweth certainly that he is to be banished into a strange country, never to return into his own again, and will not endure that his goods be transported thither, being loth to want them for that little while rather than ever to enjoy them after, may well be thought a mad man; so are they out of their wits, who enticed with vain affections to keep their goods always about them, and neglective to give alms for fear of wanting, cannot endure to have these goods sent before them to heaven, when as they know most assuredly that they shall enjoy them always there with all plenty, and with a double reward.

To ease his thoughts when he was in prison, he imagined that all the world was but a prison, out of which every day some one or other was called to execution, that is to death.

In his daily talk he used also many witty sayings, as: That it is an easy matter in some cases for a man to lose his head, and yet to have no harm at all.

Good deeds, the world being ungrateful is wont never to recompense, neither can it, though it were grateful.

Speaking of heretics, he would say: they have taken away hypocrisy but they have placed impudence in the room thereof; so that they which before feigned themselves to be religious, now do boast of their wickedness.

He prayed thus: O Lord God, grant, that I endeavour to get those things, for which I am to pray unto thee.

When he had any at his table speaking detraction, he would interrupt them, thus: Let any man think as he pleaseth, I like this room very well, for it is well contrived and fairly built.

Of an ungrateful person he would say, that they wrote good turns done unto them in the dust; but even the least injuries in marble.

He compareth reason to a handmaid, which if she be well taught, will obey; and faith to the mistress which is to keep her in awe: " captivans intellectum in obsequium fidei."

To seek for the truth amongst heretics, is like to a man wandering in a desert, and meeting with a company of lewd fellows, of whom he asketh his way, they all turning back to back, each pointeth right before him, and assureth him that that is his true way; though never so contrary one to the other.

He saith, that he were a mad man that would drink poison to take a preservative after that; but he is a wise man, that spilling the poison, leaveth the antidote for him that hath need thereof.

As it is an easier thing to weave a new net rather than to sew up all the holes of an old; even so it is a less labour to translate the Bible anew than to mend heretical versions.

He is not wise that eateth the bread which is poisoned by his enemies, although he should see a friend of his scrape it away never so much, especially having other bread to eat not poisoned.

He was wont to say, that he may well be admitted to heaven who was very desirous to see God; but on the contrary side, he that doth not desire earnestly shall never be admitted thither.

Against an heretic he speaketh thus: that if monastical life be against the Gospel, as you seem to say it must needs be, that the Gospel be contrary unto it; and that were to say, that Christ taught us to pamper ourselves carefully, to eat well, to drink well, to sleep well, and flow in all lust and pleasure.

If faith cannot be without good works, why then babble you so much against good works, which are the fruits of faith.

That people should fall into bad life and lust, is as great a miracle, he saith, as stones to fall downwards.

Whereas, he saith, you inveigh against school divinity, because truth is there called in doubt, not without danger; we inveigh against you, because false matters are held by you undoubtedly for truth itself.

These good fellows (speaking of heretics) will rather hang out of God's vineyard, than suffer themselves to be hired into it.

Heretics' writings, seeing they conclude no good thing are altogether tedious, be they never so short.

And again: As none can run a shorter race than he that wants both his feet; so none can write shorter than he that hath not any good matter nor fit words to express it.

When an heretic told him, that he should not write against heretics unless he could convert them; he said, that it was like as if one should not find fault with burners of houses, unless he were able to build them up again at his own charge.

He telleth, that heretics use to frame catholics' arguments very weak and frivolous, that they may the more easily confute them; even as little children make houses of tyle-shardes, which they cast down with great sport again presently.

Of their contumelious speeches against himself, he saith, I am not so void of reason, that I can expect reasonable matter from such unreasonable men.

When they said his writings were nothing but jesting toys, he saith: I scarce believe that these good brethren can find any pleasant things in my books; for I write nothing in them that may be pleasing unto them. When the heretic

Constantine had broken prison in his house,* he bad his man go lock the door fast and see the place mended sure, lest he should come back again; and when the heretics reported, that he was so sorry for this, that he could not for anger eat in three days, he answered that he was not so harsh of disposition to find fault with any man for rising and walking when he sate not at his ease.

* Here is an indirect but positive testimony to what has been charged upon More, that he sometimes converted his house into a prison for the restraint of those whom he called heretics. Of Barnham, another Reformer, Fox relates, that " he was carried out of the Middle Temple to the chancellor's house at Chelsey, where he continued in free prison awhile, till the time that Sir Thomas More saw that he could not prevail in perverting of him to his sect. Then he cast him into prison in his own house, and whipped him at the tree in his garden called the Tree of Troth, and after sent him to the Tower to be racked." Mart. vol. ii. p. 279.

In More's defence of himself in respect of his treatment of the Reformers, he admits the imprisonment, but denies the ill-treatment of them, except in two cases, not ill-defended. That defence ought to be read by all who speak of More. See it in Cayley's Memoirs of him, p. 137. He distinctly denies the story of the " Tree of Troth." " The lies are neither few nor small which many of the blessed brethren have made, and daily yet make by me. Divers of them have said, that of such as were in my house while I was chancellor, I used to examine them with torments, causing them to be bounden to a tree in my garden, and there piteously beaten," &c.

All his English works were set out together in a great volume, whilst Queen Mary reigned, by Judge Rastall, Sir Thomas' sister's son, by which works one may see that he was very skilful in school divinity and matters of controversy, for he argueth sharply, he confirmeth the truth profoundly, and citeth both Scriptures and fathers most aptly; besides he urgeth for the adverse part more a great deal than any heretic ever did that wrote before him.

But to see how he handleth Luther, under the name of one Rosse, would do any man good, feigning that Rosse wrote his book from Rome, against the most ridiculous and scurrilous pamphlet which Luther had made against King Henry the Eighth, who of good zeal had set out with great praise a book in defence of the seven sacraments and the pope's authority, for which Pope Leo the Tenth gave him the title of Defender of the Faith. Wherefore in defence of his sovereign, whom Luther had most basely railed at, calling him often Thomistical ass, and that he would bewray the king's crown,* with many other scurrilous speeches; Sir Thomas painteth out the foul-mouthed fellow in his lively colours, and made him so enraged, that it stung

* Here the printed copy adds, " who was not worthy to wipe his shoes."

him more than any other book that ever was set out against him.

Finally, in every one of his books, whensoever he toucheth any controversy, he doth it so exactly that one may see, that he had diligently read many great divines; and that he was well seen in S. Thomas the father of all divinity, this may be an evident sign, which his secretary John Harris, a man of sound judgment and great piety, reported of him, that on a time an heretical book, newly printed and spread abroad, was brought to Sir Thomas, which when he read, being in his boat, going from Chelsey to London, he shewed certain of the author's arguments with his finger to Mr. Harris saying: Lo here how the knave's argument is taken out of the objections of S. Thomas in 2. 2. in such and such an article; but the lewd fellow might have seen the solutions, which are presently added there. He maintained also in a learned disputation with Father Alphonsus the Franciscan, Queen Catherine's ghostly father, Scotus' opinion of attrition and contrition as more safely to be followed than that of Occham; by all which it may be gathered, that he had great insight in the diversity of scholastical opinions.

He wrote also a book in Latin against Pomeran the heretic, and indeed laboured very much rather to reduce such men unto the catholic faith than to punish them for their revolt: wherefore in his epitaph he sayeth of himself, that he was to thieves, murderers and heretics grievous; yet Simon Grineus, a Lutheran, boasteth in his translation of Proclus dedicated to my grandfather, how courteously Sir Thomas his father used him when he was in England.

CHAPTER VII.

WHILE Sir Thomas More was chancellor of the duchy, the see of Rome chanced to be vacant; and Cardinal Wolsey, a man of unsatiable ambition, who had crept up in the favour of Charles the Fifth, so that the emperor, still writing unto him, called him father, and the other called him son, hoped now, by his means, to attain to the popedom; but perceiving himself of that expectation frustrate and disappointed, because the emperor, in the time of their election, had highly commended another to the whole college of the cardinals, called Adrian, who was a Fleming, and had been sometime his schoolmaster, a man of rare learning and singular virtue; who thereupon, although absent and little dreaming of it, was chosen pope; and then forthwith going from Spain, where he was then resident, came on foot to Rome. Before he entered into the city, putting off his hose and shoes, bare-foot and bare-legged he passed through the streets towards his palace, with such humility and devotion, that all the people, not without cause, had him in great reverence and admiration; but, as I said, Cardinal Wolsey, a man of contrary qualities, waxed therewith so wroth, and stomached so the emperor for it ever after, that he studied still how he might revenge himself any ways against him; which, as it was the beginning of a lamentable tragedy, so the end thereof we cannot yet see, although there have been almost one hundred years sithence. This Wolsey, therefore, not ignorant of King Henry's unconstant and mutable disposition, inclined to withdraw his affections upon every light occasion from his own most noble, virtuous, and lawful wife, Queen Catherine, the emperor's own aunt, and to fix his amorous passions upon other women, nothing comparable unto her either in birth, wisdom, virtue, favour, or external beauty; this irreligious prelate meaning to make the king's lightness an instrument to bring about his unconscionable intent, endeavoured, by all the means he could, to allure the king to cast his fancy upon one of the French king's sisters; the king being fallen in love already, he not suspecting any such thing, with the lady Anne Bullen, a woman of no nobility, no nor so much as of any worthy fame.

This French match he thought to plot to spite the emperor, because at that time there was great wars and mortal enmity between the French King and Charles the Fifth. For the better compassing whereof, the cardinal requested Longland, Bishop of London, who was the king's ghostly father, to put a scruple into King Henry's head, that he should, as it were another Saint John the Baptist, (though the case were nothing like,) tell his majesty that it was not lawful for him, like another Herod, to marry his brother's wife.

And although King Henry's conscience had been quiet now above twenty years together, yet was he not unwilling to hearken thereunto; but entertaining it, opened his scruples to Sir Thomas More, whose counsel he required herein, showing him certain places of Scripture, that somewhat seemed to serve the turn and his appetite; which when Sir Thomas had seriously perused, and had excused himself, saying, he was unfit to meddle with such matters, being one that never had professed the study of divinity: the king, not satisfied with this answer, knowing well his judgment to be sound in whatsoever he would apply himself unto, pressed him so sore, that in conclusion he condescended to his majesty's request, being as it were a command; and for that the cause was of such weight and importance, having need of great deliberation, he besought his majesty to give him sufficient respite advisedly to consider of it; with which the king, very well satisfied, said that Tunstall and Clarke, two worthy bishops, one of Durham the other of Bath, with others the learnedest of his privy council, should be his coadjutors therein.

Sir Thomas taking his leave of the king, went and conferred with them about those places of Scripture, adding thereto, for their better means to search out the truth, the expositions of the ancient fathers, and doctors of the church; and at his next coming to the court, talking with the king about this matter, he spake thus; " To deal sincerely with your majesty, neither my Lord of Durham, nor my Lord of Bath, though I know them both wise, virtuous, learned, and honourable prelates, nor myself with the rest of your council, being all your grace's own servants and subjects, for your manifold benefits daily bestowed upon us so much bound unto your highness; none of us, I say, nor we all together are in my judgment meet counsellors for your majesty herein; but if your princely disposition purpose to understand the very truth hereof, you may have such counsellors, as neither for respect of their own worldly commodity, nor fear of your princely authority, will be inclined to deceive you;" and then he named Saint Hierome and Saint Austin, and divers others, both Greek and Latin fathers; showing him moreover, what authorities he had gathered out of them, that he need not have any further scruple thereof, and that marrying of a new wife, whilst his own was alive, was wholly repugnant to their doctrine, and the meaning of the Scriptures. All which, though King Henry did not very well like of, because it was disgustful to his passionate lust, yet the manner of Sir Thomas's discourse and collection was so wisely tempered by his discreet communication, that he took them at that present in good part, and often had conference of them again.

By which manner of Sir Thomas's counsel and sincere carriage, one may easily gather what unspotted conscience this upright man had, who for no hope of gain, or any fear of disgrace, would once swerve from the true dictamen of his conscience; and if the rest of King Henry's council had been as backward to hinder this beginning of dissolution as Sir Thomas was, no alteration of religion had, by all likelihood, happened in England; for from this only spring of King Henry's intemperance proceeded all the succeeding calamities, which have daily increased, and yet have not any hope of amendment.

All which change Sir Thomas More either like a very wise man foresaw long before, or rather like a prophet prophesied thereof to my uncle Roper, who on a time out of a certain joy began to commend to his father-in-law the happy estate of this realm, that had so Catholic and zealous a prince, that no heretic durst show his face; so learned and virtuous a clergy, so grave and sound a nobility, such loving and obedient subjects, all agreeing together in one faith and dutifulness, as though they had, " cor unum et animam unam," but one heart and one soul; Sir Thomas thus replied again : " Truth it is indeed, son Roper, as you say," and going through all estates with his commendations of them, he went far beyond my uncle; " and yet son," quoth he, " I pray God that some of us, as high as we seem to sit now upon the mountains, treading heretics under our feet like ants, do not live to see the day that we gladly would wish to be at league with them, to suffer them to have their churches quietly to themselves, so that they would be content to let us have ours peaceably to ourselves." When mine uncle Roper had told him many reasons why he had no cause to say so, " Well," said he, " I pray God some of us live not till that day;" and yet showed he no reason for all these his speeches, whereat my uncle said in a rage, " By my troth, sir, it is very desperately spoken; I cry God mercy," said my uncle, (he used unto him that very word,)* by which speech Sir Thomas, perceiving him to be somewhat angry, said, merrily, "Well, son Roper, it shall not be so; it shall not be so." But yet himself found the prediction too true; for he lived until the fifteenth year of Queen Elizabeth's reign, when he saw religion turned topsy turvy, and no hope of any amendment.

This spirit of prophecy, no doubt, was a sign of God's love unto Sir Thomas, being so dear in his sight, that he would make him partaker of some part of his secrets; but that which he wrought in the conversion of this his son-in-law, was not a sign only, but an evident demonstration of God's great favour unto him. For when Mr. William Roper was a young man, he used austerity to himself more than discretion afforded; and by this means grew weary of the Catholic fasts and religious discipline; and hearing of a new and easy way to heaven, which the preachers of novelties did promise to their

---

* This passage is not clearly expressed, either in the MS. or in the printed copies. But in Roper's own work, from which More borrowed it, the passage stands thus: "To whom I said, 'By my troth, sir, it is very desperately spoken.' That vile term, 'I cry God mercy,' did I give him; who, by these words, perceiving me in a fume, said merrily unto me," &c.

followers, he began to read diligently the books of heresies, which came over, and were spread in every place of England; insomuch, that being weary of auricular confession, fasting the lent and vigils, he grew vehement in his new opinions, and zealous in breaking of them to others; so as that he would be always talking, what a ready way to heaven was now found out, nobody needing to sue either to saints' or other men's prayers; but God's ear was open still to hear, and his mercy ready to forgive any sinner whatsoever, when he shall call to him by faith, which was only necessary to salvation; and having that only, which he assured himself of, he needed not doubt but that he was an elect and saved soul, so that it was impossible for him to sin, or fall out of God's favour. Of this dangerous poison of security, he having drunk a full draught, he came on a time to Sir Thomas to request him, because he was highly in the king's favour, that he would get him a licence to preach what the spirit had taught him; for he was assured that God had sent him to instruct the world; not knowing (God wot) any reason of this his mission, but only his private spirit; to whom Sir Thomas, in a smiling manner, replied, " Is it not sufficient, son Roper, that we that are your friends should know that you are a fool, but that you would have your folly proclaimed to the world?" After this, he often disputed with him about matters of religion; yet never could he bring him to hearken to any reason, every day seeming more obstinate than other, until at length he said in sober sadness, " I see, son, no disputation will do thee good; henceforth therefore I will dispute with thee no more, only will I pray for thee, that God will be so favourable as to touch thy heart;" and so committing him to God, they parted. And he earnestly poured out his devotions before the divine mercy for that intent. And behold, my uncle, not long after, being inspired with the light of grace, began to detest his heresies; and as another Saint Austin, was wholly converted; so that ever after he was not only a perfect Catholic, but lived and died a stout and valiant champion thereof, whose alms in charitable uses were so great, that, it is said, that he bestowed every year, to the value of five hundred pounds, especially in his latter days, in which he enjoyed an office of great gain and commodity; and after his death I have heard it reported by them that were servants in his house, that whilst his body lay unburied for three or four days, there was heard once a day, for the space of a quarter of an hour, the sweetest music that could be imagined; not of any voices of men, but angelical harmony, as a token how gracious that soul was to Almighty God, and to the quires of angels.

Now this was a more special favour, which God granted to Sir Thomas's devout prayers, than the raising of a dead man to life, by how much more the death of the soul is of more danger than the death of the body; yet it is certain also, that this glorious man begged also corporal life for some of his dear friends. On a time his daughter Margaret, wife to this William Roper, fell sick of the sweating sickness, of which many died at that time; who, lying in so great extremity of the disease, that by no inventions nor devices that any cunning physician could use at that time, having continually about her the most learned, wise, and expert that could be gotten, she could by no means be kept from sleep; so that every one about her had just cause to despair of her recovery, giving her utterly over. Her father, as he that most loved her, being in no small heaviness, at last sought for remedy of this her desperate case from God. Wherefore going, as his custom was, into the new buildings, there in his chapel, upon his knees most devoutly, even with many tears, besought Almighty God, unto whom nothing was impossible, of his goodness, if it were his blessed will, that at his mediation he would vouchsafe gra-

ciously to hear this his humble petition; where presently came into his mind that a glister was the only way to help her; which when he told the physicians, they confessed that it was the best remedy indeed, much marvelling at themselves they had not remembered it, which was immediately ministered unto her sleeping, for else she would never have been brought to that kind of medicine. And although when she awaked thoroughly, God's marks (an evident and undoubted token of death) plainly appeared upon her, yet she, contrary to all expectation, was, as it were, miraculously, and by her father's fervent prayer, restored to perfect health again; whom if it had pleased God at that time to have taken to his mercy, her father solemnly protested that he would never have meddled with any worldly matters after; such was his fatherly love and vehement affection unto his jewell, who most nearly of all the rest of his children expressed her father's virtues, although the meanest of all the rest might have been matched with any other of their age in England, either for learning, excellent qualities, or piety, they having been brought up, even from their infancy with such care and industry, and enjoying always most virtuous and learned masters.

So that the school of Sir Thomas More's children was famous over the whole world; for that their wits were rare, their diligence extraordinary, and their masters most excellent men, as above the rest Doctor Clement, an excellent Grecian and physician, who was after reader of the physic-lecture in Oxford, and set out many books of learning. After him one William Gunnell, who read after with great praise in Cambridge; and besides these, one Drue, one Nicholas, and after all one Richard Hart, of whose rare learning and industry in this behalf, let us see what may be gathered out of Sir Thomas's letters unto them, and first to Mr. Gunnell thus:

"I have received, my dear Gunnell, your letters, such as they are wont to be, most elegant and full of affection. Your love towards my children I gather by your letter; their diligence by their own; for every one of their letters pleaseth me very much, yet most especially I take joy to hear that my daughter Elizabeth hath showed as great modesty in her mother's absence, as any one could do, if she had been in presence; let her know that that thing liked me better than all the epistles besides; for as I esteem learning which is joined with virtue more than all the treasures of kings; so what doth the fame of being a great scholar bring us, if it be severed from virtue other than a notorious and famous infamy, especially in a woman, whom men will be ready the more willingly to assail for their learning, because it is a hard matter, and argueth a reproach to the sluggishness of a man, who will not stick to lay the fault of their natural malice upon the quality of learning, supposing that their own unskilfulness by comparing it with the vices of those that are learned, shall be accounted for virtue: but if any woman on the contrary part (as I hope and wish by your instruction and teaching all mine will do) shall join many virtues of the mind with a little skill of learning, I shall account this more happiness than if they were able to attain to Crœsus' wealth joined with the beauty of fair Helen; not because they were to get great fame thereby, although that inseparably followeth all virtue, as shadow doth the body, but for that they should obtain by this the true reward of wisdom, which can never be taken away as wealth may, nor will fade as beauty doth, because it dependeth of truth and justice, and not of the blasts of men's mouths, than which nothing is more foolish, nothing more pernicious; for as it is the duty of a good man to eschew infamy, so it is not only the property of a proud man, but also of a wretched and ridiculous man to frame their actions only for praise; for that man's mind must needs be full of unquietness, that always wavers for fear of other men's judgments between joy and sadness. But amongst other the notable benefits which learning bestoweth upon men, I account this one of the most profitable, that in getting of learning we look not for praise, to be accounted learned men, but only to use it in all occasions, which the best of all other learned men, I mean the philosophers those true moderators of men's actions have delivered unto us from hand to hand, although some of them have abused their sciences, aiming only to be accounted excellent men by the people. Thus have I spoken, my Gunnell, somewhat the more of the not coveting of vain glory, in regard of those words in your letter, whereby you judge that the high spirit of my daughter Margaret's wit is not to be dejected, wherein I am of the same opinion that you are, but I think (as I doubt not but you are of the same mind) that he doth deject his generous wit, whosoever accustometh himself to admire vain and base objects, and he raiseth well his spirits, that embraceth virtue and true good. They are base minded indeed, that esteem the shadow of good things (which most men greedily snatch at, for want of discretion to judge true good from apparent) rather than the truth itself. And therefore seeing I hold this the best way for them to walk in, I have not only requested you, my dear Gunnell, whom of yourself I know would have done it out of the entire affection you bear unto them; neither have I desired my wife alone, whom her motherly piety by me often and many ways tried doth stir them up thereto, but also all other my friends I have entreated many times to persuade all my children to this, that avoiding all the gulphs and downfalls of pride, they walk through the pleasant meadows of modesty, that they never be enamoured of the glistering hue of gold and silver, nor lament for the want of those things which by error they admire in others, that they think no better of themselves for all their costly trimmings, nor any meaner for the want of them; not to lessen their beauty by neglecting it, which they have by nature, nor to make it any more by unseemly art, to think virtue their chief happiness, learning and good qualities the next, of which those are especially to be learned, which will avail them most, that is to say, piety towards God, charity towards all men, modesty and Christian humility in themselves, by which they shall reap from God the reward of an innocent life, by certain confidence thereof they shall not need to fear death, and in the mean while enjoying true alacrity, they shall neither be puffed up with the vain praises of men, nor dejected by any slander of disgrace; these I esteem the true and solid fruits of learning; which as they happen not I confess to all that are learned, so those may easily attain them, who begin to study with this intent; neither is there any difference in harvest time, whether he was man or woman, that sowed first the corn; for both of them bear name of a reasonable creature equally, whose nature reason only doth distinguish from brute beasts, and therefore I do not see why learning in like manner may not equally agree with both sexes; for by it, reason is cultivated, and (as a field) sowed with the wholesome seed of good precepts, it bringeth forth excellent fruit. But if the soil of woman's brain be of its own nature bad, and apter to bear fern than corn (by which saying many do terrify women from learning) I am of opinion therefore that a woman's wit is the more diligently by good instructions and learning to be manured, to the end, the defect of nature may be redressed by industry. Of which mind were also many wise and holy ancient fathers, as, to omit others, S. Hierome and S. Augustine, who not only exhorted many noble matrons and honourable virgins to the getting of learning, but also to further them therein, they diligently expounded unto them many hard places of Scriptures; yea wrote many letters unto tender maids, full of so great learning, that scarcely our old and greatest professors of divinity can well read them, much less be able to understand them perfectly; which holy saints' works you will endeavour, my learned Gunnell, of your courtesy, that my daughters may learn, whereby they may chiefly know, what end, they ought to have in their learning, to place the fruits of their labours in God, and a true conscience; by which it will be easily brought to pass, that being at peace within themselves, they shall neither be moved with praise of flatterers, nor the nipping follies of unlearned scoffers. But methinks I hear you reply, that though these my precepts be true, yet are they too strong and hard for the tender age of my young wenches to hearken to: for what man, be he never so aged or expert in any science, is so constant or staid, that he is not a little stirred up with the tickling vanity of glory? And for my part, I esteem that the harder it is to shake from us this plague of pride, so much the more ought every one to endeavour to do it from his very infancy. And I think there is no other cause, why this almost inevitable mischief doth stick so fast in our breasts, but for that it is ingrafted in our tender minds even by our nurses, as soon as we are crept out of our shells; it is fostered by our masters, it is nourished and perfected by our parents, whilst that no body propoundeth any good thing to children, but they presently bid them expect praise as the whole reward of virtue; whence it is, that they are so much accustomed to esteem much of honour and praise, that by seeking to please the most, who are always the worst, they are still ashamed to be good with the fewest. That this plague may the farther be banished from my children, I earnestly desire, that you, my dear Gunnell, their mother and all their friends, would still sing this song unto them, hammer it always in their heads, and inculcate it unto them upon all occasions, that vain glory is abject, and to be despised, neither any thing to be more worthy or excellent, than that humble modesty, which is so much praised by Christ; the which prudent charity will so guide and direct, that it will teach us to desire virtue rather than to upbraid others for their vices, and will procure rather to love them who admonish us of our faults, than hate them for their wholesome counsel. To the obtaining whereof nothing is more available, than to read unto them the wholesome precepts of the fathers, whom they know not to be angry with them, and they must needs be vehemently moved with their authorities, because they are venerable for their sanctity. If therefore you read any such thing unto Margaret and Elizabeth besides their lessons in Sallust, for they are of riper judgment, by reason of their age, than John and Cecily, you shall make both me and them every day more bound unto you; moreover you shall hereby procure my children being dear by nature, after this more dear for learning, but by their increase of good manners most dear unto me. Farewell. From the Court this Whitsun-eve."

Another epistle of Sir Thomas More to his children.

"Thomas More to his whole school sendeth greeting:—

"Behold how I have found out a compendious way to salute you all, and make spare of time and paper, which I must needs have wasted in saluting every one of you particularly by your names, which would be very superfluous, because you are all so dear unto me, some in one respect, some in another, that I can omit none of you unsaluted. Yet I know not, whether there can be any better motive why I should love you than because you are scholars, learning seeming to bind me more straitly unto you, than the nearness of blood. I rejoice therefore that Mr. Drue is returned safe, of whose safety you know I was careful. If I loved you not exceedingly, I should envy this your so great happiness, to have had so many great scholars for your masters. For I think Mr. Nicolas is with you also, and that you have learned of him much astronomy; so that I hear you have proceeded so far in this science, that you now know not only the pole-star or dog, and such like of the common constellations, but also (which argueth an absolute and cunning astronomer,) in the chief planets themselves, you are able to discern the sun from the moon. Go forward therefore with this your new and admirable skill, by which you do thus climb up to the stars, which whilst you daily admire, in the mean while I admonish you also to think of this holy fast of Lent, and let that excellent and pious song of Boethius* sound in your ears, whereby you are taught also with your minds to penetrate heaven, lest when the body is lifted up on high, the soul be driven down to the earth with the brute beasts. Farewell. From the Court this 23rd of March."

Another.

"Thomas More to his best beloved Children, and to Margaret Giggs, whom he numbereth amongst his own, sendeth greeting:—

---

* Boethius was a favourite author in the More family. In one of the paintings of the family his work is introduced. The particular song to which Sir Thomas alludes is probably the first of the fourth book:

"Sunt enim pennæ volucres mihi
　　Quæ celsa conscendant poli:
Quas sibi cum velox mens induit
　　Terras perosa despicit,
Aeris immensi superat globum
　　Nubesque post tergum videt," &c.

"The merchant of Bristow brought unto me your letters the next day after he had received them of you, with the which I was exceedingly delighted. For there can come nothing, yea though it were never so rude, never so meanly polished, from this your shop, but it procureth me more delight than any other's works, be they never so eloquent; your writing doth so stir up my affection towards you; but excluding this, your letters may also very well please me for their own worth, being full of fine wit, and of a pure Latin phrase: therefore none of them all, but joyed me exceedingly; yet to tell you ingenuously what I think, my son John's letter pleased me best, both because it was longer than the other, as also for that he seemeth to have taken more pains than the rest. For he not only painteth out the matter decently, and speaketh elegantly, but he playeth also pleasantly with me, and returneth my jests upon me again very wittily; and this he doth not only pleasantly, but temperately withal, shewing that he is mindful with whom he jesteth, to wit, his father, whom he endeavoureth so to delight, that he is also afeared to offend. Hereafter I expect every day letters from every one of you; neither will I accept of such excuses, as you complain of, that you had no leisure, or that the carrier went away suddenly, or that you have no matter to write; John is not wont to alledge any such things; nothing can hinder you from writing, but many things may exhort you thereto; why should you lay any fault upon the carrier, seeing you may prevent his coming, and have them ready made up, and sealed two days before any offer themselves to carry them. And how can you want matter of writing unto me, who am delighted to hear either of your studies, or of your play: whom you may even then please exceedingly, when having nothing to write of, you write as largely as you can of that nothing, than which nothing is more easy for you to do, especially being women, and therefore prattlers by nature, and amongst whom daily a great story riseth of nothing. But this I admonish you to do, that whether you write of serious matters, or of trifles, you write with diligence and consideration, premeditating of it before; neither will it be amiss, if you first indite it in English, for then it may more easily be translated into Latin, whilst the mind free from inventing is attentive to find apt and eloquent words. And although I put this to your choice, whether you will do so or no, yet I enjoin you by all means, that you diligently examine what you have written, before you write it over fair again; first considering attentively the whole sentence, and after examine every part thereof, by which means you may easily find out, if any solecisms have escaped you; which being put out, and your letter written fair, yet then let it not also trouble you to examine it over again; for sometimes the same faults creep in at the second writing, which you before had blotted out. By this your diligence you will procure, that those your trifles will seem serious matters. For as nothing is so pleasing but may be made unsavory by prating garrulity; so nothing is by nature so unpleasant, that by industry may not be made full of grace and pleasantness. Farewell my sweetest children. From the Court this 3rd of September."

Another letter to his daughter Margaret only:—

"Thy letters (dearest Margaret) were grateful unto me, which certified me of the state of Shaw; yet would they have been more grateful unto me, if they had told me, what your and your brother's studies were, what is read amongst you every day, how pleasantly you confer together, what themes you make, and how you pass the day away amongst you in the sweet fruits of learning. And although nothing is written from you, but it is most pleasing unto me, yet those things are most sugared sweet, which I cannot learn of but by you or your brother." And in the end: "I pray thee, Meg, see that I understand by you, what your studies are. For rather than I would suffer you, my children, to live idly, I would myself look unto you, with the loss of my temporal estate, bidding all other cares and businesses farewell, amongst which there is nothing more sweet unto me than thyself, my dearest daughter. Farewell."

It seemeth also by another letter of his, how careful he was that his children might be learned and diligent, and he praiseth them for it thus:

"Thomas More sendeth greeting to his most dear daughters Margaret, Elizabeth and Cecily; and to Margaret Giggs as dear to him as if she were his own. I cannot sufficiently express, my best beloved wenches, how your eloquent letters have exceedingly pleased me; and this is not the least cause that I understand by them, you have not in your journeys, though you change places often, omitted any thing of your custom of exercising yourselves, either in making of declamations, composing of verses, or in your logick exercises; by this I persuade myself, that you dearly love me, because I see you have so great a care to please me by your diligence in my absence as to perform these things, which you know how grateful they are unto me in my presence. And as I find this your mind and affection so much to delight me, so will I procure that my return shall be profitable unto you.

And persuade yourselves that there is nothing amongst these my troublesome and careful affairs that recreateth me so much, as when I read somewhat of your labours, by which I understand those things to be true, which your most loving master writeth so lovingly of you, that unless your own epistles did show evidently unto me, how earnest your desire is towards learning, I should have judged that he had rather written of affection than according to the truth: but now by these that you write, you make him to be believed, and me to imagine those things to be true of your witty and acute disputations, which he boasteth of you almost above all belief; I am therefore marvellous desirous to come home, that we may hear them, and set our scholar to dispute with you, who is slow to believe, yea out of all hope or conceit to find you able to be answerable to your master's praises. But I hope, knowing how steadfast you are in your affections, that you will shortly overcome your master, if not in disputing, at least in not leaving of your strife. Farewell, dear wenches."

And thus you may conjecture how learned his daughters were; to whom, for this respect, Erasmus dedicated his Commentary upon Ovid " de Nuce." Lewis Vives also writeth great commendations of this school of Sir Thomas More's

in his book to Queen Catherine of England.*
And both Erasmus dedicated Aristotle in Greek,
and Simon Grineus, who, although an heretic,
yet in respect of his learning, had been kindly
used by Sir Thomas More, as he writeth himself,
did dedicate Plato, and other books in Greek,
unto my grandfather, John More, as to one that
was also very skilful in that tongue. See what
Grineus speaketh unto him: " There was a
great necessity why I should dedicate these
books of Proclus (full of marvellous learning,
by my pains set out, but not without the singular benefit of your father effected,) unto you, to
whom by reason of your fatherlike virtues all the
fruit of this benefit is to redound, both because
you may be an ornament unto them, and they
also may do great good unto you, whom I know
to be learned, and for these grave disputations
sufficiently provided and made fit by the continual conversation of so worthy a father, and by
the company of your sisters, who are most expert in all kind of sciences. For what author
can be more grateful to those desirous minds of
most goodly things, such as you and the muses
your sisters are, whom a divine heat of spirit to the
admiration and a new example of this our age,

---

* " De Institutione Feminæ Christianæ: Libri iii." Bruges
1523.

hath driven into the sea of learning so far, and so happily, that they see no learning to be above their reach, no disputations of philosophy above their capacity. And none can better explicate entangled questions, none sift them more profoundly, nor conceive them more easily, than this author."

Let us see another letter to his daughter Margaret. "You ask money, dear Meg, too shamefully and fearfully of your father, who is both desirous to give it you, and your letter hath deserved it, which I could find in my heart to recompence, not as Alexander did by Cherilus, giving him for every verse a Philippine of gold; but if my ability were answerable to my will, I would bestow two crowns of pure gold for every syllable thereof. Here I send you as much as you requested, being willing to have sent you more; but that as I am glad to give, so I am desirous to be asked and fawned on by my daughters, thee especially, whom virtue and learning hath made most dear unto me. Wherefore the sooner you have spent this money well, as you are wont to do, and the sooner you ask me for more, the sooner know you will do your father a singular pleasure. Farewell, my most beloved daughter."

This daughter was likest her father, as well in favour as wit, and proved a most rare woman for learning, sanctity, and secrecy, and therefore he trusted her with all his secrets. She wrote two declamations in English, which her father and she turned into Latin so elegantly, as one could hardly judge which was the best. She made also a treatise of the Four Last Things; which her father sincerely protested that it was better than his, and therefore, it may be, never finished his. She corrected by her wit a place in Saint Cyprian corrupted, as Pamelian and John Coster testify, instead of " nisi vos sinceritatis," restoring " nervos sinceritatis."* To her Erasmus wrote an epistle, as to a woman not only famous for manners and virtue, but most of all for learning. We have heretofore made mention of her letter that Cardinal Pole so liked, that when he had read it, he would not believe it could be any woman's; in answer whereof Sir Thomas did send her the letter, some part whereof we have seen before; the rest is this, which though there were no other testimony of her extraordinary learning, might suffice: " In the mean time," saith her father, " I thought with myself how true I found that

* For Pamelian, read Pamelius. The passage referred to is in his notes upon the thirty-first Epistle of Saint Cyprian. See also Costerius's Observations upon the Commonitory of Vincentius Lerinensis, p. 47. This note is from the edition of 1726.

now, which once I remember I spoke unto you in jest, when I pitied your hard hap, that men that read your writings would suspect you to have had help of some other man therein, which would derogate somewhat from the praises due to your works; seeing that you of all others deserve least to have such a suspicion had of you, or that you never could abide to be decked with the plumes of other birds. But you, sweet Meg, are rather to be praised for this, that seeing you cannot hope for condign praise of your labours; yet for all this you go forward with this your invincible courage, to join with your virtue the knowledge of most excellent sciences, and contenting yourself with your own pleasure in learning, you never hunt after vulgar praises, nor receive them willingly, though they be offered you. And for your singular piety and love towards me, you esteem me and your husband a sufficient and ample theatre for you to content you with; who, in requital of this your affection, beseech God and our Lady, with as hearty prayers as possible we can pour out, to give you an easy and happy childbirth, to increase your family with a child most like yourself, except only in sex; yet if it be a wench, that it may be such a one as would, in time, recompence by imitation of her mother's learning and virtues, what by the condition of her sex may be wanting; such a wench I should prefer before three boys. Farewell, dearest daughter."

But see, I pray you, how a most learned bishop in England was ravished with her learning and wit, as it appeareth by a letter, which her father wrote unto her to certify her thereof. "Thomas More sendeth hearty greeting to his dearest daughter Margaret: I will let pass to tell you, my sweetest daughter, how much your letter delighted me; you may imagine how exceedingly it pleased your father, when you understand what affection the reading of of it raised in a stranger. It happened me this evening to sit with John, Lord Bishop of Exeter, a learned man, and by all men's judgment, a most sincere man. As we were talking together, and I taking out of my pocket a paper, which was to the purpose we were talking of, I pulled out, by chance, therewith your letter. The handwriting pleasing him, he took it from me and looked on it; when he perceived it by the salutation to be a woman's, he began more greedily to read it, novelty inviting him thereunto; but when he had read it, and understood that it was your writing, which he never could have believed if I had not seriously affirmed it;

'such a letter'—I will say no more—yet why should not I report that which he said unto me—'So pure a style, so good Latin, so eloquent, so full of sweet affections'—he was marvellously ravished with it. When I perceived that, I brought forth also an oration of your's, which he reading, and also many of your verses, he was so moved with the matter so unlooked for, that the very countenance and gesture of the man, free from all flattery and deceit, betrayed that his mind was more than his words could utter, although he uttered many to your great praise; and forthwith he drew out of his pocket a portegue, which you shall receive inclosed herein. I could not possibly shun the taking of it, but he would needs send it unto you, as a sign of his dear affection towards you, although by all means I endeavoured to give it him again; which was the cause I showed him none of your other sister's works; for I was afraid lest I should have been thought to have showed them of purpose, because he should bestow the like courtesy upon them; for it troubled me sore, that I must needs take this of him; but he is so worthy a man, as I have said, that it is a happiness to please him thus. Write carefully unto him, and as eloquently as you are able, to give him thanks therefore. Farewell. From the court, this 11th of September, even almost at midnight."

She made an oration to answer Quintilian, defending that rich man which he accused for having poisoned a poor man's bees, with certain venomous flowers in his garden, so eloquent and witty, that it may strive with his. She translated Eusebius out of Greek, but it was never printed, because Christopherson at that time had done it exactly before. Yet one other letter will I set down of Sir Thomas to this his daughter, which is thus: " Thomas More sendeth greeting to his dearest daughter Margaret. There was no reason, my dearest daughter, why thou shouldst have deferred thy writing unto me one day longer, for fear that thy letters being so barren, should not be read of me without loathing. For though they had not been most curious, yet in respect of thy sex, thou mightest have been pardoned by any man; yea, even a blemish in the child's face, seemeth often to a father beautiful. But these your letters, Meg, were so eloquently polished, that they had nothing in them, not only why they should fear the most indulgent affection of your father More, but also they needed not to have regarded even Momus's censure, though never so testy. I greatly thank Mr. Nicolas, our dear friend (a most expert man in astronomy), and do congratulate your happiness, whom it may fortune within the space of one month, with a small labour of your own, to learn so many and such high wonders of that mighty and eternal workman, which were not found but in many ages, by watching in so many cold nights under the open skies, with much labour and pains, by such excellent, and, above all other men's understanding wits. This which you write pleaseth me exceedingly, that you had determined with yourself to study philosophy so diligently, that you will hereafter recompence by your diligence, what your negligence hath heretofore lost you. I love you for this, dear Meg, that whereas I never have found you to be a loiterer (your learning, which is not ordinary, but in all kind of sciences most excellent, evidently shewing how painfully you have proceeded therein), yet such is your modesty, that you had rather still accuse yourself of negligence than vainly boast of diligence; except you mean by this your speech that you will be hereafter so diligent, that your former endeavours, though indeed they were great and praiseworthy, yet in respect of your future diligence, may be called negligence. If it be so that you mean (as I do verily think you do), I imagine nothing can happen to me more fortunate, nothing to you, my dearest daughter, more happy; for, as I have earnestly wished that you might spend the remainder of your life in studying physic and holy Scriptures, by the which there shall never be helps wanting unto you, for the end of man's life; which is to endeavour that a sound mind be in a healthful body, of which studies you have already laid some foundations, and you shall never want matter to build thereupon; so now I think that some of the first years of your youth, yet flourishing, may be very well bestowed in human learning and the liberal arts, both because your age may best struggle with those difficulties, and for that it is uncertain whether, at any time else, we shall have the commodity of so careful, so loving, and so learned a master; to let pass, that by this kind of learning our judgments are either gotten, or certainly much helped thereby. I could wish, dear Meg, that I might talk with you a long while about these matters, but behold, they which bring in supper interrupt me, and call me away. My supper cannot be so sweet unto me as this my speech with you is, if I were not to respect others more than myself. Farewell, dearest daughter, and commend me kindly to your husband, my loving son, who maketh me rejoice for that he studieth the same things you do; and whereas I am wont always to counsel you to give place to your husband, now on the other side, I give you licence to strive to master him in the knowledge of the sphere. Farewell again and again. Commend me to all your schoolfellows, but to your master especially." And having, upon this occasion of speaking of Sir Thomas's children, how tenderly he loved them, how earnestly he sought to make them scholars, and with their scholarship to have them join virtue, made somewhat a longer digression than I thought; we will return as we had begun, to speak of the alteration of religion in our country, and how thereupon Sir Thomas More fell into trouble.*

* This last clause from " And having upon this occasion, &c." is wanting in the manuscript.

CHAPTER VIII.

WHILST this unlucky divorce was so hotly pursued by the king, it happened that my uncle Roper, walking with his father along by the Thames side, near Chelsey, amongst other talk, Sir Thomas said, "Now, would to our Lord, son Roper, that upon condition three things were established in Christendom, I were put into a sack, and here presently cast into the Thames." "What great things are those, good Sir," said he, "that should move you so to wish?" "Wouldst thou know them, son Roper?" "Yea, marry, Sir, with a good will," said he, "if it would please you." "In faith, son, they be these: First, that where the most part of Christian princes be at mortal war, they were at an universal peace. Secondly, whereas the church of Christ is at this time sore afflicted with many errors and heresies, it were settled in a perfect uniformity of religion. Thirdly, that whereas the matter of the king's marriage is come in question, it were to the glory of God, and quietness of all parties, brought to a good conclusion." Whereby one might well gather that otherwise he judged this would be a disturbance to a great part of Christendom. The first he saw in some sort granted him by his means; the other two are this day to be seen, what tragedies they have raised in England and elsewhere.

Thus did he by his words and deeds, show throughout the whole course of his life, that all his thoughts, travails, and pains, were only for the honour of God, without respect either of his own glory, or of any earthly commodity; for it may be seen by many things, as well deeds as letters, how much he contemned the honours which were heaped upon him daily by his prince's especial bounty and favour towards him, and my uncle Roper testifieth from his own mouth, in his latter days, that he professed unto him, that he never asked of the king, for himself, the value of one penny. The like may be said of his contempt of riches and worldly wealth; but a fitter place to speak thereof may be had hereafter. All which excellent endowments of his mind proceeded, no doubt, from his confidence in God, and his godly exercises to attain to perfection and all virtues.

He built a chapel in his parish church at

Chelsey, where the parish had all ornaments belonging thereunto abundantly supplied at his charge, and he bestowed thereon much plate, often speaking those words: Good men give it and bad men take it away.

A little before he was preferred to the dignity of chancellorship, there were questions propounded to many, whether the king in the case of his first marriage needed have any scruple at all; and if he had, what way were best to deliver him from it. The most part of his council were of opinion, that there was good cause of scruple, because Queen Catherine was married before to Prince Arthur, King Henry's elder brother; wherefore she was not to be wife to two brothers; and therefore to ease the king's mind, suit was to be made to the pope and the see of Rome, where the king hoped by liberal gifts to obtain what he desired; but in this, as after it appeared, he was far deceived.

After this there was a commission procured from Rome for trial and examination of this marriage; in which the Cardinals Wolsey and Campegius, were joined together; who for the determination hereof sate at the Black Friars in London. A libel was put in for the annulling of the former matrimony, alleging that that marriage was utterly unlawful; but on the other side for proof that it was lawful and good, a dispensation was brought forth, which was of very good force as touching the power which the pope had to dispense in a law that was neither contrary to God's positive law in the Old Testament, but rather agreeable thereto, nor to the law of nature; and it is commanded in Leviticus, that if the brother died without issue, the next in kindred to him should be in a manner enforced to marry his wife. But there was found an imperfection in the dispensation; yet that same was lawfully supplied by a public instrument or brief found in the treasury of Spain, which was sent immediately to the commissioners in England, and so should judgment have been given by the pope accordingly, that the first marriage stood in force, had not King Henry upon intelligence thereof, before the judgment was pronounced, appealed to the next general council. " Hinc illæ lachrymæ;" hence came the deadly enmity between the king and the pope; hence proceeded that bitterness of King Henry, that he commanded none should appeal to Rome, nor none should so much as go thither; no bishops nor spiritual men should have any bulls or authority from thence; all spiritual jurisdiction began now, never before thought of, to be invested from God immediately upon the imperial crown of England; but this not all at once: yea, he grew afterwards unto such height of malice, that he caused the name of the pope to be razed out of every book that could be found either printed or written. He caused St. Thomas of Canterbury to be attainted of high treason after he had been three hundred years accounted a blessed martyr of the whole church; yea so acknowledged by King Henry the Second, who was the cause of his death; but this king most barbarously cast his sacred bones out of his renowned shrine, after numbers of miracles, and caused them to be burnt. This was the strange pass King Henry was brought unto doting on Anne Bullen, though, God knows, she had no qualities wherefore he should so dote on her, as appeared evidently when for foul matters he after a short time cut off her head, and proclaimed himself in open parliament to be a cuckold; which no doubt he never had been, if he had kept himself to his first virtuous wife Queen Catherine; but all these things happened a good while after, and many other extreme violences and ensuing miseries, as we may see and feel.

Whilst those things were a doing, as is before said, about the king's divorce, and nothing yet brought to any conclusion,* the king sent Tunstal,

---

* The manuscript here varies remarkably from the printed copy. "When the imperfection of the dispensation was supplied, the king seemed to take the matter as ended, and meaning no farther to proceed, he assigned Tunstal, bishop of Durham, and Sir Thomas More, to go embassadors to Cambray."

bishop of Durham, and Sir Thomas More, embassadors to Cambray, to treat of a peace between him, the French king, and Charles the emperor: in which journey Sir Thomas so worthily behaved himself that he procured in our league with the said princes far more benefits to our realm than at that time was thought possible by the king and all his council; insomuch that his majesty caused it afterwards openly to be declared to the people, when he was made chancellor, how much all England was bound to Sir Thomas More. And now at his return the king again was very earnest with him to have him agree to his second marriage; for which cause also it is thought, and Cardinal Pole testifieth it in a letter, he made him the rather his lord chancellor; telling him, that though the dispensation was good in respect of the laws of the church, yet now it was found out to have been against the law of nature, in which no dispensation could be had, as Doctor Stokeley, (whom for that quirk found out he had lately preferred to the bishoprick of London,) was able to instruct him, with whom he willed Sir Thomas to confer in that point. But for all the conferences he could have with him, Sir Thomas could no way induce himself to change his former opinion therein. Yet the bishop relating to the king their conference, so favourably reported of Sir Thomas More's carriage therein, that he said, he found him very toward and desirous to find out good matter, whereby he might truly serve his grace to his contentment, but yet he could not.

This bishop having been lately by the cardinal in the Star-chamber openly disgraced and awarded to the Fleet, not brooking this contumely, sought by all means to wreak his anger against the cardinal: and picked a quarrel at him to the king, because he began to wax cold in the divorce. For so it was, that Wolsey was sent over into France to treat of a marriage between King Henry and the king of France's sister: and finding their favourable acceptance, it was likely to come to that issue, which he hoped for. Yet God so wrought to cross him, that this very invention, which he had first plotted to revenge himself on Charles the emperor, the same was the pit wherein he fell, and whereby all his dignity, credit, and wealth was taken away; so that of him it may be well be said: "incidit in foveam quam fecit." For whilst he was contriving for the king a marriage in France, the king himself little to his knowledge had knit the knot in England with a mean woman in respect of a prince, a private knight's daughter, and of meaner conditions than any gentlewoman of worth.

Wherefore when Wolsey upon his return found his embassage crossed, he began to repine at the king for disgracing him so much, and now wished that he had never began to put such scruples into Longland's head; which Stokeley soon finding, and himself having devised a new knot in a rush, to bring the king in better liking of himself for his forwardness, and into more dislike of the cardinal, so wrought with his majesty, that he sent for the cardinal back, being now on his way gone to be installed in the archbishoprick of York: so that by Sir William Kingston he was arrested of high treason, having confiscated all his goods before, so that he that had been one of the greatest prelates of Christendom, had not now one dish to be served in at the table; who if he had loved God half so well as he adored his prince, could never have come to such misery; for that he died either with sorrow or poison shortly after.

But the king caused in his place of chancellor Sir Thomas More to be placed, that with that bait (saith Cardinal Pole,) corrupted, he might the more easily be brought to the bent of the king's bow; who behaved himself so excellently in that place as one may say, that none ever before him did better; although he was the first lay-man that ever possessed that room, as Cardinal Pole noteth; yea Wolsey himself hearing that Sir Thomas More should have it, though he was very loath to lose it himself, and withal bore Sir Thomas no more good will than needs he must,* yet professed he to many, that he thought none in England more worthy of it than Sir Thomas; such was his fame, that none could envy it, though it were never so unaccustomed a case.

The manner how Sir Thomas More was installed in this high office, how the king did extraordinarily grace him therein, and how modestly notwithstanding he accepted thereof, is very remarkable. For being led between the Dukes of Norfolk and Suffolk through Westminster Hall up to the Star-chamber, and there honourably placed in the high judgment seat of chancellor, the Duke of Norfolk, who was the chief peer and lord treasurer of England, by the king's order, spoke thus unto the people, there with great applause and joy gathered together:—
"The king's majesty (which I pray God may prove happy and fortunate to the whole realm of England) hath raised to the most high dignity of chancellorship, Sir Thomas More, a man for his extraordinary worth and sufficiency well-known to himself and the whole realm, for no

* This clause is wanting in the manuscript; and the account which follows of the manner in which Sir Thomas More was installed in his office of Chancellor, is related in the manuscript with less particularity than in the printed text, which has here been followed. In the speeches of the Duke of Norfolk and Sir Thomas More the printed text has been used with very trifling departures from it.

other cause or earthly respect, but for that he hath plainly perceived all the gifts of nature and grace to be heaped upon him, which either the people could desire, or himself wish for the discharge of so great an office. For the admirable wisdom, integrity and innocency, joined with most pleasant facility of wit, that this man is endued withal, have been sufficiently known to all Englishmen from his youth, and for these many years also to the king's majesty himself. This hath the king abundantly found in many and weighty affairs, which he hath happily dispatched both at home and abroad; in divers offices, which he hath borne in most honourable embassages, which he hath undergone, and in his daily counsel and advises upon all other occasions. He hath perceived no man in his realm to be more wise in deliberating, more sincere in opening to him what he thought, nor more eloquent to adorn the matter which he uttered. Wherefore because he saw in him such excellent endowments, and that of his especial care he hath a particular desire that his kingdom and people might be governed with all equity and justice, integrity and wisdom: he of his own most gracious disposition hath created this singular man lord chancellor; that by his laudable performance of this office, his people may enjoy peace and justice, and honour also and fame may redound to the whole kingdom. It may perhaps seem to many a strange and unusual matter, that this dignity should be bestowed upon a lay-man, none of the nobility, and one that hath wife and children; because heretofore none but singular learned prelates, or men of greatest nobility, have possessed this place; but what is wanting in these respects, the admirable virtues, the matchless gifts of wit and wisdom of this man, doth most plentifully recompense the same. For the king's majesty hath not regarded how great, but what a man he was; he hath not cast his eyes upon the nobility of his blood, but on the worth of his person; he hath respected his sufficiency, not his profession; finally he would show by this his choice, that he hath some rare subjects amongst the gentlemen and lay-men, who deserve to manage the highest offices of the realm, which bishops and noblemen think they only can deserve: which the rarer it is, so much he thought it would be to you the more acceptable, and to the whole kingdom most grateful. Wherefore receive this your chancellor with joyful acclamations, at whose hands you may expect all happiness and content."

Sir Thomas More according to his wonted modesty was somewhat abashed at this the duke's speech, in that it sounded so much to his praise; but recollecting himself as that place and time would give him leave, he answered in this sort:—" Although, most noble duke, and you right honourable lords, and worshipful gentlemen, I know all these things which the king's majesty, it seemeth, hath been pleased should be spoken of me at this time and place, and your grace hath, with most eloquent words thus amplified, are as far from me as I could wish with all my heart they were in me for the better performance of so great a charge : and although this your speech hath caused in me greater fear than I can well express in words, yet this incomparable favour of my dread sovereign, by which he showeth how well, yea how highly he conceiveth of my weakness, having commanded that my meanness should be so greatly commended, cannot be but most acceptable unto me; and I cannot chuse but give your most noble grace exceeding thanks, that what his majesty hath willed you briefly to utter, you of the abundance of your love unto me, have, in a large and eloquent oration, dilated. As for myself, I can take it no otherwise but that his majesty's incomparable favour towards me, the good will and incredible propension of his royal mind (wherewith he hath these many years favoured me continually,) hath alone, without any desert of mine at all, caused both this my new honour, and these your undeserved commendations of me; for who am I, or what is the house of my father, that the king's highness should heap upon me, by such a perpetual stream of affection, these so high honours? I am far less than any the meanest of his benefits bestowed on me; how can I then think myself worthy or fit for this so peerless dignity? I have been drawn by force, as the king's majesty often professeth, to his highness's service, to be a courtier; but to take this dignity upon me, is most of all against my will; yet such is his highness's benignity, such is his bounty, that he highly esteemeth the small dutifulness of his meanest subjects, and seeketh still magnificently to recompense his servants; not only such as deserve well, but even such as have but a desire to deserve well at his hands. In which number I have always wished myself to be reckoned, because I cannot challenge myself to be one of the former; which being so, you may all perceive with me, how great a burden is laid upon my back, in that I must strive in some sort with my diligence and duty to correspond with his royal benevolence, and to be answerable to that great expectation which he and you seem to have of me; wherefore those so high praises are by so much the more grievous unto me, by how much I know the greater charge I have to render myself worthy of, and the fewer means I have to make them good. This weight is hardly suitable to my weak shoulders; this honour is not correspondent to my poor deserts; it is a burthen, not glory; a care, not a dignity; the one therefore I must bear as manfully as I can, and discharge the other with as much dexterity as I shall be able. The earnest desire which I have always had, and do now acknowledge myself to have, to satisfy by all means I can possible the most ample benefits of his highness, will greatly excite and aid me to the diligent performance of all; which I trust also I shall be more able to do, if I find all your good wills and wishes both favourable unto me, and conformable to his royal munificence; because my serious endeavours to do well, joined with your favourable acceptance, will easily procure that whatsoever is performed by me, though it be in itself but small, yet will it seem great and praiseworthy, for those things are always achieved happily which are accepted willingly; and those succeed fortunately which are received by others courteously. As you therefore do hope for great matters, and the best at my hands, so though I dare not promise any such, yet do I promise truly and affectionately to perform the best I shall be able."

When Sir Thomas had spoken these words, turning his face to the high judgment seat of the chancery, he proceeded in this manner: "But when I look upon this seat, when I think how great and what kind of personages have possessed this place before me, when I call to mind who he was that sat in it last of all; a man of what singular wisdom, of what notable experience, what a prosperous and favourable fortune he had for a great space, and how at last dejected with a heavy downfall he hath died inglorious; I have cause enough, by my predecessor's example, to think honour but slippery, and this dignity not so grateful to me as it may seem to others; for both it is a hard matter to follow with like paces or praises a man of such admirable wit, prudence, authority, and splendour, to whom I may seem but as the lighting of a candle when the sun is down; and also the sudden and unexpected fall of so great a man as he was doth terribly put me in mind that this honour ought not to please me too much, nor the lustre of this glistering seat dazzle mine eyes. Wherefore I ascend this seat as a place full of labour and danger, void of all solid and true honour; the which by how much the higher it is, by so much greater fall I am to fear, as well in respect of the very nature of the thing itself, as because I am warned by this late fearful example. And truly I might even now at this very first entrance stumble, yea faint, but that his majesty's most singular favour towards me, and all your good wills, which your joyful countenance doth testify in this most honourable assembly, doth somewhat recreate and refresh me; otherwise, this seat would be no more pleasing to me than that sword was to Damocles, which hung over his head, tied only by a hair of a horse's tail, when he had store of delicate fare before him, seated in the chair of state of Denis, the tyrant of Sicily; this, therefore, shall be always fresh in my mind; this will I have still before mine eyes, that this seat will be honourable, famous, and full of glory unto me, if I shall with care and diligence, fidelity and wisdom endeavour to do my duty, and shall persuade myself, that the enjoying thereof may chance to be but short and uncertain; the one whereof my labour ought to perform, the other my predecessor's example may easily teach me. All which being so, you may easily perceive what great pleasure I take in this high dignity, or in this most noble duke's praising of me."

All the world took notice now of Sir Thomas' dignity, whereof Erasmus writeth to John Fabius, Bishop of Vienna, thus: "Concerning the new increase of honour lately happened to Thomas More, I should easily make you believe it, if I should show you the letters of many famous men, rejoicing with much alacrity, and congratulating the king, the realm, himself, and also me, for More's honour, in being made Lord Chancellor of England."

Now it was a comfortable thing for any man to behold, how two great rooms of Westminster Hall were taken up, one with the son, the other with the father, which hath as yet never been heard of before or since; the son to be Lord Chancellor, and the father, Sir John More, to be one of the ancientest judges of the King's Bench, if not the eldest of all, for now he was near ninety years old. Yea what a grateful spectacle was it to see the son go to ask the father blessing, every day upon his knees, before he sat in his own seat; a thing expressing rare humility, exemplar obedience, and submissive piety.

Shortly began every one to find a great alteration between the intolerable pride of the precedent chancellor, Wolsey, who would scarce look or speak to any, and into whose only presence none could be admitted, unless his fingers were tipped with gold; and on the other side, this chancellor, the poorer and the meaner the suppliant was, the more affably he would speak unto him, the more attentively he would hearken to his cause, and with speedy trial dispatch him; for which purpose he used commonly, every afternoon, to sit in his open hall, so that if any person whatsoever had any suit unto him, he might the more boldly come unto him, and there open to him his complaints.

Which his open manner of extraordinary favour to all, my uncle Dauncy, his son-in-law, seemed merrily on a time to find fault with, saying, that when Cardinal Wolsey was chancellor, not only divers of his inner chamber, but such as were but his doorkeepers, got great gains by him; and "sith I have married one of your daughters, I might of reason look for some commodity; but you are so ready to do for every poor man, and keep no doors shut, that I can find no gains at all, which is to me a great discouragement, whereas else, some for friendship, some for profit, and some for kindred, would gladly use my furtherance to bring them to your presence; and now if I should take any thing of them, I should do them great wrong, because they may daily do as much for themselves; which thing, though it is in you, Sir, very commendable, yet to me I find it nothing profitable." Which word Sir Thomas answered thus: "I do not mislike, son, that your conscience is so scrupulous; but there be many other ways wherein I may both do yourself good, and pleasure your friends; for, sometime, by my word I may stand your friend in stead; sometime I may help him greatly by my letter; if he hath a cause depending before me, I may hear it before another, at your entreaty; if his cause be not all the best, I may move the parties to fall to some reasonable end, by arbitrement: but this one thing I assure thee, on my faith, that if the parties will at my hands call for justice and equity, then, although it were my father, whom I reverence dearly, that stood on the one side, and the devil, whom I hate extremely, were on the other side, his cause being just, the devil of me should have his right."

What a saying was this to express the love to justice which he always bore; and his deeds showed it so, that no malicious tongue ever could pick the least quarrel against him for the least touch of injustice, as shall be more at large spoken of, when every light matter comes to be sifted narrowly, after he fell from the king's favour; and that he would for no respect of alliance digress one jot from equity, well appeared by another son-in-law of his, my uncle Heron; for when he, having a cause in the Chancery, before Sir Thomas, and presuming too much on his favour, because he ever showed himself the most affectionate father to his children that was in the world; by reason whereof he would by no means be persuaded to agree to any indifferent order, at last Sir Thomas made a flat decree against him, wherein he lively expressed the practice of his former saying.

Now at his coming to this office, he found the Court of Chancery pestered and clogged with many and tedious causes, some having hung there almost twenty years, which was a great misery for poor suitors. Wherefore to prevent the like, first he caused Mr. Crooke, chief of the Six Clerks, to make a docket, containing the whole number of all injunctions, as either in his time had already passed, or at that time depended in any of the king's courts at Westminster. Then bidding all the judges to dinner, he, in the presence of them all, showed sufficient reason why he had made so many injunctions, that they all confessed that they themselves, in the like case, would have done no less. Then he promised them besides, that if they themselves, to whom the reformation of the rigour of the law appertained, would, upon reasonable considerations, in their own discretion (as he thought in conscience they were bound), mitigate and reform the rigour of the law, there should then from him no injunctions be granted; to which when they refused to condescend, " then," said he, " forasmuch as yourselves, my lords, drive me to this necessity, you cannot hereafter blame me, if I seek to relieve the poor people's injuries." After this, he said to his son Roper secretly, " I perceive, son, why they like not this; for they think that they may, by a verdict of a jury, cast off all scruple from themselves upon the poor jury, which they account their chief defence; wherefore I am constrained to abide the adventure of their blame."

He took great pains to hear causes at home, as is said before, arbitrating matters for both the parties' good; and lastly, he took order with all the attornies of his court, that there should no subpœnas go out, whereof in general he should not have notice of the matter, with one of their hands unto the bill; and if it did bear sufficient cause of complaint, then would he set his hand, to have it go forward; if not, he would utterly quash it, and deny a subpœna. And when on a time, one of the attornies, whose name was Mr. Tubbe, had brought unto Sir Thomas the sum of the cause of his client, requesting his hand unto it; Sir Thomas reading it, and finding it a matter frivolous, he added, instead of his name thereto, these words, "A tale of a;" and "Tubbe" was joined thereto: for which the attorney, going away, as he thought, with Sir Thomas' name unto it, found, when his client read it, to be only a jest.

Shortly after his entry into the chancellorship, the king again importuned him to weigh and consider his great matter, thinking that now he had so bound him unto him, that he could not have gainsaid him; but he, valuing more the quiet of his conscience, and the justice of the cause, than any prince's favour in the world, fell down upon his knees before his majesty, and humbly besought him to stand his gracious sovereign, as he had ever found him since his first entrance into his princely service; adding, that there was nothing in the world had been so grievous to his heart, as to think that he was not able (as he gladly would, with the loss of one of his chiefest limbs,) to find any thing in that matter, whereby, with integrity of his conscience, he might serve his grace to his contentment; and he always bore in mind those most godly words that his highness spoke unto him, when he first admitted him into his royal service, the most virtuous lesson that ever prince gave unto his servant, whereby he willed him, first to look to God, and, after God, to him; as, in good faith, he said he did, and would; or else might his majesty account him for his most unworthy vassal. Whereto the king courteously answered, that if he could not therein with his conscience serve him, he was contented to accept his service otherwise; and use in this matter the advice of other his learned council, whose consciences could well agree thereto: yet he would, notwithstanding, continue his accustomed favour towards him, and never after, molest his conscience therewith. But how well he performed his promise, may be seen by the discourse following. And indeed there is no prince, be he bent to never so much wickedness, but shall find counsellors enough that will always seek to please his humours; but to find one that will not agree to what the king is bent to have wrongfully brought to pass, these are very rare, and therefore most to be admired.

About this time it happened Sir John More to fall sick of a surfeit of grapes, as I have heard; who, though he was very old, yet had he till then been more lusty than his years afforded him. In his sickness, his son, whom now he had seen Lord Chancellor,* often came and visited him, using many comfortable words unto him; and at his departure out of this miserable world, with tears taking him about the neck, most lovingly kissed and embraced him, commending his soul devoutly to the merciful hands of his Creator and Redeemer; so with a heavy heart departed from him, who left

* The father and the son were contemporaries in their high seats of justice for about a year. One of the few ascertained dates in the life of Sir Thomas More is that of the delivery to him of the great seal. This was on October 25, 1529. Sir John More died in the course of the next year; for his will (which was made on Feb. 20, 1520) was proved on December 5, 1530. It is to be found in the Prerogative Office, London. Jankyn, f. 24.

him now bettered with a very small increase of estate, because his chief house and lands at Gubbins in Hertfordshire his last wife enjoyed, who outlived Sir Thomas some ten years, and therefore Sir Thomas never enjoyed almost any inheritance from his father; insomuch that he affirmed in his Apology, which he wrote about this time, that all his revenues and pensions, except that which had been granted by letters patent from the king of his mere liberality, to wit, the manors of Duckington, Frinckford, and Barlypark, in Oxfordshire, all the rest, he saith, amount not to above fifty pound by the year, as those which he had from his father or by his wife, or by his own purchase. Surely a rare saying, that one of the king's council, who had gone through many offices for almost twenty years should not be able to purchase one hundred pound land; when as now a private attorney by his own practice will leave his child five hundred pound land of inheritance. Therefore in so great an officer this showeth an admirable contempt of worldly commodities, a bountiful hand to spend liberally and abundantly upon the poor, his own kinsfolk and family, the church, and upon hospitality. And as for ready money, he had not in all the world, when he gave up his office, above one hundred pound either in gold or silver; which is as strange as the former. All which doth demonstrate his uprightness, his munificence, his singular perfections, and his divine wisdom. For what could millions of gold have stood him in stead, but to cumber his conscience, when he lost all from himself and his posterity by reason of the malice of a spiteful queen, who pursued him and his to death, to their utter temporal overthrow, showing perfectly that saying, "non est malitia super malitia mulieris." For the king could not by his fall promise himself any great increase of goods, as he had gotten by the cardinal's overthrow.

Now the bishops of England at this time considering with themselves, that for all his prince's favour he was neither a rich man, nor in yearly revenues advanced as his worthiness deserved, and weighing with themselves what pains and travails he had taken in writing many learned books for the defence of the true catholic faith, against many heresies secretly sown abroad in the realm, to whose pastoral charge the reformation of them principally appertained, there being not one clergyman that had matched his writings either in the greatness of the volumes, the soundness of the arguments to convince the adversaries, or the pains taken to reduce them. They called therefore a convocation together, whither most of the clergy came, where they concluded to offer unto him the sum of four thousand pounds at the least, thereby to recompense in part his travails therein sustained. To the payment whereof every bishop, abbot, and the rest of the clergy, after the rate of their abilities, were liberal contributors, hoping that this sum would content him. Wherefore his dear friends, Tunstal, bishop of Durham, and Clarke, bishop of Bath, and, as is supposed, Veysey of Exeter, came to Sir Thomas and spoke thus unto him; how that they held themselves bound to consider him for his pains taken and bestowed to discharge them in God's quarrel; and albeit they could not according to his deserts requite him so worthily as they willingly would, but must refer that only to the goodness of God: yet for a small part of recompence, in respect of his estate so unequal to his worth, they presented unto him that sum in the name of the whole convocation, desiring him to take it in good part. And though this were a bountiful deed in respect of those prelates; yet little knew they Sir Thomas's magnificent disposition, who answered them in this manner: "That like as it was no small comfort unto him, that so wise and learned men accepted so well of his simple doings, for which he never purposed to receive any reward, but at the hands of God alone, to whom the thanks thereof was chiefly to be ascribed; so gave he most humble thanks unto their honours all, for their so bountiful and friendly consideration; but he purposed not to receive any thing from them." And when they with great importunity pressed still upon him, that few would have supposed he could have refused it, they could not for all that fasten any whit upon him. Then they besought him that he would be content they might bestow it upon his wife and children. "Not so, my lords, (quoth he,) I had rather see it cast all into the Thames than I or any of mine should have thereof one penny. For though your offer, my lords, is indeed very honourable, yet set I so much by my pleasure and so little by my profit, that I would not in good faith for much more money have lost the rest of so many nights' sleep as was spent upon the same: and yet for all this I could wish that upon condition all heresies were suppressed, all my works were burnt, and my labour utterly lost." Thus they were fain to depart, and restore to every one his own again. By which wise and virtuous answer, every one may see that all his pains that he took, were only in respect of God's honour, and not for either vain glory or any earthly commodity.

Yea he cared not what any said of him, contemning the people's dispraise as a blast of wind. For the heretics having gotten it by the end, that the clergy had offered him a great sum of money, and measuring other men by their own covetous humours, reported and wrote in pamphlets that he was bribed by the clergy to write, whom he answered mildly by a flat denial, that he was not made richer by one penny from the clergy; yet some of them had spent him somewhat: and besides he being bigamus, twice married, could never hope for any spiritual promotion.

The water bailiff of London, who had been sometimes his servant, hearing (where he had been at dinner) certain merchants somewhat drunk with this new poison, liberally to rail against Sir Thomas, in that he was so bitter against Lutherans, waxed sore discontented therewith, knowing well, that he little deserved any evil report; wherefore he hastily came to Sir Thomas and told him what he had heard: " And were I, Sir, (said he,) in such favour and authority with my prince, as you are, such men should not be suffered so villainously and falsely to misreport and slander me. Wherefore you may do well, Sir, to call them before you, and to their shame to punish them for their undeserved malice." But Sir Thomas smiling on him said: " Why Mr. Water-bailiff, would you have me punish those by whom I reap more benefit than by all you that are my friends: let them in God's name speak as lewdly of me as they list, and shoot never so many bolts at me, as long as they hit me not, what am I the worse: but if they should once hit me, then would it not a little grieve me; howbeit I trust by God's grace and help, there shall none of them all be able to touch me. I have more cause, I assure thee, to pity them than to be angry with them." Lo, to what height of perfection had he now attained, that he was neither allured by hopeful gains, nor deterred one jot from his duty by evil tongues or slanders, always carrying one and the same alacrity in all his crosses and adversities;

When that one of the house of the Manners, by the king's favour was come lately to a noble dignity, who had been before a great friend to Sir Thomas; but perceiving that the world began somewhat to frown upon him for that he was not so forward as other men to egg the king to the divorce, and being desirous to pick a quarrel against him said unto him: "My lord, 'Honores mutant mores.'" Sir Thomas readily, after his merry fashion replied, "It is so indeed, my lord; but 'mores' signifieth in English 'Manners' and not 'More;'" he was therewith so put out of countenance that he wist not what to say.

In like manner he wittily twitted another man, whom he had lent money unto: of whom asking his due, he bad him remember that he should die, God knoweth how soon, and then he should have little use of money, adding the sentence in Latin, to please Sir Thomas the more, "Memento morieris;" whereto readily Sir Thomas said, "What say you, Sir, methinks you put yourself in mind of your duty herein saying 'Memento Mori æris,' remember More's money." Thus was he continually in his discourses full of witty jests, that though his countenance was always grave, yet none could converse with him, but he would make them laugh exceedingly; tempering all serious matters with some witty device or other.

It happened on a time that a beggar-woman's little dog, which she had lost, was presented for a jewel to my Lady More, and she had kept it some se'nnight very carefully; but at last the beggar had notice where her dog was, and presently she came to complain to Sir Thomas, as he was sitting in his hall, that his lady withheld her dog from her; presently my lady was sent for, and the dog brought with her; which Sir Thomas taking in his hands, caused his wife, because she was the worthier person, to stand at the upper end of the hall, and the beggar at the lower end, and saying, that he sat there to do every one justice, he bad each of them call the dog; which when they did, the dog went presently to the beggar, forsaking my lady. When he saw this, he bad my lady be contented, for it was none of hers; yet she repining at the sentence of my lord chancellor, agreed with the beggar, and gave her a piece of gold, which would well have bought three dogs, and so all parties were agreed; every one smiling to see his manner of enquiring out the truth.

A certain friend of his had taken great pains about a book, which he would have set out, thinking well of his own wit, which no other would praise. And because he would have Sir Thomas to oversee it, before it was printed, he brought it to him to view; who perusing it, and finding no matter therein worth the print, said with a grave countenance: if it were in verse, it were more worth: upon which words he went and turned it into verse, and after brought it again to Sir Thomas; who looking thereon, said, soberly, "Yea, marry, now it is somewhat; for now it is rhyme; before it was neither rhyme nor reason."

And although he never left his mirth in outward appearance, yet still did he use the like mortifications which he was wont; yea he exercised acts of humility that he made most worldly men to wonder at him. On the Sundays, even when he was lord chancellor, he wore a surplice, and sung with the singers at the high mass and matins in his parish church of Chelsey; which the Duke of Norfolk on a time finding, said:—
" God body, God body, my lord chancellor a

parish clerk: you disgrace the king, and your office." "Nay, (said Sir Thomas, smilingly,) your grace may not think I dishonour my prince in my dutifulness to his lord and ours;" having in his mind that saying of David in the like case dancing before the ark of God, when his wife Michal laughed at him "Vilior fiam in oculis meis;" I will still think meanly of myself, whatsoever others shall think of me. He often would also in public processions carry the cross before the rest, thinking himself happy, if he could any way show love and readiness in Almighty God's service; and when many counselled him in the long processions in rogation week to use a horse for his dignity and age, he would answer: it beseemed not the servant to follow his master prancing on cockhorse, his master going on foot. He never undertook any business of importance, but he prepared himself first by confession and receiving the blessed sacrament devoutly, trusting more on the grace of God derived to us by these holy sacraments, than he did to his own wit, judgment and practice; yet every of them was in him extraordinary, so that he lived a most worthy life in all the course of his actions: never changed with any prosperity, nor dismayed with any adversity.

As when his barns of corn and hay were burnt, he never altered his countenance or showed the least sign of sorrow, only saying: "Fiat voluntas Dei; he hath bestowed much more upon us, and therefore may take away what he pleaseth:" besides he wrote a most patient letter to my lady, which is thus;—

"Mrs. Alice, I commend me unto you: having heard by my son Heron, that ours and some of our neighbours' barns with all the corn in them are burnt; although we may be sorrowful for the loss of so much good corn, abstracting from God's holy disposition; yet seeing that it hath been his divine pleasure to suffer it, we ought not only patiently but also willingly to receive this gentle scourge. God gave us all that we have; and seeing he hath taken part of it away by this chance, his blessed will be done: let us neither murmur nor grudge for this accident, but take it in good part, and give God thanks as well in adversity as in prosperity. Perhaps this loss may be a greater benefit of God than the gain of so much would have been; for he knoweth what is most expedient for us. Be therefore of good courage I pray thee, and taking all our family with you, go to the church and give God thanks as well for those things which he hath given us, as for those which he hath taken away, and for all that which he hath left us, which he can easily increase, when he seeth it fittest for us; and if he pleaseth to take more from us, his blessed will be fulfilled. Let it be diligently enquired out, what our neighbours have lost, and desire them not to be sad for any thing, for I will not see any of them endamaged by any mischance of my house, although I should thereby not leave myself so much as one spoon. I pray thee be cheerful with all my children and family. Also take counsel of our friends, how corn is to be provided for that which is needful for you, and for seed corn this next year, if perhaps it be fit that we sow any fields ourselves; and, whether that be fitting or no, I do not think it expedient, presently to give over all care of husbandry and let out our farm to others, until we have better and at more leisure considered of it. If we have more workmen in our house than we have need of, such may be dismissed, if they can be commodiously placed with other masters; but I will not suffer any to be sent away to run at random, without a place to dwell in. At my return to the king, I see things go so, as it is likely I shall stay with him a good while; yet because of this misfortune, perhaps I shall get leave to come and see you some time this next week, when we will confer more at leisure about these our household affairs. Farewell. From the Court at Woodstock, 13 Sept. 1529."*

* Both in the MS. and printed copies the date of this letter is 1539, which is a palpable mistake. Mr. More no

But mark how God rewarded this his patience: for it was in October next that he was made lord chancellor; by which office he might easily have purchased many fair houses, if his mind had aimed at worldly riches, and not rather thirsted after heavenly rewards. Some have not stuck to say, that if Sir Thomas had been so happy as to have died of his natural death about this time, he had been a very fortunate man, living and dying in all men's favour, in the highest judgments of the world, and prosperous also to his posterity; for he had left them a fair and great inheritance, especially by the king's gracious gift; yea, no doubt, a saint of God, because the whole course of his life was so virtuous and innocent. But in my mind they are all carnally wise that affirm this, and no way have tasted of heavenly wisdom. For the last scene of this tragedy is the best, and not to be wished to have been omitted for all the land King Henry enjoyed, though you add the abbey-lands and all, after which now his fingers' ends began to itch: for that Cardinal Wolsey had showed already a precedent thereof, by getting leave of the pope to dissolve certain small abbeys for the building

doubt wrote 1529, which is the true date, as Sir Thomas was made chancellor in the October of that year, soon after his return from Cambray. The barns destroyed were at Chelsey.

and maintenance of his great college of Christ church in Oxford, which for that cause, as I think, is St. Peter's work, and lieth still unfinished.

Though in all his life time Sir Thomas had showed lively examples of many excellent virtues, as piety, zeal of God's honour, wisdom, justice, liberality, contempt of the world and of worldly riches, yea what not? yet his most heroical virtues towards his end he hath expressed more lively and exactly, as magnanimity, contempt of honours, of wife, children, possessions, life itself, and whatsoever can be of us desired, and in stead thereof hath chosen disgraces, extreme adversities, imprisonment, loss of dignities, goods, and inheritance, and hath taken up his cross and followed Christ in shedding of his blood to his honour. "No champion is crowned till he hath gotten the victory;" and behold he most gloriously triumpheth over the flesh by forsaking his life and leaving it; the world, by despising it; and the devil by resisting manfully all his temptations.

CHAPTER IX.

WHEN Sir Thomas had behaved himself in his office of the chancellorship for the space of two years and a half so wisely that none could mend his doings, so uprightly that none could take exception against him or his just proceedings, and so dexterously that never any man did before or since that which he did; for he had taken such order for the dispatching of all men's causes, that on a time sitting as judge there, and having finished one cause, he called for the next to be heard; whereto was answered, that there was not one cause more depending. This he caused to be set down upon record; whereas at this day there are little fewer than a thousand, if not more; whereof some lie in the suds by the space of divers years.

When (as I say) Sir Thomas had deserved high commendations of every one, and now perceived that the king was fully determined to proceed to the unfortunate marriage of Anne Boleyn, and for that cause a parliament was called, wherein Sir Thomas being the chief officer of the higher house, was with divers bishops and noble men commanded by the king, to go down to the lower house to show unto them, both what many universities beyond the seas, and Oxford and Cambridge at home, had done in that behalf, with their public seals testifying the same. All which matters at the king's command he opened to the lower house, not showing his mind therein, yet doubting, (as good cause he had) lest further attempts should after follow, which, contrary to his conscience, by reason of his office, he was likely to be put unto; he made great suit to the Duke of Norfolk, his singular good friend, that he would be a means to the king that he might be discharged, with his majesty's favour, of the chancellorship; wherein for certain infirmities of his body he pretended himself unable any longer to serve. The duke being often thereto by Sir Thomas solicited, at length obtained of the king, when at a time convenient, by his majesty appointed, Sir Thomas repaired to the king to yield up unto him the great seal of England; which his majesty courteously received at his hands, with great praise and thanks for his worthy service in that office, at which time it pleased his highness to say thus unto him; "That for the service he had hitherto done unto him, in any suit that he should hereafter have unto him, that either should concern Sir Thomas's honour (that very word it liked his highness to use unto him) or that should appertain to his profit, he should not fail to find him a good and gracious lord." But how true these words proved, let others be judges, when the king not only not bestowed upon him the value of one penny, but took from him and his posterity all that ever he had, either given him by himself, or left him by his father, or purchased by himself.

The next morning being holiday, few yet knowing what had been done, he went to Chelsey church with my lady and his children and family; and, after mass was done, because it was a custom that one of my lord's gentlemen should then go to my lady's pew, and say, "his lordship is gone;" then did he himself come unto her, and, making a courtesy with his cap in his hand, said, " May it please your ladyship, my lordship is gone:" which she imagining to be but one of his jests, as he used many unto her, he sadly affirmed unto her, that it was true; for he had resigned up his office, and the king had graciously accepted it. This was the way that he thought fittest to break this matter unto his wife; who was full sorry to hear it; and it may be she spoke then those words, which I have rehearsed before, " Tilli vally; what will you do Mr. More? will you sit and make goslings in the ashes: it is better to rule than to be ruled." But to requite her brave mind, he began to find fault with her dressing, for which she chiding her daughters that none of them could espy it, they still saying they could find none; Sir Thomas merrily said, " Do you not perceive that your mother's nose standeth somewhat awry?" At which words she stept away from him in a rage. All which he did to make her think the less of her decay of honour, which else would have troubled her sore.

Shortly after this he called all his servants together, many of whom were gentlemen of good sort and fashion, and told them, that he could not maintain them as he gladly would, and therefore demanded them, what course of life they would betake themselves to; and if they purposed to serve any nobleman, he would undertake to place them to their contentment, who with eyes full of tears affirmed, that they had rather serve him for nothing, than most men for a great stipend: but when to this he would not agree, he settled them all in places most fit for their turns, either with bishops or noblemen. His barge he gave to my Lord Audley, who succeeded him in his office, and with it his eight watermen: his fool,* Pattison, he gave to the lord mayor of London, upon this condition,

* This ancient appendage to the households of the great appears in Holbein's painting of the More family. One anecdote of Pattison has been often related. When Sir Thomas scrupled to take the oath of the king's supremacy, Pattison expressed his surprise, adding, " Why, what eyleth him that he will not sweare? Whereupon should he styck to swere, I have sworne the oath myself." Another anecdote, which shows that whatever sport might be afforded to our ancestors by the simplicity of these unfortunate beings, they were sometimes found to be a real annoyance, is to be found in the " Il Moro" before quoted. In the course of the dialogue, Sir Thomas relates that, " Pattison was yesterday standing by the table while we were at dinner, and seeing a gentleman among the company with an unusually large nose, after he had gazed for some time upon the gentleman's face, he said aloud, to my great annoyance, ' What a terrific nose that gentleman has got.' As we all affected not to hear him, that the good man might not be abashed; Pattison perceived that he had made a mistake and endeavoured to set himself right by saying, ' How I lyed in my throat, when I said that gentleman's nose was so monstrously large: on the faith of a gentleman it really is rather a small one.' At this, all being greatly inclined to laugh, I made signs that the fool should be turned out of the room. But Pattison not wishing for his own credit's sake that this should be the termination of the affair (because he was always accustomed to boast, as above every other merit he possessed, that whatever he commenced he brought to a happy conclusion,) to bring this affair to a good end, he placed himself in my seat at the head of the table, and said aloud, ' There is one thing I would have you to know: that gentleman there has not the least atom of a nose.' "

that he should every year wait upon him that should have that office. After this he called before him all his children, and asking their advice, how he might now in the decay of his ability so impaired by the surrender of his office, that he could not hereafter as he had done and gladly would bear out the whole charges of them all himself (for all his children with their children had hitherto dwelt with him) so that they could not be able to continue together as he could wish they should: when he saw them all silent and none to show him their opinion therein, " Then will I (said he) show unto you my mind: I have been brought up at Oxford, at an Inn of Chancery, at Lincoln's-Inn, and in the king's court, from the lowest degree to the highest; and yet have I in yearly revenues at this present little left me above a hundred pounds by the year: so that now if we look to live together, you must be content to be contributories together. But my counsel is, that we fall not to the lowest fare first; we will not therefore descend to Oxford fare, nor to the fare of New-Inn; but we will begin with Lincoln's-Inn diet, where many right worshipful men of great account and good years do live full well; which if we find ourselves the first year not able to maintain, then will we the next year come down to Oxford fare, where many great learned and ancient fathers and doctors are continually conversant; which if our purses stretch not to maintain neither, then may we after with bag and wallet go a begging together, hoping that for pity some good folks will give us their charity, and at every man's door to sing a 'Salve Regina,' whereby we shall still keep company and be merry together." O worthy resolution! see how he expresseth his love towards his children, but more towards God, taking patiently whatsoever might befal him. And he that provideth for the worst, will be the better prepared to endure lesser crosses. But what an admirable thing is this, that whereas he was by the king taken into his majesty's service from a very worshipful living, as I have said, four hundred pounds by the year, to deal in the greatest and weightiest causes that concerned his highness and the realm, he had spent with painful cares, travels and troubles as well beyond the seas, as within this kingdom, in effect the whole substance of his life; yet with all the gain he got thereby (being never himself a wasteful spender) he was not now able after the resignation of his offices, to find for himself and those who necessarily belonged unto him, sufficient meat, drink, fuel, apparel, and such needful charges; all the lands, which he ever purchased being, as my uncle Roper well knew, not above the value of twenty marks by the year, and after his debts paid, he had not of my uncle's own knowledge (his chain excepted) in gold and silver left him the worth of one hundred pounds. Wherefore his children went to their own livings, all but my uncle Roper and my aunt, who lived in the house next unto him.

And how really he had desired himself to resign up his place of chancellorship, partly for the above mentioned consideration, and partly also for his own content and quiet enjoying of himself, may well appear in that he so much liked and highly commended the like deed in William Warham, that worthy archbishop of Canterbury, immediately before Cardinal Wolsey; as by this letter unto him is to be seen:* " I have always esteemed your most reverend fatherhood happy in your courses, not only when you executed with great renown the office of chancellorship; but also more happy now, when being rid of that great care you have betaken yourself to a most wished quietness, the better to live to yourself, and to serve God more easily; such a

* This sentence stands thus in the manuscript: " Now having performed by his earnest suit, that which long before this Cassiodorus had obtained from his prince, and the same which William Warham, that worthy Archbishop of Canterbury, had done immediately before Cardinal Wolsey; see how Sir Thomas praiseth him for that very deed, writing unto him in one of his epistles thus."

quietness I say that is not only more pleasing than all these troublesome businesses, but also more honourable far in my judgment, than all those honours which you then enjoyed. For many men, and amongst those some wicked men also, may oftentimes be raised to great offices: but when you had that high office of chancellorship, which, as all others of the like kind are, is of that nature, that the more authority and power one hath whilst he doth bear it, the more slanders he is subject unto having left it, to resign such an office voluntarily (which yet your fatherhood could scarce get leave to do with all the means you could use) none but a modest minded man would, nor any but a guiltless man dare, do. Wherefore many, and amongst them myself do applaud and admire this your act, which proceeded from a mind I know not whether more modest in that you would willingly forsake so magnificent a place, or more heroical in that you could contemn it, or more innocent in that you feared not to depose yourself from it, but surely most excellent and prudent it was to do so; for which your rare deed I cannot utter unto you how I rejoice for your sake, and how much I congratulate you for it, seeing your fatherhood to enjoy so honourable a fame, and to have obtained so rare a glory, by sequestering yourself far from all worldly businesses, from all tumult of causes, and to bestow the rest of your days with a peaceable conscience for all your life past, in a quiet calmness, giving yourself wholly to your book and to true Christian philosophy; which pleasing and contented state of yours, my own misery causeth me daily more and more to think of; who although I have no businesses worth the talking of (and yet he was then one of the king's privy counsel, treasurer of the exchequer, and employed in many embassages) yet because weak forces are easily oppressed with small matters, I am so troubled daily with businesses, that I have not as much as once leisure to visit your fatherhood, or to excuse myself therefore by letter, and scarcely was I able to write this unto you, by which I was to commend this my little book of Utopia unto your most reverend fatherhood, which an Antwerpian friend of mine (love swaying his judgment) hath thought fit to be published, and hath put it in print without my privity, being rather huddled up than polished, which I was emboldened to send to you, though it be unworthy of your learning, experience and dignity, relying on your courteous nature, which is wont to conster to the best every man's endeavours, also trusting in your tried love towards me, by which I hope, though the work itself should not like you, that yet for the author's sake you will favour it. Farewell, most honourable prelate."

A little after this time he wrote thus to Erasmus: "I have a good-while expected, if any man could accuse me of any thing, since the deposing myself of the chancellorship: and as yet no man hath come forth to complain of any my injustice: either I have been so innocent or so crafty that my adversaries must needs suffer me to glory, in the one, if they cannot abide I should do so in the other. Yea this the king's majesty also, as well in private discourse often, as also twice in public hath witnessed, for that (which shamefacedness will not suffer me to speak of myself) he commanded the most noble Duke of Norfolk high treasurer of England, when my successor an excellent man was settled in my place to testify this to all the assembly, that he had hardly at my earnest intreaty suffered me to let the office go; and not content with that singular favour in my behalf he caused the same again to be spoken of in his own presence when in the audience of a public meeting of the nobility and people my successor recited his first speech, as the custom is, in the assembly of all the estates, which we call the parliament."

He writeth also to Erasmus in another letter thus:—"That which I have from a child unto this day almost continually wished (my most dear Desiderius) that being freed from the troublesome businesses of public affairs, I might live somewhile only to God and myself, I have now by the espècial grace of Almighty God, and the favour of my most indulgent prince, obtained." And then having spoken somewhat of the weakness of his health, he goes on, saying: " Having these things often in my head, either that I was to depose myself of the office, or that I should fail in the performance of my duty therein, seeing that I could not dispatch those affairs, but that I must endanger my life, and so dispatch myself of the office howsoever, I purposed at the last to forego the one rather than both. Wherefore, because I would as well be careful of the public welfare as of mine own health, I was an earnest suitor to my prince, and at last have obtained by his singular courtesy, that because I began to grow weary and even ready to lie under my burden, I might be rid of that though a most honourable office, whereto his favour had raised me above all my deserving as it was wholly without my seeking. I beseech therefore all the saints in heaven, that by their intercession Almighty God would recompence this most favourable affection of the king's towards me, and that he would give me grace to spend the rest of my age in his service, profitably and not idly or vainly, affording me health of body, that I maybe the better able to take pains."

And to Cochleus he writeth thus:—" I have been lately sore sick for some months together not so much to the sight of others, as to mine own feeling, which infirmity I can scarce shake off now, when I have left off my office; for then I could not exercise my function of chancellor, unless I should endanger my health daily. The care of my recovery, but especially the due respect I had not to hinder public justice, moved me thereto, which I thought I should greatly hinder if being sickly I should be constrained to undertake businesses as I did when I was stronger. That leisure, which the favourable benignity of my most gracious prince hath vouchsafed to grant me I have purposed to dedicate wholly to my study and the honour of God."

And as for his contempt of worldly honour he writeth thus to Erasmus: "You will not believe how unwillingly I undertake embassages; neither can there be any thing more displeasing unto me than the function of an embassador." Of his Utopia he writeth, that he judged the book no better worthy than to lie always hidden in his own island, or else to be consecrated to Vulcan. Of his poetry he saith, "My epigrams never pleased my mind as you well know, my Erasmus, and if other men had not better liked them than myself they should never have been put out in print."

The year immediately before his troubles, he spent most in spiritual exercises, and in writing of books against heretics; of whom in another letter he speaketh thus: " That which I profess in my epitaph, that I have been troublesome to heretics, I have done it with a little ambition; for I so hate these kind of men, that I would be their sorest enemy that possibly they could have if they will not repent; for I find them such men, and so to increase every day, that I even greatly fear the world will be undone by them." Yet for all his hatred to them, no heretics suffered death whilst he was lord chancellor, as Erasmus confesseth in the above-mentioned letter. And indeed it seemeth he would not have them suffer death, because he writeth to that effect in the laws of his Utopia. Writing another time to Cochlie, he saith, " I would to God, my Cochlie, I had such skill in holy Scriptures and divinity, that I were able to write against these plagues of the world fruitfully and with good effect." Erasmus also confesseth that he hated those seditious opinions, with the which the world was then cruelly shaken.

He would often talk with his wife and children of the exceeding joys in heaven, and terrible pains of hell, of the lives of holy martyrs, what torments they endured for the love of God, of their marvellous patience and deaths, which they suffered most willingly rather than they would offend God's divine majesty; and what an honourable thing it was for the love of our

Lord Jesus Christ to abide imprisonment, loss o goods, lands, and life; adding also what a comfort it would be to him, if he might find that his wife and children would encourage him to die in a good cause; for it would cause him for joy thereof merrily to run to death; besides, as prophesying of his future troubles, he would tell them what miseries might chance to happen unto him. With which virtuous discourses he had so encouraged them, that when these things after fell upon him indeed, their misery seemed the more tolerable unto them, because shafts foreseen hurt not so much.

Within a while after the resigning of his office, Mr. Cromwell (now highly in the king's favour) came of a message from the king to Sir Thomas; wherein when they had thoroughly talked together, before his going away Sir Thomas said unto him, " Mr. Cromwell, you are entered into the service of a most noble, wise, and liberal prince: if you will follow my poor advice, you shall in your counsel-giving to his majesty, ever tell him what he ought to do, but never what he is able to do; so shall you show yourself a true and faithful servant, and a right worthy counsellor; for if a lion knew his own strength, hard were it for any man to rule him." But Cromwell never learned this lesson; for he ever gave that counsel to his prince, which he thought would best please him, and not what was lawful. For it was he that was the mischievous instrument of King Henry to pull down all abbies and religious houses, yea to ruinate religion utterly; whereby you may see the difference between King Henry a just prince, whilst he followed Sir Thomas More's counsel, and after a cruel tyrant and bloodsucker, when he practised Thomas Cromwell's plots and devices; and also we may see the issue of both these counsellors, the one having gotten great fame for his just deserts, the other having purchased eternal infamy, yea the overthrow of himself and his family. For though he attained to be Lord Cromwell, yea afterwards Earl of Essex, yet his honour and life was soon taken away from him most justly; and now there is scarce any of his posterity left, his lands are all sold, yea such was his grandchild's misery, that he complained very lamentably to some gentlemen that he had not bread to put into his mouth; whereas Sir Thomas More's great grandchildren, though they live not in great abundance, yet have they, God be blessed, sufficient to maintain the estate of poor* gentlemen; which God of his mercy continue.

Now had King Henry also chosen an archbishop of Canterbury for his own tooth, pro-

---

* In the printed copies the word 'honest' is substituted for 'poor.'

moted by the king, as I have heard say, at a bear-baiting, soon after Warham's death; his name was Thomas Cranmer, Anne Bullen's chaplain, a man wholly bent to fulfil the king's pleasure in all things: by his counsel Queen Mary was after disinherited, and all men were to swear to the succession of Queen Anne's issue, and to renounce the pope's authority, by acknowledging King Henry and his successors supreme heads of the church of England.

Unto this man there was a commission granted under the great seal to determine the marriage, who had a conscience large enough to put in execution, what the king did fancy; and sitting at St. Albans about this new match, all things were easily accorded. The king pretended that he could get no justice at the pope's hands; wherefore from thenceforth he sequestered himself and his kingdom from the see of Rome, marrying Queen Anne in private; for she was not solemnly carried through London, before she was great with child of Queen Elizabeth.

Thus every man may see the cause of our breach from Rome, the union whereof had continued more than nine hundred years, ever since holy Pope Gregory first converted us, and would have remained God knows how long, if that either King Henry would not have cast his liking upon a wanton damsel, or else the pope's conscience could have stretched to dispense with a king to have two wives together; for the king still would praise his former wife, and term her a virtuous woman; only forsooth scruple of conscience was pretended; but he could not see any cause of scruple in breaking his promise upon his appeal; whereby he professed he would stay until the determination of a general council, to which from the pope he had already appealed.

As soon as Sir Thomas had heard that King Henry was married, he said to my uncle Roper, "God give grace, son, that these matters within a while be not confirmed with oaths." My uncle then, although he saw no likelihood thereof, yet fearing always that that would fall out, which Sir Thomas foretold, waxed for these words very sore grieved. For he had many times had experience, that he spoke prophetically of divers things.

Before that Queen Anne should be carried in triumph from the Tower to Westminster through the streets of London, with many pageants and sumptuous shows, which proved after but a May-game, Sir Thomas received a letter from three great bishops, Durham, Winchester, and Bath, requesting him both to keep them company to her coronation, and also to take twenty pounds, which by the bearer thereof they had sent him, to buy him a gown; the money he thankfully received; yet stayed he still at home, and at their next meeting he said merrily thus unto them:— "In the letter, my lords, which you lately sent me, you requested two things of me; the one whereof I was well content to grant you, that the other I might the bolder deny; and like as the one, because I took you for no beggars, and myself I knew to be no rich man, I thought the rather to fulfil: so the other put me in mind of an emperor, that ordained a law, that whosoever had committed a certain offence, which now I remember not, except she were a virgin, should suffer death for it, such reverence had he to virginity. Now it happened that the first that offended in that crime was a virgin, which the emperor hearing of, was in a perplexity; as he that by some example would fain have that law put in execution. Whereupon when his counsel had sat long debating this case very solemnly, suddenly rose there up one plain man of the counsel, and said, 'why make you so much ado, my lords, about so small a matter? Let her be deflowered, and after devoured.' So, though your lordships have, in the matter of this marriage, hitherto kept yourselves virgins, yet take heed you keep your virginity still; for some there be, that by procuring your lordships first to be present at the coronation, next to preach for the setting forth thereof, and finally to write books in defence of it, are desirous to deflower you; and when they have deflowered you, they will not fail soon after to devour you. As for myself, it lieth not in my power, but that they may devour me, but God being my good Lord, I will provide so that they shall never deflower me." In which speech he most lively prophesieth both of all the bishops' fall to schism, which after befell; and his own death, which followed not long after.

These words of his, it is probable, came to Queen Anne's ears; who as impatient as an Herodias, not abiding that any in the realm should find fault with her great catch, she incensed King Henry more against Sir Thomas More than any other man; and a month after this solemnity was not past, but she got him to be sent prisoner to the Tower, little knowing that her fortune's wheel would soon turn after.

When the king perceived he could not win Sir Thomas to the bent of his lust by no manner of benefits, then lo, the fair sunshine day of his favours became overcast, and there ensued a terrible storm; he now going about by terrors and threats to drive him to consent unto it; full little imagining that he was a steady rock, against which no waves of his rage could prevail.

But mark how Sir Thomas prepared himself

for this valiant combat; having given over his office of chancellorship, he never busied himself in state matters any more, but gave himself wholly, during that year, which was between that and his troubles, not only to confute heretics, as I have said, but also addicted himself to great acts of mortification, prayer, and piety; he lessened his family, placing his men in other services; he sold his household stuff, to the value of one hundred pounds; he disposed his children into their own houses. As he lay by his wife's side, many nights he slept not for thinking the worst that could happen unto him, and by his prayers and tears he overcame the frailty of his flesh, which, as he confesseth of himself, could not endure a fillip. He hired a pursuivant to come suddenly to his house, when he was one time at dinner, and knocking hastily at his door, to warn him the next day to appear before the commissioners; to arm his family the better to his future calamity; imitating herein the act of Saint John the alms-giver, who hired a man to to come to him at meals, to tell him that his grave was not yet finished, and that he should take order for it, for the hour of death was uncertain.

But see how the beginning of this trouble grew first by occasion of a certain nun, called Elizabeth Berton, dwelling in Canterbury, who for her virtue and holiness was not a little set by amongst the common people; unto whom, for that cause, many religious persons, doctors of divinity, and divers laymen of good worship, used to resort; she affirming to them constantly, that she had revelations oftentimes from God, charging her to give the king warning of his wicked life, and of his abuse of the sword and authority committed from Almighty God unto him. She moreover, knowing that my Lord of Rochester, Bishop Fisher, was of a singular and rare virtuous life, and of admirable learning, repaired to Rochester, and there disclosed unto him all her revelations, desiring his advice and counsel therein; which the holy bishop perceiving might well stand with the laws of God, and his holy church, advised her (as she before had warning to do, and intended it) to go to the king herself, and let him understand all the circumstances thereof; which she performed stoutly, telling him all the revelations, and so returned to her cloister again.

In a short space after, she making a journey to the nuns of Sion, by means of one Father Reynold, a priest of that house, there she happened to enter into talk with Sir Thomas More concerning such secrets as had been revealed unto her, some part thereof touching deeply the matter of the king's supremacy, which shortly after this followed, and about the unlawfulness of the king's marriage. Sir Thomas, though he might well at that time, without danger of any law (of which there was then none) freely talk with her therein: yet notwithstanding, he demeaned himself so discreetly in all his talk with her, that he deserved no blame, but rather great commendations, as it was proved after most evidently, when it was sore laid to his charge.

After the divorce was pronounced, there was set out a book by authority from the council, which laid down the reasons why this divorce was done; wherein amongst other matters it was said, that therefore the king would not stay for the pope's sentence, because he had already appealed from him to the next general council. Straight after it was rumoured abroad, that Sir Thomas More had answered and refuted this book, of which slander Sir Thomas purged himself, by a letter to Mr. Cromwell, now secretary, and in the king's great favour, showing by many arguments that he neither would nor could confute that book; which letter is at large in the latter end of Sir Thomas's works.

But for all his purging himself, accusations still came thick and threefold upon him. For the king, by threats, and sifting of his former deeds, would either win him to his mind, or else find some occasion to except against his doings; and had he not been a man of singular integrity, free from all bribes and corruption in all his offices, every light matter would have been laid now heavy upon him; as of some things he was indeed accused, which added more to his honour and reputation. There was one Parnell, that grievously complained against Sir Thomas, because, when he was Lord Chancellor, at the suit of one Mr. Vaughan, his adversary, he had made a decree against him; for which, at his wife's hands, Sir Thomas had taken a great gilt cup as a bribe. For the clearing of which accusation, Sir Thomas being called before the body of the council, the whole matter was in grievous manner laid to his charge; and when Sir Thomas confessed the taking thereof, saying, that forasmuch as that cup was given him, long after the decree, for a new year's gift, he, at her importunity, of courtesy refused not to take it. Then the Earl of Wiltshire, Queen Anne's father, who was the preferrer of the suit, and hated Sir Thomas both for his religion, and for that he had not consented to his daughter's marriage, with much joy said unto the other lords, "Lo! did I not tell you, that you should find the matter true?" Whereupon Sir Thomas desired their honours, as they had courteously heard him tell the one part of his tale, so they would vouchsafe to hear the other with indifferent ears; which being granted, he further declared unto them, that albeit at her urging, he had indeed received the cup, yet immediately thereupon he caused his butler to fill it with wine, and therein drunk to her; which when he had done, and she pledged him, then he as freely as her husband bestowed it upon him, did even as willingly bestow the same upon her again, for her new year's gift; and so forced her to receive it, though much against her will; all which herself and many others there then present, deposed before that honourable assembly. Thus his accusers were put to shame enough, and he with honour acquitted.

At another time on a new year's day also, there came unto him Mrs. Coaker, a very rich woman, for whom, with no small pains, he had made a decree in chancery against the Lord of Arundel, (never fearing in acts of justice, any nobility of blood, or greatness of personage,) who presented him with a pair of gloves, and four score angels in them; he thankfully received the gloves of her, but refused the money, saying, " Mistress, seeing it were against good manners to refuse a gentlewoman's new year's gift, I am content to take your gloves; but as for the lining, I utterly refuse it," and so caused her to take her money again.

One Mr. Gresham likewise, having at the same time a cause depending before him in the chancery, sent him for a new year's gift, a fair gilt cup, the fashion whereof he very well liked; wherefore he caused the messenger to take one of his own cups, which was in value better, though the fashion pleased him not so well, and deliver it to his master in recompence of the other; and under no other condition would he receive it; wherefore he was fain so to do.

Many like unto those acts did he, which declared how clean his hands were from taking of any bribes, which I could set down, but to avoid tediousness they shall be omitted; for these are enough to show any man how little he gained, yea how little he cared, for all transitory wealth, esteeming virtues of the mind his richest treasure, and Christ naked on the cross his chief desire; which holy pleasure of his, Almighty God before his death fulfilled, when for his love he lost all that might be most dear unto worldly men, separation from wife and children, loss of all liberty, and the utter overthrow of all his goods and estate; yet by losing these things he gained better; for, instead of temporal, he achieved eternal, in lieu of transitory, he hath purchased permanent, in room of deceitful trash, he hath bought to himself a crown of glory; " Centuplum accepit, et vitam æternam possidet." He was a true merchant, that by selling all he had, bought the precious margarite spoken of by Christ in St.

Matthew, than which there can be imagined nothing more precious, which, without doubt, he enjoyeth for all eternity.

Now there was another parliament called, wherein there was a bill put into the Lower House to attaint the nun, and many other religious men of high treason, and Bishop Fisher with Sir Thomas More of misprision of treason; which bill the king supposed would be so terrible to Sir Thomas, that it would force him to relent, and condescend unto him; but therein he was much deceived; for first Sir Thomas sued, that he might be admitted into the parliament, to make his own defence personally; which the king not liking of, granted the hearing of this cause to my Lord of Canterbury, the Lord Chancellor, the Duke of Norfolk, and Mr. Cromwell, who appointing Sir Thomas to appear before them; my uncle Roper requested his father earnestly to labour unto them, that he might be put out of the parliament bill; who answered then that he would; but at his coming thither, he never once entreated them for it; when he came into their presence, they entertained him very courteously, requesting him to sit down with them, which in no case he would; then the Lord Chancellor began to tell him, how many ways the king's majesty had showed his love and favour towards him, how gladly he would have had him continue in his office, how desirous he was to have heaped still more and more benefits upon him, and finally, that he could ask no worldly honour and profit at his highness's hands, but that it was probable that he should obtain it; hoping by these words, declaring the king's affection towards him, to stir Sir Thomas up to recompence the king with the like, by adding his consent unto the king's, which the parliament, the bishops, and many universities had already consented unto.

Whereunto Sir Thomas mildly made this answer, " that there was no man living that would with better will do any thing which should be acceptable to his highness than he, who must needs confess his manifold bounty, and liberal gifts plentifully bestowed upon him; howbeit he verily hoped that he should never have heard of this matter any more; considering that from the beginning he had so plainly and truly declared his mind unto his majesty; which his highness, of his benign clemency had ever seemed, like a gracious prince, very well to accept of; never minding, as he said unto him, to molest him any more therewith; since which time," said he, " I never found any further matter to move me to any change; and if I could," said he, " there is not one in the whole world, which would have been more joyful for it."

Many speeches having passed to and fro on both sides, in the end, when they saw evidently, that they could not remove him from his former determination, by no manner of persuasion, then began they more terribly to threaten him, saying, the king's majesty had given them in command expressly, if they could by no gentle means win him, that they should in his name with great indignation charge him, that never there was servant so villainous to his sovereign, nor any subject so traitorous to his prince as he; for, by his subtle and sinister sleights, he had most unnaturally procured and provoked the king to set forth a book of the assertion of the seven sacraments, and for the maintenance of the pope's authority, so that he had caused his majesty to put a sword into the pope's hands to fight against himself, to his great dishonour, in all the parts of Christendom.

Now when they had displayed all their malice and threats against him, "My lord," said Sir Thomas, "these terrors be frights for children, and not for me; but to answer that, wherewith you chiefly burthen me, I believe the king's highness of his honour will never lay that book to my charge; for there is none that can in that point say more for my discharge than himself; who right well knoweth that I never was procurer, promoter, nor counsellor of his majesty thereunto; only, after it was finished, by his grace's appointment, and the consent of the makers of the same, I only sorted out, and placed in order the principal matters therein; wherein when I had found the pope's authority highly advanced, and with strange arguments mightily defended, I said thus to his grace, 'I must put your highness in remembrance of one thing, and that is this: the pope, as your majesty well knoweth, is a prince, as you are, in league with all other Christian princes; it may hereafter fall out, that your grace and he may vary upon some points of the league, whereupon may grow breach of amity and war between you both; therefore I think it best that that place be amended, and his authority more slenderly touched.' 'Nay,' quoth his grace, 'that shall it not; we are so much bound to the see of Rome, that we cannot do too much honour unto it.' Then did I further put him in mind of our statute of præmunire, whereby a good part of the pope's authority and pastoral cure was pared away; to which his majesty answered, whatsoever impediment be to the contrary, we will set forth that authority to the uttermost; for we have received from that see our crown imperial;' which till his grace with his own mouth so told me, I never heard before. Which things well considered, I trust when his majesty shall be truly informed thereof, and call to his gracious remembrance my sayings and doings in that behalf, his highness will never speak more of it, but will clear me himself." With which words they with great displeasure dismissed him, and parted.

Then took Sir Thomas his boat to Chelsey, wherein by the way he was very merry, and my uncle Roper was not sorry to see it; hoping that he had gotten himself discharged out of the bill. When he was landed and come home, they walked in his garden, where my uncle said unto him, " I trust, Sir, all is well, because you are so merry." " It is so, indeed son, I thank God." " Are you then, Sir, put out of the parliament bill?" said my uncle. " By my troth, son, I never remembered it." " Never remembered that!" said he, " that toucheth you and us all so near? I am very sorry to hear it; for I trusted all had been well when I saw you so merry." " Wouldest thou know, son, why I am so joyful? In good faith, I rejoice that I have given the devil a foul fall; because I have with those lords gone so far, that without great shame I can never go back." This was the cause of his joy, not the ridding himself of troubles, but the confidence he had in God, that he would give him strength willingly to suffer any thing for Christ's sake, that he might say with Christ Jesus, " Desiderio desideravi," &c. I thirst greatly to drink of the cup of Christ's passion; and with St. Paul, " Cupio dissolvi, et esse cum Christo." But these speeches, though they liked Sir Thomas well, yet pleased they my uncle Roper but a little.

Now after the report made of this their examination of Sir Thomas to the king, by the Lord Chancellor and the rest, King Henry was so highly displeased with Sir Thomas More, that he plainly told them, that he was resolutely determined, that the foresaid parliament bill should undoubtedly proceed against them. Yet to this the Lord Chancellor and the rest said, that they had perceived that all the Upper House was so powerfully bent to hear Sir Thomas speak in his own defence, that if he were not put out of the bill, it would utterly be overthrown, and have no force against the rest. Which words, although the king heard them speak, yet needs would he have his own will therein, adding, that he would be personally present himself at the passing of it. But the Lord Audley and the rest, seeing him so vehemently bent upon it, fell down upon their knees, and besought his majesty not to do so; considering that if he in his own person should be confronted, and receive an overthrow, it would not only encourage his subjects ever after to contemn him, but also redound to his dishonour for ever throughout all Christendom; and they doubted not, in time, but to find some other fitter matter against him; for in this case of the nun, they said, all men accounted him so clear and innocent, that for his behaviour therein every one reckoned him rather worthy of praise than of reproof. At which words of theirs, the king was contented, at their earnest persuasion, to condescend to their petition; yet was not his displeasure against Sir Thomas any whit assuaged, but much more incensed.

On the next morning, Mr. Cromwell meeting my uncle Roper in the Parliament House, told him that his father was put out of the bill, which message he sent presently to Chelsey; and when my aunt Roper told her father thereof, he answered, " In faith, Megg, quod differtur, non aufertur," knowing, as it were, the very bottom of the king's heart, and all his counsels, imagining that this was not any favour done unto him, but that they might find a fitter matter to work on, as it shortly after proved.

Within a while after the Duke of Norfolk fell into familiar talk with Sir Thomas, and amongst other speeches, he said unto him, " By the mass, Mr. More, it is perilous striving with princes; therefore, I could wish you as a friend to incline to the king's pleasure; for by God's body, Mr. More, indignatio principis mors est."—" Is that all, my lord, (said Sir Thomas,) why, then, there is no more difference between your grace and me, but that I shall die to-day, and you to-morrow. If, therefore, the anger of a prince causeth but a temporal death, we have greater cause to fear the eternal death, which the king of heaven can condemn us withal, if we stick not to displease him, by pleasing an earthly king."

Now in this parliament, in the year 1534, when as Queen Elizabeth had been born the September before, and Queen Anne had been proclaimed queen the 12th of April before that, and Queen Catherine declared the widow only of Prince Arthur, there was, I say, at this parliament an oath framed, whereby all English subjects should both renounce the pope's authority, and swear also to the succession of Queen Anne's children, accounting the Lady Mary illegitimate; within a month or thereabouts after the enacting of this statute, all the clergy, as well bishops as priests, yet no layman but Sir Thomas More, were summoned to appear at Lambeth, before the Lord Archbishop Cranmer, the Lord Chancellor Audley, Mr. Secretary Cromwell, the

Abbot of Westminster, with others appointed commissioners by the king, to tender this oath unto them.

On the same morning that Sir Thomas was to go thither, as he was accustomed before he took any matter of importance in hand, he went to Chelsey church, and there was confessed, and received at mass devoutly the blessed sacrament; and whereas ever at other times, before he parted from his wife and children, they used to bring him to his boat, and there kissing them, bade them farewell; at this time he suffered none of them to follow him forth of his gate, but pulled the wicket after him, and with a heavy heart, as by his countenance appeared, he took boat with his son Roper, and their men, in which sitting sadly a while, as it were with Christ in his agony in the garden, at the last suddenly he rounded my uncle in the ear, and said, " I thank our Lord, son, the field is won." Whereto my uncle answered at random, as not knowing then his meaning; " I am very glad thereof." But one may easily know what he meant, and so my uncle afterward perceived, that the burning love of God wrought in him so effectually, that it now had conquered all carnal affections; trusting to that saying of our Saviour, " Behold, and have confidence; I have conquered the world."

How wisely he behaved himself at Lambeth, may be seen in a letter of his sent after to my aunt Roper, which is set out in print in the latter end of his English works, with other his most singular letters, wherein he lively describeth to his children all his troubles, and showeth what a heavenly spirit he had to endure all for God's sake, trusting still chiefly to God's goodness, not to his own strength, the effect whereof is this:—
" After he was called before them, he requested of them to see the oath, which when he had read unto himself he answered, that he neither would find fault with the oath, nor with the authors of it, nor would blame the conscience of any man that had taken it, but for himself he could not take it without endangering his soul of eternal damnation; which if they doubted of, he would swear unto them, that that was the chief cause of his refusal; in which second oath, if they doubted to trust him, how then could they trust him in the former?" Which he having said, my Lord Chancellor replied, that all there were heartily sorry, he should make such an answer; for they constantly affirmed that he was the first man that denied to take it; which would greatly aggravate the king's displeasure against him; and forthwith they showed him a catalogue of the nobility and many others who had taken it, and had subscribed their names thereunto.

Yet because he would not blame any man's conscience therein, he was commanded to walk into the garden awhile; and presently all the clergymen, some bishops, many doctors, and priests were called in, who all took it, except Bishop Fisher, and one Doctor Wilson, without any scruple, stop, or stay; and the vicar of Croydon, saith Sir Thomas, called for a cup of beer at the buttery bar, " quia erat notus Pontifici," and he drunk " valde familiariter."*

---

* This notice of the vicar of Croydon is not in Stapleton, from whom More has translated in this part of the Life, but is taken from a letter of Sir Thomas More addressed to Margaret Roper, 17 April 1534. It was first published in the Works of Sir Thomas More, p. 1429; but may be found with other valuable illustrations of the life of More in Mr. Singer's edition of Roper's Life, p. 122. Neither has Cresacre More reported faithfully what his ancestor had said of this person. His words are these: " I hard also that Maister Vicare of Croydon, and all the remenant of the priestes of London that were sent for, wer sworne: and that they had such favour at the counsels' hande, that they were not lingered, nor made to dance any long attendance to their travaile and cost, as sutours were somtime wont to be, but were spedde a pace to their gret comfort: so farre forth that Maister Vicar of Croidon, either for gladnes or for drines, or els that it might be sene, ' quod ille notus erat pontifici,' went to my lorde's buttry barre, and called for drinke, and dranke ' valde familiariter.'" In the margin of Robinson's edition of the Utopia, this vicar of Croydon is again mentioned. " It is thought of some that here is unfainedly meant the late famous vicar of Croydon in Surrey." It is against that passage

After all these had soon dispatched the matter, for which they were sent for, Sir Thomas was called in again, and the names of all that had taken the oath, were showed him; whereto for himself he answered as before; then they often objected unto him obstinacy; because he would neither take it, nor give any reason, why he refused it; to which he replied, that his denial only would provoke the king's indignation sufficiently against him, and therefore he was loath any further to aggravate his displeasure, showing what urgent necessity drew him unto it; howbeit, if his majesty would testify that his expressing the causes, wherefore he refused it, would not provoke against him his further anger, he would not stick to set them down in writing; and if any man could satisfy those reasons to the content of his conscience, he would take the oath most willingly.* Then Cranmer, my lord archbishop

in 'The Epistle' in which it is said, that one virtuous and godly man and a professor of divinity was exceedingly desirous to go to Utopia to perfect the conversion of so amiable a people to Christianity. There is other evidence that this fine political romance was taken by many for reality.

* An important circumstance is here omitted, to be found in Sir Thomas More's own letter, which contains so full an account of all these proceedings. It is surprising, that Mr. More omitted it, as it tends to clear his ancestor from the charge of obstinacy, in not declaring his reasons for refusing

urged him, that seeing he was not certain of his conscience, but that it was a thing certain, that he must obey his prince, therefore was he to reject that doubtful conscience of his, and stick to the latter, which was undoubted. Yet if this argument were of any force, then in all controversies of religion we may soon be resolved to follow whatsoever any king commandeth us.

And when the Abbot of Westminster had said, that he might very well suspect his own conscience to be erroneous, because he alone would seem to control all the wisdom of the whole realm, who had made and taken it: thereto Sir Thomas answered, that if he alone should stand against so worthy a kingdom, he had great cause to fear his own conscience; but if that of his side he could produce a far greater number of as learned men as they, he thought himself "not then bound to conform his conscience to follow the consent of one kingdom against the general received opinion of the whole Christian world." When Mr. Secretary seemed greatly to

---

the oath. To his last remark it was answered, that though the king should give him licence to speak, under his letters patent, yet would it not serve against the statute. To this Sir Thomas More replied, that if he had the king's letters patent, he would trust to his honour for the rest. What more could have been expected?

pity him, Sir Thomas added, if any hard thing happened unto himself, he could not prevent it, without he should endanger his own soul.

Then asked they him, whether he would swear to the succession; to which he answered, that he was willing enough to do that, if the oath were set down in such words as he might safely take it; thereto my Lord Chancellor said, "See, Mr. Secretary, he will not swear to that neither, but under a certain form of words." "No truly, (replied Sir Thomas,) except I find that I may swear it without danger of perjury, and with a safe conscience."

When he had thus behaved himself, he was committed to the custody of the Abbot of Westminster for the space of four days; during which time the king consulted with his council, what order were meet to be taken with him. And at first albeit they were resolved, that, he swearing an oath not to be known whether he had sworn to the supremacy or no, nor what he thought thereof, he should be discharged; yet did Queen Anne by her importunate clamours so exasperate the king to proceed against him, contrary to his former resolution (but indeed for the greater honour of God and his martyr) the king caused again the oath of supremacy to be ministered unto him; who although again he made thereto a discreet qualified answer, nevertheless he was forthwith committed to the Tower; when as he went thither, wearing a chain of gold about his neck, Sir Richard Wingfield, who had the charge of his conveyance thither, advised him to send home his chain by his wife, or some of his children; "Nay, Sir, (said he,) that I will not; for if I were taken in the field by mine enemies, I would they should fare somewhat the better for me:" rather choosing to have it lost in the Tower, than that the king's officers should get it at home, when he should lose all; or else esteeming nothing lost but gained, which was lost for Christ. At his landing Mr. Lieutenant was ready to receive him at the Tower gate; where the porter demanded of him his upper garment: "Marry, porter, (said he,) here it is," and gave him off his cap; saying, "I am sorry it is no better for thee." "Nay, Sir, (quoth he,) I must have your gown;" which forthwith he gave him; and then was conveyed to his lodging, where he called unto him, John Wood, his man, there appointed to attend him, who could neither write nor read, and sware him before Mr. Lieutenant, that if he should hear or see him at any time speak or write any thing against the king, the council, or the state of the realm, he should open it to Mr. Lieutenant, that he might straightways reveal it again to the council. This was his peaceable and constant carriage in adversity, bearing all his troubles with great alacrity, that both God was much pleased with his willingness, and every man admired much his patience: for if adversity will try men's wisdom and true fortitude, surely Sir Thomas was a most wise man, that nothing happened unto him, which he did not in a manner foresee, and truly stout, that nothing could daunt his courage or abate his magnanimity.

When he had remained with great cheerfulness about a month's space in the Tower, his daughter Margaret, longing sore to see her father, made earnest suit, and at last got leave to go to him; at whose coming after they had said together the seven Psalms, and Litanies (which he used always to say with her when she came thither, before he would fall in talk of any worldly matters, to the intent he might commend all his words to Almighty God's honour and glory,) amongst other speeches he said thus unto her, "I believe, Megg, that they who have put me here, think they have done me a high displeasure; but I assure thee on my faith, mine own good daughter, that if it had not been for my wife and you my children, whom I account the chief part of my charge, I would not have failed long ere this to have closed myself in as strait a room as this, and straiter too; now since I am come hither without mine own desert,

I trust that God of his goodness will discharge me of my care, and with his gracious help supply the want of my presence amongst you; and I find no cause, I thank God, to reckon myself here in worse case, than in mine own house; for methinks God by this imprisonment maketh me one of his wantons, and setteth me upon his lap and dandleth me, even as he hath done all his best friends, St. John Baptist, St. Peter, St. Paul, and all his holy apostles, martyrs, and his most especial favorites, whose examples God make me worthy to imitate."

By which discourse of his it appeareth most evidently, that all the troubles, which ever happened unto him, were no painful punishments, but by his admirable patience and alacrity most profitable exercises. My aunt Roper contrary-wise, either because she would have more familiar access unto her father, or else because indeed she would really persuade him to follow the king's fancy, began to divert him from such zealous discourses, and forcibly to urge him with many reasons and motives to the taking of this oath, that they might enjoy his presence at his house at Chelsey; first, because he was more bound to the king than any man in England, and therefore ought the rather to obey his will in a case that was not evidently repugnant to God's law; secondly, it seemed not credible, that so many wise and learned men, as were in England, should all impugn the will of God; thirdly, that he should beware how he pinned his soul upon Bishop Fisher, being one of the meanest bishops in England; fourthly, that there were so many bishops, doctors, and learned men, that had taken it, so that he being a lay-man seemed bound, in her judgment, to accommodate his conscience to theirs; and lastly, every one thought him bound in conscience to approve that, which a whole parliament of the realm had so uniformly enacted; for which reasons many have condemned you, father, said she, either of inconsideration, rashness, or obstinacy. To the first Sir Thomas answered, as may appear by a letter of my aunt Roper's yet extant, which containeth all this their discourse, and by that letter of Sir Thomas's written to Mr. Cromwell, " that he had not slightly considered of this matter, but for these seven years' space, since the time that King Henry had written against Luther, he had diligently read over all the fathers both Greek and Latin, who all from Ignatius (St. John Evangelist's disciple) even to these late divines, with one consent, do agree of the pope's supremacy, which hath been also accepted of throughout all Christendom, these thousand years and more; and he saw not how one member of the church, as England was, could withdraw itself from the whole body;" yet when he saw this controversy began to be disputed of, he always had tempered his speeches against Tindall, that, 'ex professo,' he never argued upon that theme; but now being put to his choice, whether he should offend his conscience or the king, whether he should fall into temporal danger or eternal hazard of his soul, I cannot, saith he, resolve otherwise, than any wise man would.

To the second, he said he would not condemn any body for taking it; "For some," saith he, "may do it upon temporal hopes, or fear of great losses, for which I will never think any hath taken it; for I imagine nobody is so frail and fearful as myself; some may hope that God will not impute it unto them for a sin, because they do it by constraint; some may hope to do penance presently after; and others are of opinion that God is not offended with our mouth, so our heart be pure; but as for my part, I dare not jeopard myself upon these vain hopes."

To the third he saith, it was altogether improbable, because he refused this oath before it was tendered to Bishop Fisher, or before he knew whether he would refuse it or no.

To the fourth, "Though there were never so many learned prelates within this realm, that should take it, yet being many more in other parts of Christendom which think as I do, I am not bound to conform myself to these alone, having the doctors of the church on my side, who could not be drawn neither for hopes nor fears."

Finally, to the last, he wisely answered, that " Although to deny the decree of a general council were a damnable act, yet to withstand a statute of one realm's making, which contradicteth the constant opinion of the whole church, is neither a rash deed, nor an obstinate, but most laudable and Christian-like." All which disputation my aunt Roper set down in a letter to her sister Allington, printed together with Sir Thomas's letters.

After all this, my aunt Roper sought to fright him with the danger of death, which might perhaps move him to relent, when he cannot hinder his mishaps, but now he might prevent all, it being not too late; whereunto how humbly he speaketh of his own frailty; and how confidently he relieth upon God's mercy may be seen at large; whose words are so humble, so zealous, so godly, that they are able to pierce any man's heart, that will read them, in the latter end of his works; they breathe out an angelical spirit far different from the presumptuous speeches of either heretic or desperate man: " Lord help me! If God, for my many and grievous sins, will suffer me to be damned, his justice shall be praised in me; but I hope he will procure for me, that his mercy shall have the upper hand; nothing can happen, but that which God pleaseth; and what that is, though it should seem evil unto us, yet it is truly the best."

At another time, when he had questioned with my aunt Roper of his wife, children, and state of his house in his absence, he asked her at last how Queen Anne did. "In faith, father," said she, "never better; there is nothing else in the court but dancing and sporting." "Never better," said he; " alas, Meg, alas! it pitieth me to remember unto what misery, poor soul, she will shortly come. These dances of her's will prove such dances, that she will spurn our heads off like foot-balls; but it will not be long ere her head will dance the like dance." And how prophetically he spoke these words, the end of her tragedy proved.

Mr. Lieutenant coming into his chamber to visit him, rehearsed the many benefits and friendships that he had often received from him, and therefore that he was bound to entertain him friendly, and make him good cheer; but the case standing as it did, he could not do it without the king's displeasure; wherefore he hoped that he would accept of his good will, and of the poor fare he had; whereto he answered, "I verily believe you, good Mr. Lieutenant, and I thank you most heartily for it; and assure yourself I do not mislike my fare; but whensoever I do, then spare not to thrust me out of your doors."

Now whereas the oath of supremacy and marriage was comprised in few words in the first statute; the Lord Chancellor and Mr. Secretary did, of their own heads add more words unto it, to make it seem more plausible to the king's ears; and this oath, so amplified, they had exhibited to Sir Thomas and others; of which their deed Sir Thomas said to his daughter, "I may tell thee, Meg, that they who have committed me hither, for refusing an oath not agreeable with their own statute, are not able, by their own law, to justify mine imprisonment; wherefore it is great pity, that any Christian prince should be drawn to follow his affections by flexible counsel, and by a weak clergy lacking grace, for want of which they stand weakly to their learning, and abuse themselves with flattery most shamefully." Which words coming to the council's ears, that " they could not justify his imprisonment," they caused another statute, espying their oversight, to be enacted with all these additions.

Another time, looking out of his window, to behold one Mr. Reynolds, a religious, learned, and virtuous father of Sion, and three monks of the Charter-house, going forth of the Tower to their execution (for now King Henry began to be fleshed in blood, having put to death the nun, and divers others, and many after, for the supremacy and his marriage), Sir Thomas, as one that longed to accompany them in that journey, said to his daughter, then standing beside him, "Lo! dost not thou see, Meg, that these blessed fathers be now as cheerfully going to death, as if they were bridegrooms going to be married? Whereby, good daughter, thou mayest see what a great difference there is between such as have in effect spent all their days in a straight, hard, and penitential life, religiously, and such as have in the world, like worldly wretches (as thy poor father hath done), consumed all their time in pleasure and ease licentiously. For God, considering their long continued life in most sore and grievous penance, will not suffer them any longer to remain in this vale of misery, but taketh them speedily hence, to the fruition of his everlasting deity; whereas thy silly father, who hath most like a wicked caitiff, passed forth most sinfully the whole course of his miserable life, God thinketh him not worthy to come so soon to that eternal felicity, but leaveth him still in the world, further to be plunged and turmoiled with misery." By which most humble and heavenly meditation, we may easily guess what a spirit of charity he had gotten by often meditations, that every sight brought him new matter to practice most heroical resolutions.

Within a while after this, Mr. Secretary coming to him from the king (who still gaped more for Sir Thomas's relenting, than all his other subjects), pretended much friendship towards Sir Thomas, and for his comfort told him, that the king was his good and gracious lord, and minded not to urge him to any matter, wherein he should have any cause of scruple from thenceforth to trouble his conscience. As soon as Mr. Secretary was gone, to express what comfort he received of his words, he wrote with a coal, (as he did usually many other letters, because all his ink had been taken from him by the king's express commandment), certain excellent witty verses, which are printed in his book.

CHAPTER X.

ALL the while Sir Thomas was in the Tower, he was not idle, but busied himself in writing (with a coal,* for the most part,) spiritual treatises, as the "Three Books of Comfort in Tribulation," where, in dialogue-manner, under the names of two Hungarians, fearing the Turks running over their country, who had made great preparations therefore, he painteth out in lively colours, both the danger that England stood then in to be overwhelmed with heresy, and how good Catholics should prepare themselves to lose liberty, life, and lands, and whatsoever can be most dear unto them, rather than to forsake their faith. It is a most excellent book, full of spiritual and forcible motives, expressing lively Sir Thomas's singular resolution to apply all those wholesome medicines to himself, now being ready to practice in deed, what he setteth down in words.

* A stick of charcoal. The clause is not in the manuscript, and is probably not genuine.

When he had remained a good while in the Tower, my lady, his wife, obtained leave to see him, that he might have more motives to break his constancy; who at the first coming to him, like a plain rude woman and somewhat worldly withall, in this manner began bluntly to salute him, "What the goodyear, Mr. More, I marvel that you, who have been hitherto always taken for a wise man, will now so play the fool, as to lie here in this close filthy prison, and be content to be shut up thus with mice and rats, when you might be abroad at your liberty, with the favour and good will both of the king and his council, if you would but do as all the bishops and best learned of his realm have done; and seeing you have at Chelsey a right fair house, your library, your books, your gallery, your garden, your orchard, and all other necessaries so handsome about you; where you might, in company with me your wife, your children, and household, be merry. I muse what a God's name you mean, here still thus fondly to tarry." After he had a good while heard her, he said unto her, with a cheerful countenance, " I pray thee, good Mrs. Alice, tell me one thing." " What is that?" saith she. " Is not this house as near heaven as mine own?" She answering after her custom, " Tilly vally, tilly vally!" he replied, " How sayest thou, Mrs. Alice, is it not so indeed?" " Bone Deus, man, will this gear never be left?" " Well, then, Mrs. Alice, if it be so, I see no great cause why I should much joy either of my fair house, or any thing belonging thereunto, when if I should be but seven years buried under the ground, and rise and come hither again," (he might have said but seven months,) " I should not fail to find some therein that would bid me get out of doors, and tell me plainly, that it were none of mine; what cause have I then to like such a house as would so soon forget his master? Again, tell me, Mrs. Alice, how long do you think we may live and enjoy it?" " Some twenty years," said she. " Truly," replied he, " if you should say a thousand years, it were somewhat; and yet he were a very bad merchant that would put himself in danger to lose eternity for a thousand years; how much the rather, if we are not sure to enjoy it one day to an end." And thus her persuasions moved him but a little, thinking of those words of Job to his wife, tempting him, " Quasi una ex stultis mulieribus locuta es."*

* We have, in the " Il Moro," a story illustrative of the character of Lady More, who appears to have been but an unsuitable companion for Sir Thomas. " Wherefore," says one of the speakers, " to your opposition I will only reply, that it is exactly similar to a fine trait of your lady, Sir Thomas More, which I have several times wished to relate to you. You were reading to your daughters on the nature of a line, and

Not long after this came there to him, at two several times, the Lord Chancellor, the Dukes of Norfolk and Suffolk, with Mr. Secretary, and certain others of the privy council, to procure him by all means and policies they could, either to confess precisely the king's supremacy, or plainly to deny it. Here we may see that those very men, which seemed to cry before unto him, "Osanna, benedictus, qui venit in nomine Domini," say here, " Tolle, tolle, crucifige eum." This is the fickleness of the world and worldly men. But to this as appeareth by the examinations set out at the end of his English works, they could never bring him, because he was loth to aggravate the king's displeasure against himself, saying only, that the statute was like a two edged sword; if he should speak against it, he should procure the death of his body; and if he should

taking great pains to make them understand that it consisted only of length, without breadth or thickness. When you had done, your lady called your daughters into the hall, and said to them, ' How very clever you are, children! Where was the necessity for your father to puzzle his brains for a whole hour to show you what a line is? Look here, stupid children as you are, here is a line,' pointing at the same time to a beam which crossed the hall." " Tilli vally" occurs in Shakspeare. Lady More, however, appears to some advantage in her letter to Cromwell, written about this time, which is given in the Appendix.

consent unto it, he should procure the death of his soul.

After all these examinations, came Mr. Rich, afterwards made the Lord Rich for his good service done in this point, then newly made the king's solicitor, Sir Richard Southwell, and one Mr. Palmer, Mr. Secretary's man, sent by the king to take away all his books; and while Sir Richard and Mr. Palmer were busy in trussing up the books, Mr. Rich, pretending to talk friendly with Sir Thomas, said thus unto him, (as it proved after of set purpose), " Forasmuch as it is well known, Mr. More, that you are a man both wise and well learned in the laws of this realm, and in all other studies, I pray you, Sir, let me be so bold as of good will to put unto you this case: admit there were an act of parliament made, that all the realm should take me for king, would not you, Mr. More, take me for king?" " Yes, Sir,' said Sir Thomas, " that I would." " I put the case further," said Mr. Rich, " that there were an act of parliament, that all the realm should take me for pope, would not you then take me for pope?" " For answer," said Sir Thomas, " to your first case, the parliament may well, Mr. Rich, meddle with the state of temporal princes; but to make answer to your other case, suppose the parliament should make a law, that God should not be God, would you then, Mr. Rich, say so?" "No, Sir," said he, "that I would not; for no parliament can make such a law." "No more," reported he, that Sir Thomas should say (but indeed he made no such inference, as he avouched after to Mr. Rich's face,) "could the parliament make the king supreme head of the church;" and upon this only report of Mr. Rich, Sir Thomas was shortly after indicted of high treason, upon the new statute of the supremacy. At this time, Mr. Lieutenant reported after to Sir Thomas that Mr. Rich had so vile a smell about him that he could scarce endure him, which Sir Thomas also felt.

He had, a little before this, begun a divine treatise of the passion of Christ; but when he came to expound those words of the Gospel, "And they laid hands upon him, and held him;" these gentlemen took from him all his books, ink, and paper, so that he could write no more. Which being done, he applied himself wholly to meditation, keeping his chamber windows fast shut, and very dark; the occasion whereof Mr. Lieutenant asking him, he said, "When all the wares are gone, the shop windows are to be shut up." Yet still, by stealth, he would get little pieces of paper, in which he would write divers letters with a coal, of which my father left me one, which I account as a precious jewel, afterwards drawn over by my grandfather with ink.*

What respect Sir Thomas had not to displease the king, in any of his deeds and answers, may be seen by his discreet behaviour in all his proceedings: for, first, in his books he never handled exactly the pope's supremacy, though urgent occasion were given him by the books which he took in hand to confute; secondly, whatsoever writings he had, touching that controversy, he either made them away, or burnt them, before his troubles; as a book, which the Bishop of Bath had written of that matter; thirdly, he would never take upon him to advise any man in that point, though much urged thereto by letters, especially of Doctor Wilson, his fellow-prisoner in the Tower, knowing himself, being a layman, not to be bound to persuade a clergyman, much less a doctor of divinity; fourthly, when he was brought from the Tower to Westminster to answer his indictment, and thereupon arraigned at the King's Bench bar,

---

* This passage is corrupted in the printed copies, where it stands thus: " Yet still, by stealth, he would gett little peeces of paper, in which he would write diuerse letters with a coale: of which my father left me one, which was to his wife; which I accounte as a precious iewell, afterwards drawen ouer by my grand-fathers sonne with inke."

where he had often asked his father's blessing; he openly told the judges, that he would have abidden in law, and demurred upon the indictment, but that he should have been driven thereby to confess, of himself, that he had denied the king's supremacy, which he protested he never had done. And indeed the principal fault there laid to his charge was, that he maliciously, traitorously, and diabolically would not ntter his mind of that oath. Whereto Sir Thomas pleaded not guilty, and reserved to himself advantage to be taken of the body of the matter after verdict, to avoid that indictment, adding moreover, that if only those odious terms were taken out, he saw nothing that could charge him of any treason.

After that the king had endeavoured, by all means possible, to get Sir Thomas's consent unto his laws, knowing that his example would move many, being so eminent for wisdom and rare virtues, and could by no means obtain his desire, he commanded him to be called to his arraignment at the King's Bench bar, having been a prisoner in the Tower somewhat more than a twelvemonth, for he was committed about mid April, 1534, and this happened the 7th of May, 1535. He went thither leaning on his staff, because he had been much weakened by his imprisonment, his countenance cheerful and constant; his judges were Audley, the lord chancellor; Fitzjames, the lord chief justice; Sir John Baldwin, Sir Richard Leicester, Sir John Port, Sir John Spelman, Sir Walter Luke, Sir Anthony Fitzherbert, where the king's attorney reading a long and odious indictment, containing all the crimes that could be laid against any notorious malefactor, so long, as Sir Thomas professed, he could not remember a third part of that which was objected against him; but the special fault was that of the refusal of the oath, as is before spoken, for proof whereof his double examination in the Tower was alleged; the first before Cromwell, Thomas Beadle, John Tregunnell, &c. to whom he professed that he had given over to think of titles, either of popes or princes, although all the whole world should be given him, being fully determined only to serve God; the second before the Lord Chancellor, Duke of Suffolk, Earl of Wiltshire, and others, before whom he compared that oath to a two-edged sword, for if he should take it, his soul should be wounded; if he refused it, his body. That he had written letters to Bishop Fisher to persuade him therein, because their answers were alike; upon all which it was concluded, that Sir Thomas was a traitor to his prince and realm, for denying the king's supreme jurisdiction in ecclesiastical government. Presently after this indictment was read, the Lord Chancellor and the Duke of Norfolk spoke to this effect unto him: " You see now how grievously you have offended his majesty. Yet he is so merciful, that if you will lay away your obstinacy, and change your opinion, we hope you may obtain pardon of his highness." Whereto the stout champion of Christ replied, " Most noble lords, I have great cause to thank your honours for this your courtesy; but I beseech Almighty God that I may continue in the mind I am in, through his grace, unto death." By which three words he exercised the acts of three virtues, humanity, piety, and fortitude, showing himself a civil man, a godly Christian, and a noble confessor of Christ's truth.

After this he was suffered to say what he could in his own defence, and then he began in this sort: " When I think how long my accusation is, and what heinous matters are laid to my charge, I am stroken with fear, lest my memory and wit both, which are decayed together with the health of my body, through an impediment contracted by my long imprisonment, so as I shall not be able to answer these things on the sudden, as I ought, and otherwise could." After this there was brought him a chair, in which when he was sate, he began again thus:

"There are four principal heads, if I be not deceived, of this my indictment, every of which I purpose, God willing, to answer in order; to the first that is objected against me, to wit, that I have been an enemy of a stubbornness of mind to the king's second marriage; I confess that I always told the king my opinion therein, as my conscience dictated unto me, which I neither ever would, nor ought to have concealed; for which I am so far from thinking myself guilty of high treason, as that of the contrary, I being demanded my opinion by so great a prince in a matter of such importance, whereupon the quietness of a kingdom dependeth, I should have basely flattered him against mine own conscience, and not uttered the truth as I thought, then I should worthily have been accounted a most wicked subject, and a perfidious traitor to God; if herein I had offended the king, if it can be an offence to tell one's mind plainly, when our prince asketh us, I suppose I have been already punished enough for this fault, with most grievous afflictions, with the loss of all my goods, and committed to perpetual imprisonment, having been shut up already almost these fifteen months.

"My second accusation is, that I have transgressed the statute in the last parliament, that is to say, being a prisoner, and twice examined by the lords of the council, I would not disclose unto them my opinion, out of a malignant, perfidious, obstinate and traitorous mind, whether the king were supreme head of the church or no; but answered them, that this law belonged not to me, whether it were just or unjust, because I did not enjoy any benefice from the church; yet I then protested, that I never had said or done any thing against it, neither can any one word or action of mine be produced, to make me culpable; yea this I confess was then my speech unto their honours, that I hereafter would think of nothing else, but of the bitter passion of our blessed Saviour and of my passage out of this miserable world. I wish no harm to any; and if this will not keep me alive, I desire not to live; by all which I know that I could not transgress any law, or incur any crime of treason; for neither this statute nor any law in the world can punish any man for holding his peace; for they only can punish either words or deeds, God only being judge of our secret thoughts."

Of which words, because they were urgent indeed, the king's attorney interrupted him and said: "Although we have not one word or deed of yours to object against you, yet have we your silence, which is an evident sign of a malicious mind, because no dutiful subject being lawfully asked this question, will refuse to answer." To which Sir Thomas replied, saying: " My silence is no sign of any malicious mind, which the king himself may know by many of my dealings, neither doth it convince any man of breach of your law. For it is a maxim amongst the civilians and canonists, ' Qui tacet, consentire videtur;' he that holdeth his peace, seemeth to consent. And as for that you say, no good subject will refuse to answer directly, I think it verily the duty of a good subject, except he be such a subject as will be an evil Christian, rather to obey God than man, to have more care of offending his conscience, than of any other matter in the world, especially if his conscience procure neither heavy scandal nor sedition to his prince or country, as mine hath not done; for I here protest unfeignedly, that I never revealed it to any man living.

" I now come to the third capital matter of my indictment, whereby I am accused, that I maliciously attempted, traitorously endeavoured, and perfidiously practised against this statute, as the words thereof affirm, because I wrote eight sundry packets of letters, whilst I was in the Tower, unto Bishop Fisher, by which I exhorted him to break the same law, and induced him to the like obstinacy; I would have these letters produced and read against me, which may either free me or convince me of a lie. But because you say the bishop burnt them all, I will here tell the truth of the whole matter; some were only of private matters, as about our old friendship and acquaintance; one of them was in answer to his, whereby he desired of me to know how I had answered in my examinations to this oath of supremacy; touching which, this only I wrote unto him again, that I had already settled my conscience; let him settle his to his own good liking; and no other answer I gave him, God is my witness, as God shall, I hope, save this my soul; and this I trust is no breach of your laws.

" The last objected crime is, that being examined in the Tower I did say, that this law was like a two-edged sword; for in consenting thereto, I should endanger my soul; in refusing it, I should lose my life: which answer, because Bishop Fisher made the like, it is evidently gathered, as you say, that we both conspired together. Whereto I reply, that my answer there was but conditional, if there be danger in both either to allow or disallow this statute; and therefore, like a two-edged sword, it seemeth a hard thing, that it should be offered to me, that never have hitherto contradicted it either in word or deed. These were my words. What the bishop answered, I know not. If his answer were like mine, it proceeded not from any conspiracy of ours, but from the likeness of our wits and learning. To conclude, I unfeignedly avouch, that I never spake word against this law to any living man; although perhaps the king's majesty hath been told the contrary."

'To this full answer the attorney did not reply any more, but the word, malice, was in the mouth of all the court; yet could no man produce either word or deed to prove it; yet for all this clearing of himself, for a last proof to the jury that Sir Thomas was guilty, Mr. Rich was called forth to give evidence unto them upon his oath, which he did forthwith, affirming that which we have spoken of before in their communication in the Tower, against whom, now sworn and forsworn, Sir Thomas began in this wise to speak, "If I were a man, my lords, that did not regard an oath, I needed not at this time in this place, as is well known unto every one, to stand as an accused person. And if this oath, Mr. Rich, which you have taken be true, then I pray, that I never see God in the face: which I would not say, were it otherwise, to gain the whole world."

Then did he recite their whole communication in the Tower, according as it was, truly and sincerely, adding this: "In good faith, Mr. Rich, I am more sorry for your perjury, than for mine own peril; and know you, that neither I nor any man else to my knowledge ever took you to be a man of such credit, as either I or any other would vouchsafe to communicate with you in any matter of importance. You know that I have been acquainted with your manner of life and conversation a long space, even from your youth to this time; for we dwelt long together in one parish,* where as yourself can well tell (I am sorry you compel me to speak it) you were always esteemed very light of your tongue, a great dicer and gamester, and not of any commendable fame either there or at your house in the Temple, where hath been your bringing up. Can it therefore seem likely to your honourable lordships, that in so weighty a cause I should so unadvisedly overshoot myself as to trust Mr. Rich, a man always reputed of me for one of so little truth and honesty, so far above my sovereign lord, the king, to whom I am so deeply indebted for his manifold favours, or any of his noble and grave counsellors, that I would declare only to Mr. Rich the secrets of my conscience touching the king's supremacy; the special point, and

* The parish of St. Lawrence in the Jewry, in which parish Sir John More lived, and by his last will directed that he should be buried in the church. Several of the Riches were buried in that church, as may be seen in Stowe, p. 277.

only mark, so long sought for at my hands, which I never did, nor never would reveal after the statute once made, either to the king's highness himself, or to any of his noble counsellors, as it is well known to your honours, who have been sent for no other purpose, at sundry times, from his majesty's person to me, in the Tower; I refer it to your judgments, my lords, whether this can seem a thing credible unto any of you.

"And if I had done as Mr. Rich hath sworn, seeing it was spoken but in familiar secret talk, affirming nothing but only in putting of cases, without any unpleasing circumstances, it cannot justly be taken to be spoken maliciously, and where there is no malice there can be no offence. Besides this, my lords, I cannot think that so many worthy bishops, so many honourable personages, and so many worshipful, virtuous, and well learned men as were in the parliament assembled at the making of that law, ever meant to have any man punished by death in whom there could be found no malice, taking 'malitia' for 'malevolentia;' for if 'malitia' be taken in a general signification for any sin, no man there is that can excuse himself thereof. Wherefore this very word 'maliciously' is as material in this statute, as the word 'forcible' is in the statute of forcible entry; for in that case, if any enter peaceably, and put his adversary out forcibly, it is no offence; but if he enter forcibly, he shall be punished by that statute.

"Besides all the unspeakable goodness of the king's highness towards me, who hath been so many ways my singular good lord and gracious sovereign, he, I say, who hath so dearly loved and trusted me, even from my first coming into his royal service, vouchsafing to grace me with the dignity of being one of his privy council, and hath most liberally advanced me to offices of great credit and worship, finally, with the chief dignity of his majesty's high chancellor, the like whereof he never did to any temporal man before, which is the highest office in this noble realm, and next to his royal person, so far above my merits and qualities, honouring and exalting me, of his incomparable benignity, by the space of these twenty years and above, showing his continual favours towards me, and now at last it hath pleased his highness, at mine own humble suit, to give me licence, with his majesty's favour, to bestow the residue of my life in the service of God, for the better provision of my soul, to discharge and disburthen me of that weighty dignity, before which he had still heaped honours more and more upon me; all this his highness's bounty so long and so plentifully poured upon me, were in my mind matter sufficient to convince this slanderous accusation so wrongfully by this man surmised and urged against me, which I commit to your lordship's honourable considerations, whether this oath be likely or not to be true."

Mr. Rich, seeing himself so evidently to be disproved, and his credit so foully defaced, caused Sir Richard Southwell and Mr. Palmer, who, in the time of their communication, were in the same chamber with them, to be there sworn, what words had passed between them. Whereupon Mr. Palmer, upon his deposition, said, that he was so busy in the trussing up Sir Thomas's books in a sack, that he took no heed to their talk. Sir Richard Southwell also said, likewise, that because he was appointed only to look to the conveying of these books, he gave no ear unto them. And after all this, Sir Thomas alleged many other reasons in his own defence, to the utter discredit of Mr. Rich's foresaid evidence, and for proof of the clearness of his own conscience.

But for all that ever he could do or say, the jury of twelve men, whose names were Sir Thomas Palmer, Sir Thomas Pierte, George Lovell, esquire; Thomas Burbage, esquire; Geoffrey Chamber, gentleman; Edward Stockmore, gentleman; William Browne, gentleman; Jaspar Leake, gentleman; Thomas Billington, gentleman; John Parnel, gentleman; Richard Bellamy, gentleman; George Stoakes, gentleman. These, I say, going together, and staying scarce one quarter of an hour, (for they knew what the king would have done in that case) returned with their verdict, guilty.

Wherefore the Lord Chancellor, as chief judge in that matter, began presently to proceed to judgment; which Sir Thomas perceiving, said unto him, " My lord, when I was towards the law, the manner in such cases was, to ask the prisoner, before sentence, whether he could give any reason why judgment should not proceed against him." Upon which words the Lord Chancellor, staying his sentence, wherein he had already partly proceeded, asked Sir Thomas what he was able to say to the contrary, who forthwith made answer in this sort: " Forasmuch as, my lords, this indictment is grounded upon an act of parliament directly repugnant to the laws of God, and his holy church, the supreme government of which, or of any part thereof, no temporal person may, by any law, presume to take upon him, that which rightfully belongeth to the see of Rome, which by special prerogative was granted by the mouth of our Saviour Christ himself to Saint Peter, and the Bishops of Rome his successors only, whilst he lived, and was personally present here upon earth; it is therefore, amongst Catholic Christians, insufficient in law to charge any Christian man to obey it." And for proof of this sound assertion, he declared, amongst many reasons and sound authorities, that " like as this realm alone being but one member, and a small part of the church, might not make a particular law disagreeing with the general law of Christ's universal Catholic church, no more than the city of London, being but one member in respect of the whole realm, may enact a law against an act of parliament, to bind thereby the whole kingdom. So showed he further that this law was even contrary to the laws and statutes of this our realm, not yet repealed, as they might evidently see in Magna Charta, where it is said that ' Ecclesia Anglicana libera sit, et habeat omnia jura integra et libertates suas illæsas.' And it is contrary also to that sacred oath, which the king's highness himself, and every other Christian prince always receive with great solemnity at their coronations. Moreover, he alleged that this realm of England might worse refuse their obedience to the see of Rome, than any child might to their natural father. For, as Saint Paul said to the Corinthians, ' I have regenerated you, my children, in Christ,' so might that worthy pope of Rome Saint Gregory the Great, say to us Englishmen, ye are my children, because I have given you everlasting salvation; for, by Saint Augustin and his followers, his immediate messengers, England first received the Christian faith, which is a far higher and better inheritance than any carnal father can leave to his children, for a son is only by generation; we are by regeneration made the spiritual children of Christ and the pope."

To these words the Lord Chancellor replied, that seeing all the bishops, universities, and best learned men of this realm had agreed to this act, it was much marvelled that he alone should so stiffly stick thereat, and so vehemently there argue against it. To which words Sir Thomas answered, that " if the number of bishops and universities were so material as his lordship seemeth to make it, then do I, my lord, see little cause why that thing in my conscience should make any change; for I do not doubt but of the learned and virtuous men that are yet alive, I speak not only of this realm, but of all Christendom about, there are ten to one that are of my mind in this matter; but if I should speak of those learned doctors and virtuous fathers, that are already dead, of whom many are saints in heaven, I am sure that there are far more, who all the while they lived, thought in this case as I think now. And therefore, my lord, I think myself not bound to conform my conscience to the council of one realm against the general consent of all Christendom."

Now when Sir Thomas had taken as many exceptions as he thought meet, for the avoiding of this indictment, and alleging many more substantial reasons than can be here set down, the Lord Chancellor having bethought himself, and being loth now to have the whole burthen of this condemnation to lie upon himself, asked openly there the advice of my Lord Chief Justice of England, Sir John Fitzjames, whether this indictment were sufficient or no; who wisely answered thus: " My lords all, by Saint Gillian," for that was ever his oath, " I must needs confess, that if the act of parliament be not unlawful, then the indictment is not, in my conscience, insufficient." An answer like that of the Scribes and Pharisees to Pilate: ' If this man were not a malefactor, we would never have delivered him unto you.' And so, with IFS and ANS, he added to the matter a slender evasion. Upon whose words my Lord Chancellor spoke, even as Caiaphas spoke to the Jewish council: ' Quid adhuc desideramus testimonium, reus est mortis.' And so presently he pronounced this sentence:—

That he should be brought back to the Tower of London, by the help of William Bingston, sheriff, and from thence drawn on a hurdle through the city of London to Tyburn, there to be hanged till he be half dead, after that cut down yet alive, his belly ripped, his bowels burnt, and his four quarters set up over four gates of the city, and his head upon London Bridge.

This was the judgment of that worthy man, who had so well deserved both of king and country, for which Paulus Jovius calleth King Henry another Phalaris.

The sentence yet was, by the king's pardon, changed afterwards only into beheading, because he had borne the greatest office of the realm; of which mercy of the king's, word being brought to Sir Thomas, he answered merrily, "God forbid the king should use any more such mercy unto any of my friends; and God bless all my posterity from such pardons."

When Sir Thomas had now fully perceived that he was called to martyrdom, having received sentence of death, with a bold and constant countenance he spoke in this manner: "Well, seeing I am condemned, God knows how justly, I will freely speak for the disburthening of my conscience, what I think of this law. When I perceived that the king's pleasure was to sift out from whence the pope's authority was derived, I confess I studied seven years together to find out the truth thereof; and I could not read in any one doctor's writings, which the church alloweth, any one saying that avouched that a layman was, or could ever be, head of the church."

To this my Lord Chancellor again : " Would you be accounted more wise, and of more sincere conscience than all the bishops, learned doctors, nobility, and commons of this realm?" To which Sir Thomas replied : " I am able to produce against one bishop, which you can bring forth of your side, one hundred holy and Catholic bishops for my opinion; and against one realm, the consent of all Christendom for more than a thousand years." The Duke of Norfolk hearing this, said, " Now, Sir Thomas, you show your obstinate and malicious mind." To whom Sir Thomas said, " Noble Sir, not any malice or obstinacy causeth me to say this, but the just necessity of the cause constraineth me for the discharge of my conscience, and I call God to witness, no other than this hath moved me thereunto."

After this the judges courteously offered him their favourable audience, if he had any thing to allege in his own defence; who answered most mildly and charitably, " More have I not to say, my lords, but that like as the blessed apostle Saint Paul, as we read in the Acts of the Apostles, was present and consenting to the death of the protomartyr Saint Stephen, keeping their clothes that stoned him to death, and yet they be now both twain holy saints in heaven, and there shall continue friends together for ever; so I verily trust, and shall therefore heartily pray, that though your lordships have been on earth my judges to condemnation, yet we may hereafter meet in heaven merrily together, to our everlasting salvation; and God preserve you all, especially my sovereign lord the king, and grant him faithful counsellors:" in which prayer he most lively imitated the example of holy Saint Stephen; "ne statuas illis hoc peccatum;" yea, of our Saviour himself, speaking on the cross, " Pater, dimitte illis, quia nesciunt quid faciunt."

All these Sir Thomas's speeches were faithfully delivered from Sir Anthony Saintleger, Richard Haywood, and John Webbe, gentlemen, with others more of good credit, who were present and heard all, which they reported to my uncle Roper, agreeing all in one discourse.*

---

* As much is said on the want of distinct information, respecting the charges on which More was tried and convicted, I annex the words of Roper, which are more express than those of our author. " Thus much touching Sir Thomas More's arraignment, being not there present myself, have I by the credible report of the Right Worshipful Sir Anthony Saintleger, and partly of Richard Haywood and John Webb, gen-

After his condemnation, he was conducted from the bar to the Tower again, an axe being carried before him with the edge towards him, and was led by Sir William Kingston, a tall, strong, and comely gentleman, constable of the Tower, and his very good friend; but presently a doleful spectacle was presented to Sir Thomas and all the standers by; for his only son, my grand-father, like a dutiful child, casteth himself at his father's feet, craving humbly his blessing, not without tears, whom he blessed and kissed most lovingly, whose love and obedience Sir Thomas after in a letter praised, saying, that this his behaviour pleased him greatly.

When Sir William had conducted Sir Thomas to the Old Swan, towards the Tower, there he bade him farewell with a heavy heart, the tears appearing down his cheeks; but Sir Thomas, with a staid gravity, seeing him sorrowful, began to comfort him with these cheerful speeches, saying, " Good Mr. Kingston, trouble not yourself, but be of good cheer, for I will pray for you, and my good lady your wife, that we may meet in heaven together; where we shall be merry for ever and ever." Soon after this Sir William, talking hereof

tlemen, with others of good credit, at the hearing thereof present themselves, as far forth as my poor wit and memory would serve me, here truly rehearsed unto you."—Singer's edition, p. 89.

to my uncle Roper, said, " In good faith, Mr. Roper, I was ashamed of myself, that at our parting I found my heart so weak and his so stout, that he was fain to comfort me, who should rather at that time have comforted him; but God, and the clearness of his conscience is a comfort, which no earthly prince can give or take away."*

When Sir Thomas was come now to the

---

* The Old Swan, the place at which Sir William Kingston parted from this illustrious victim of an unrighteous sentence is named by Roper, from whom More has the circumstance. It is, I presume, the place mentioned by Stowe, London, p. 185. If so, it was near adjoining the school of St. Anthony, the scene of More's early studies. How much might memory there supply to contrast with his present condition. How does it add to the reason we have to admire the equanimity of this genuine philosopher, as well as true Christian hero, who, at such a moment, and in such a place, could give the consolation which he seemed rather to require.

I cannot forbear, as pertinent to this circumstance in the life of More, to quote the following lines from Mr. Landor's truly philosophic work, the Imaginary Conversations of Literary Men, where they are attributed, I think erroneously, to Spenser.

> How much is lost when neither heart nor eye,
>   Rose-winged desire or fabling hope deceives;
> When boyhood, with quick throb, hath ceased to spy
>   The dubious apple in the yellow leaves.
> When springing from the turf where youth reposed,
>   We find but deserts in the far-sought shore;
> When the huge book of Faery-land lies closed,
>   And those strong brazen clasps will yield no more.

Tower-wharf, his best beloved child, my aunt Roper, desirous to see her father, whom she feared she should never see in this world after, to have his last blessing, gave there attendance to meet him; whom as soon as she had espied, after she had received upon her knees his fatherly blessing, she ran hastily unto him, and without consideration of care of herself, passing through the midst of the throng and guard of men who, with bills and halberts compassed him round, there openly in the sight of them all embraced him, took him about the neck and kissed him, not able to say any word but " Oh, my father! Oh, my father!" He liking well her most natural and dear affection towards him, gave her his fatherly blessing; telling her, that whatsoever he should suffer, though he were innocent, yet it was not without the will of God; and that he knew well enough all the secrets of his heart, counselling her to accommodate her will to God's blessed pleasure, and to be patient for her loss. She was no sooner parted from him, and had gone scarce ten steps, when she, not satisfied with the former farewell, like one who had forgot herself, ravished with the entire love of so worthy a father, having neither respect to herself, nor to the press of people about him; suddenly turned back, and ran hastily to him, took him about the neck, and divers times together kissed him; whereat he spoke not a word, but carrying still his gravity, tears fell also from his eyes; yea, there were very few in all the troop who could refrain hereat from weeping, no not the guard themselves; yet at last, with a full heavy heart, she was severed from him; at which time Margaret Giggs embraced him, and kissed him also; yea, mine aunt's maid, Dorothy Collie, did the like; of whom he said after, it was homely, but very lovingly done. All these, and also my grand-father, witnessed, that they smelt a most odoriferous smell to come from him, according to that of Isaac, " Odor filii mei, sicut odor agri pleni, cui benedixit Dominus."

Oh, what a spectacle was this, to see a woman, of nature shamefaced, by education modest, to express such excessive grief, as that love should make her shake off all fear and shame! which doleful sight, piercing the hearts of all beholders, how do you think it moved her father's? Surely his affection and forcible love, would have daunted his courage, if that a divine spirit of constancy had not inspired him to behold this most generous woman, his most worthy daughter, endowed with all good gifts of nature, all sparks of piety, which are wont to be most acceptable to a loving father, to press unto him at such a time and place, where no man could have access, hanging about his neck before he perceived, holding so fast by him, as she could scarce be plucked off, not uttering any other words but "Oh, my father!" What a sword was this to his heart! And at last, being drawn away by force, to run upon him again, without any regard, either of the weapons wherewith he was compassed, or of the modesty becoming her own sex. What comfort did he want! What courage did he then stand in need of! And yet he resisted all this most courageously, remitting nothing of his steady gravity, speaking only that which we have recited before, and at last beseeching her to pray for her father's soul.

This and other his heroical acts, made Cardinal Pole write thus of him:

"Strangers, and men of other nations, that never had seen him in their lives, received so much grief at the hearing of his death, and reading the story thereof, that they could not refrain from weeping, bewailing an unknown person, only famous unto them for his worthy acts. Yea," saith he, "I cannot hold myself from weeping as I write, though I be far off my country. I loved him dearly, who had not so many urgent causes of his love, as many others had, only in respect of his virtues and heroical acts, for which he was a most necessary member of his country. And now, God is my witness, I shed for him, even whether I would or no, so many tears that they hinder me from writing, and often blot out the letters quite, which I am framing, that I can proceed no farther."

So remained this unconquerable conqueror of the flesh, the world, and the devil, some sevennight after his judgment, in the Tower, arming himself with prayer, meditation, and many holy mortifications, for the day of his martyrdom, and walking about his chamber with a sheet about him, like a corpse ready to be buried, and using to whip himself very sore and long.

In this time there came to him a light-headed courtier, talking of no serious matter, but only urging him this, that he would change his mind; and being wearied with his importunity, he answered him that he had changed it; who presently went and told the king thereof; and being by him commanded to know wherein his mind was changed, Sir Thomas rebuked him for his lightness, in that he would tell the king of every word that he spoke in jest, " For my meaning was," said he, " that whereas I had purposed to have been shaven, that I might seem to others as I before was wont; my mind is changed, for that I intend my beard shall take such part as my head doth;"

which made the courtier blank, and the king very angry.

In this while also he wrote a most kind letter unto Mr. Anthony Bonvise, an Italian merchant, in Latin, calling him the half of his heart; which is to be seen among his other letters. Last of all, the day before he was to suffer, being the 5th of July, he wrote a most loving letter with a coal, to his daughter Margaret, sending therein his blessing to all his children, in which he writeth (knowing nothing of the time of his departure then) very affectionately in these words: "I cumber thee, daughter Margaret, very much; but I would be sorry that it should be any longer than to-morrow, for to-morrow is Saint Thomas of Canterbury's eve, and the octaves of Saint Peter; therefore to-morrow long I to go to God; it were a day very meet and convenient. I never liked your manner towards me better than when you kissed me last. For I like when daughterly love and dear charity have no leisure to look unto worldly courtesy. Farewell, dear daughter, pray for me and I will pray for you and all your friends, that we may meet together in heaven. Commend me, when you can, to my son John; his towardly carriage towards me pleased me very much. God bless him and his good wife, and their children, Thomas," (who was my father) " and Augustine," (who died unmarried) "and all that they shall have." In which words I hope, by God's help, to have some part of his blessing. But, oh good God! " voluntate labiorum ejus non fraudasti eum." For upon the eve of his special patron, and the octaves of Saint Peter, for whose supremacy he suffered martyrdom, God heard his petition, and he suffered death most courageously. Together with this letter, he sent unto her his shirt of hair, and his whip, as one that was loth to have the world know that he used such austerity. For he cunningly, all his lifetime, had with his mirth hidden from the eyes of others his severe mortifications; and now having finished his combat, he sent away his weapons, not being certain of any notice of the king's mind, but either taught by revelation, or having a firm confidence of God's great goodness, " et desiderium cordis tribuit ei Dominus."

For upon the next morning, being Tuesday the 6th of July, there came unto him Sir Thomas Pope, very early in the morning, his singular good friend, with a message from the king and the council, that he was to suffer death on that day, before nine of the clock, and therefore he should forthwith prepare himself thereto. " Mr. Pope," said he, " I most heartily thank you for your good tidings. I have been much bound to the king's highness, for the benefits and honours that he hath most bountifully bestowed upon me; yet am I more bound to his grace, I assure you, for putting me here, where I have had convenient time and space to have remembrance of my end. And so help me God, most of all I am bound unto him, that it pleaseth his majesty to rid me so shortly out of the miseries of this wretched world." " The king's pleasure further is," said Sir Thomas Pope, " that you use not many words at your execution." " Mr. Pope," answered he, " you do well to give me warning of the king's pleasure, for otherwise I had purposed at that time somewhat to have spoken; but no matter wherewith his grace, or any other should have cause to be offended; howbeit, whatsoever I intended, I am ready obediently to conform myself to his highness's command. And I beseech you, good Mr. Pope, be a means to his majesty, that my daughter Margaret may be at my burial." " The king is contented already," said he, " that your wife, children, and other your friends should have liberty to be present at it." " Oh how much am I beholding to his grace, that vouchsafeth to have so much consideration of my poor burial." Then Sir Thomas Pope taking his leave of him, could not refrain from weeping. Which Sir Thomas perceiving, comforted him in these words: "Quiet yourself, Mr. Pope, and be not discomforted; for I trust we shall once see each other full merrily, where we shall be sure to live and love together in eternal bliss." And further, to put him out of his melancholy, Sir Thomas More took his urinal in his hand, and casting his water, said merrily, "I see no danger but this man may live longer, if it please the king."

After which words they parted; and when he was gone, Sir Thomas, as one that had been invited to a solemn banquet, changed himself into his best apparel, and put on his silk camlet gown, which his entire friend, Mr. Anthony Bonvise, (a noble citizen of the state of Lucca, in Italy, to whom he wrote the letter as is late spoken of before,) gave him, whilst he was in the Tower. Mr. Lieutenant seeing him prepare himself so to his death, counselled him, for his own benefit, to put them off again, saying, that he who should have them was but a javill. "What Mr. Lieutenant," said Sir Thomas, " shall I account him a javill, who will do me this day so singular a benefit. Nay, I assure you, were it cloth of gold, I would think it well bestowed on him. For Saint Cyprian, that famous Bishop of Carthage, gave his executioner thirty pieces of gold, because he knew he should procure unto him an unspeakable good turn." Yet for all this, Mr. Lieutenant so pressed him, that at last being loth, for friendship's sake, to deny him so small a matter, he altered his gown, and put on a gown of friese; but yet he sent of that little money which was left him, one angel of gold, to the hangman, in token that he maliced him nothing, but rather loved him exceedingly for it.

He was therefore brought about nine of the clock, by Mr. Lieutenant, out of the Tower, his beard being long, which fashion he never had before used, his face pale and lean, carrying in his hands a red cross, casting his eyes often towards heaven. As he thus passed by a good woman's house, she came forth and offered him a cup of wine,* which he refused, saying, "Christ at his passion drank no wine, but gall and vinegar." There came another woman after him, crying unto him for certain books, which she had given into his custody when he was Lord Chancellor; to whom he said, "Good woman, have patience but for one hour's space, and by

* It appears to have been the practice of the times to offer meat and drink to persons condemned to die, when on the way to execution. At York a cup of ale was presented. At Paris the procession usually stopped at the Cour de Filles Dieu, where the criminal kissed the crucifix, received the aspersion, eat three morsels of bread, and drank a glass of wine. The custom might originate in a humane feeling; but it is probable that there is an allusion in it to the potion presented to our Saviour on the cross.

that time the king's majesty will rid me of the care I have of thy papers, and all other matters whatsoever." Another woman, suborned thereto, as some think, by his adversaries, to disgrace him, followed him also, crying out against him, that he had done her great injury, when he had been Lord Chancellor; to whom he gave the answer, " that he remembered her cause very well; and that if he were now to give sentence therein, he would not alter what he had already done."

Last of all there came a citizen of Winchester, who in times past, having been greatly troubled with grievous temptations of despair, was brought by a friend of his to Sir Thomas More, when he was Lord Chancellor; who, though he could not before, by any wholesome counsel alter this his mind, yet Sir Thomas More promising him to pray for him, he was for the space of three years free from all such temptations. When Sir Thomas was committed, and he could get no leave to have access unto him, his temptations grew so great, that he often sought to have been the cruel murderer of himself; but now hearing Sir Thomas was to be executed, he came to London, and ran to Sir Thomas as he was carried to execution, desiring him with great earnestness that he would help him by his prayers, for his temptation was come again unto him, and he could not possibly rid himself thereof; to whom Sir Thomas spake thus: "Go and pray for me, and I will carefully pray for you." He went away with confidence, and he never after was troubled with the like again.

Being now brought to the scaffold, whereon he was to be beheaded, it seemed to him so weak that it was ready to fall; wherefore he said merrily to Mr. Lieutenant, "I pray you, Sir, see me safe up, and for my coming down let me shift for myself." When he began to speak a little to the people, which were in great troops there to hear and see him, he was interrupted by the sheriff; wherefore briefly he desired all the people to pray for him, and to bear witness with him, that he there died in and for the faith of the holy Catholic Church, a faithful servant both of God and the king. Having spoken but this, he kneeled down, and pronounced with great devotion the "Miserere" psalm, which being ended, he cheerfully rose up, and the executioner asking him forgiveness, he kissed him, saying, "Thou wilt do me this day a greater benefit than ever any mortal man can be able to give me. Pluck up thy spirit, man, and be not afraid to do thy office; my neck is very short; take heed therefore that thou strike not awry, for saving thy honesty." When the executioner would have covered his eyes, he said, " I will cover them myself;" and presently he did so, with a cloth that he had brought with him for the purpose; then laying his head upon the block, he bade the executioner stay until he had removed his beard aside; saying, " That had never committed treason." So with great alacrity and spiritual joy, he received the fatal axe, which no sooner had severed the head from the body, but his soul was carried by angels into everlasting glory, where a crown of martyrdom was put upon him which can never fade nor decay. And then he found those words true which he had often spoken, that a man may lose his head and have no harm; yea, I say, unspeakable good and endless happiness.

When news of his death was brought to the king, who was at that time playing at tables, Anne Bullen looking on, he cast his eye upon her and said, " Thou art the cause of this man's death;" and presently leaving his play he betook himself to his chamber, and thereupon fell into a fit of melancholy; but whether this were from his heart, or to seem less cruel than he was indeed, I can hardly conjecture; for on the one side the remembrance of his faithful service, so many years employed for the whole realm's benefit, could not but make the king sorrowful;

and on the other side, his unmerciful dealing with his son and heir, his small allowance to his wife, his pitiless cruelty against all his children, showeth that he had an implacable hatred against him, because he would not consent unto his lustful courses; of which we will speak more largely, when we have discoursed of his burial.

His head was put upon London-bridge, where traitors' heads are set up upon poles;* his body was buried in the chapel of St. Peter in the Tower, in the belfrey, or as some say, as one entereth into the vestry,† near unto the body of the holy martyr Bishop Fisher, who being put to death just a fortnight before, had small respect done unto him all this while.

But that which happened about Sir Thomas' winding sheet, was reported as a miracle by my aunt Roper, Mrs. Clement, and Dorothy Collie, wife unto Mr. Harris. Thus it was: his daughter Margaret, having distributed all her money to the poor, for her father's soul, when she came to bury his body at the Tower she had forgotten to bring a sheet; and there was not a penny of

---

* The author of the " Expositio Fidelis de Morte D. Thomæ Mori," relates a horrible circumstance. " Priusquam exponeretur, aquâ ferventi decoctum est, quo plus haberet horroris." The head of Sir Thomas More! Well might a foreigner contemplating this circumstance and the punishment denounced in his sentence, brand Henry with the name of another Phalaris.

† This clause is wanting in the Manuscript.

money left amongst them all; wherefore Mrs. Harris went to the next draper's shop, and agreeing upon the price, made as though she would look for some money in her purse, and then try whether they would trust her or no; and she found in her purse the same sum for which they agreed, not one penny over or under; though she knew before, certainly, that she had not one cross about her. This the same Dorothy affirmed constantly to Doctor Stapleton, when they both lived at Doway, in Flanders, in Queen Elizabeth's reign. His shirt, wherein he suffered, all embrued with his blood, was kept very carefully by Doctor Clement's wife, living also beyond the seas, as also his shirt of hair. His head having remained about a month upon London-bridge, and being to be cast into the Thames, because room should be made for divers others, who in plentiful sort suffered martyrdom for the same supremacy, shortly after, it was bought by his daughter Margaret, lest (as she stoutly affirmed before the council, being called before them after for the same matter) it should be food for fishes; which she buried, where she thought fittest; it was very well to be known, as well by the lively favour of him which was not all this while in any thing almost diminished; as also by reason of one tooth, which he wanted whilst he lived; herein it was to be admired, that the hairs of his beard being almost grey before his martyrdom, they seemed now as it were reddish or yellow.

His glorious death and martyrdom, strengthened many to suffer courageously for the same cause, because he was an eminent man both for dignities, learning, and virtue; so that Doctor Stapleton boldly affirmeth, that he was wonderfully both admired and sought to be imitated by many, as he himself had heard, when he came first to the years of understanding and discretion. And truly German Gardiner, an excellent learned and holy layman, coming to suffer death for the same supremacy some eight years after, avouched at his end, before all the people, that the holy simplicity of the blessed Carthusians, the wonderful learning of the bishop of Rochester, and the singular wisdom of Sir Thomas More, had stirred him up to that courage; but the rest seemed not so much to be imitated of laymen, being all belonging to the clergy, as this famous man, who had been clogged with wife and children. Yea his death so wrought in the mind of Doctor Learcke, his own parish-priest, that he, following the example of his own sheep, afterwards suffered a most famous martyrdom for the same cause of supremacy.

Thus have we, according to our poor talent, laboured to set down briefly the life and death of Sir Thomas More, my most famous great-grandfather; whose prayers and intercessions I daily crave both for myself and all my little ones, who are also part of his charge, because he gave them his blessing, in his most affectionate letter: viz. " God bless Thomas and Augustine, and all that they shall have:"—immediate or mediate; those which they shall have, usque ad mille generationes, if it were needful. This hath been our comfort, that the trial thereof hath been evidently shown in that Edward, Thomas, and Bartholomew, my father's brethren, being born after my great-grandfather's death, and having not this blessing so directly, as my father and my uncle Augustine, they have degenerated both from that religion and those manners, which Sir Thomas More had left as it were a happy depositum unto his children and family. For although mine uncle Bartholomew died young of the plague in London, and therefore might have by the grace of God excuse and remorse at his end; yet Thomas the younger's courses were far different; for he lived and died a professed minister, and for all that very poor, bringing up his children, whereof his eldest son is yet living, in no commendable profession. As for mine uncle Edward, who is yet alive, although he were endowed with excellent gifts of nature, as a ready wit, tongue at will, and his pen glib; yet, God knows, he hath drowned all his talents in self-conceit in no worthy qualities, and besides burieth himself alive in obscurity, in forsaking God, and his mean and base behaviour. My father only right heir of his father and grandfather, though he not long enjoyed any of their lands, was a lively pattern unto us of his constant faith, his worthy and upright dealings, his true catholic simplicity, of whom I have a purpose to discourse unto my children more at large, that they may know in what hard times he lived, and how manfully he sustained the combat, which his father and grandfather had left unto him as their best inheritance: for all their land was taken away by two acts of parliament immediately after Sir Thomas's death; the one act was to take away lands, which the king had given him, and this was somewhat tolerable; the other most violent and tyrannical, to frustrate utterly a most provident conveyance, which Sir Thomas had made of all his lands and inheritance, which he had settled upon my father, being a child of two years old or more, without any fraud or covin, even when as yet no statute had been made about the oath of supremacy; and therefore before Sir Thomas could commit any such fault against such a statute, much less treason, having reserved to himself only an estate for term of life; yet all this was taken away contrary to all order of law, and joined to the crown: but that land, which he had conveyed to my uncle Roper and mine aunt, for term of their lives in recompence of their marriage money, that they kept still, because that was done two days before the first conveyance. The lady More also, his wife, was turned out of her house at Chelsey immediately, and all her goods taken from her, the king allotting her of his mercy a pension of twenty pounds by the year; a poor allowance to maintain a lord chancellor's lady. My grandfather was committed also to the Tower, and for denying the same oath, was condemned; yet because they had sufficiently fleeced him before, and could get little by his death, he got at last his pardon and liberty, but lived not many years after, leaving my father to the education of his mother, called before her marriage Anne Cresacre, the last of her family, by whose match he enjoyed after a competent living to keep him out of a needy life. Mine aunt Roper, because she was a woman, was not so hardly dealt withal, but only threatened very sore, both because she kept her father's head for a relic, and that she meant to set her father's works in print, yet for all that after a short imprisonment she was at last sent home to her husband. Thus all his friends felt in part the king's heavy anger for his undaunted courage.

Sir Thomas was of a mean stature, well proportioned, his complexion tending to phlegmatic, his colour white and pale, his hair neither black nor yellow, but between both; his eyes grey, his countenance amiable and cheerful, his voice neither big nor shrill, but speaking plainly and distinctly; it was not very tunable, though he delighted much in music; his body reasonably healthful, only that towards his latter time, by using much to write, he complained much of the ache of his breast. In his youth he drunk much water; wine he only tasted of when he pledged others; he loved salt meats, especially powdered beef; he loved also milk, cheese, eggs and fruit; and usually he eat coarse brown bread, which it may be he rather used to punish his taste, than for any love he had thereto; for he was singular wise to deceive the world with mortifications, only contenting himself with the knowledge which God had of his actions: " et pater ejus, qui erat in abscondito, reddidit ei."

CHAPTER XI.

NOW let us see, what most of the learned men of Christendom, not only catholics, but also protestants, thought and wrote of King Henry, for Sir Thomas More's death, who were not likely, being free from all partiality, but to speak their minds sincerely, not fearing him as his subjects, nor hating him for any private respects. First, Cardinal Pole, then living in the court of Rome, and writing to the king in the defence of ecclesiastical unity, saith thus by the figure of apostrophe, of the complaints of other men: " Thy father, oh England,* thy ornament, thy defence, was brought to his death, being innocent in thy sight; by birth, thy

---

* It is observed by the former editor, that More has been here led into a mistake, by following Stapleton. The apostrophe was not to England, but to London. The passage occurs in Cardinal Pole's " Britanniæ pro Ecclesiæ unitate Defensio." Lib. iii. p. 66-67. More has not done justice in his translation to a truly eloquent passage.

child; by condition, thy citizen, but thy **father** for the many benefits done unto thee; **for he** showed more evident signs of his fatherly love towards thee, than ever any loving father hath expressed to his only and truly beloved child; yet in nothing hath he more declared his fatherly affection, than by his end, for that he left his life for thy sake; especially lest he should overthrow and betray thy salvation. Wherefore that which we read in the ancient stories of Greece, as touching Socrates, whom the Athenians condemned most unjustly to take poison, so thou hast now seen thy Socrates, beheaded before thine eyes. A while after his death, when in a play there was recited out of a tragedy these words: 'You have slain, you have slain the best man of all Greece;' then upon these words every man so lamented the death of Socrates, calling to mind that injustice, although the poet himself dreamed least of him, that the whole theatre was filled with nothing else, but tears and howlings, for which cause the people presently revenged his death, by punishing grievously the chief authors thereof; those that were of them to be found, were put to death presently, and they that could not be found out, were banished. There was also a statue erected in his honour, in the very market-place. If they therefore at the only hearing of these words upon the stage took an occasion to be revenged of that most innocent man's slaughter; what more just cause mayst thou, London, have of compassion and revenge, hearing the like words to these, not pronounced only by any stage-player at home, but by most grave and reverend men in all places of Christendom, when as they speak most seriously, exprobating often unto thee thine ingratitude, and saying: 'You have slain, you have slain the best Englishman alive.'" This spoke this learned and wise cardinal, who could testify this of his knowledge, by reason he conversed often with the greatest states of Christendom, being a man famous amongst them for nobility of blood, for his dignity, his learning and excellent virtues, for which none have cause to suspect him to be partial.

Erasmus as may be easily guessed by the stile although he wrote it not in his own name, because he had then many friends in England saith thus, "This is evident, that neither More nor the Bishop of Rochester erred at all for any malice they had against the king, but for sincere conscience' sake: this they persuaded themselves wholly, this was infixed in their marrows, that the matter which they defended was good and lawful and honourable for the king, and wholesome for all the whole kingdom. If it had been lawful for them to have dissembled it, they would have done it willingly; but they took their death most patiently and peaceably, praying to God for the king and the whole realm's safety. In heinous offences, a simple and pure conscience, and a mind not desirous of hurting any, but of well deserving, excuseth much the fault; besides due respect and honour hath been always had, even amongst barbarous nations, to eminent learning and excellent virtue. The very name of a philosopher rescued Plato from being beheaded by the Æginetes, having transgressed the laws of their city. Diogenes, without any fear, came into Philip king of Macedonia's army, and being brought before him for a spy of their enemies, freely reproached the king to his face of madness, that being not content with his own kingdom, he would cast himself into danger to lose all; yet was he sent away without any harm at all done to him, and not only so, but had a great reward given him, for no other cause but that he was a philosopher. And as the courtesies of monarchs showed unto learned men, do get them great fame, so to have used such men hardly, hath been occasion, that they have been much hated and envied. For who doth not hate Antony, for having Cicero's head cut off! Who doth not detest Nero for putting Seneca to death; yea Octavius incurred some infamy for Ovid's banishment amongst the Getes. When Lewis the Twelfth of France, now being peaceably settled in his kingdom, would have been divorced from his wife, the daughter of Lewis the Eleventh, this matter displeased many good men, and amongst them John Standock; and his scholar Thomas, spake of it a sermon, desiring the people to pray to God, that he would inspire the king to do for the best; they were therefore accused of sedition, as men that had committed a fault against the king's edict; yet for all this they had no other punishment but banishment. They kept and enjoyed all their goods, and when the controversies were ended, they were called home again with honour. By this mildness the king both satisfied his edict, and got no great hatred for molesting two men, both divines, both accounted holy men. But every man bewaileth the death of Sir Thomas More, even they who are adversaries unto him for religion, so great was his courtesy to all men; so great his affability, so excellent was his nature. Whom did he ever send away from him, if he were any thing learned, without gifts? or who was so great a stranger unto him, to whom he did not seek to do one good turn or other? Many are favourable only to their own countrymen; Frenchmen to Frenchmen, Scottishmen to Scots. This his bounty hath so engraven More in every man's heart, that they all lament his death as the loss of their own father or brother. I myself have seen many tears come from those men who never saw More in their lives, nor never received any benefit from him; yea, whilst I write these things, tears gush from me, whether I will or no. How many souls hath that axe wounded, which cut off More's head!" &c. And a little after, pulling off his vizard, he showeth himself Erasmus in these words, " Therefore when men have congratulated me, that I had such a friend placed in such high dignities, I am wont to answer, that I would not congratulate his increase of honour, before he should command me to do so."*

John Cochleus, a most learned German, and a great divine, writing against Richard Sampson, an Englishman, who defended king Henry the

* This is translated from the Epistola Fidelis de Morte D. Thomæ Mori, et Episcopi Roffensis insignium virorum in Anglia, which was first printed at Antwerp in 1536, the year after the death of these illustrious men. It has been generally attributed to Erasmus, as it is by More. It is written, however, in the name of Courinus Nucerinus: Nomen fictum pro Erasmo ut aliqui putant, says one of its editors. But Nucerinus seems rather to guide us to Paulus Jovius as the author, who was Bishop of Nuceria. This letter, one of the most honourable tributes to the memory of More, forms the twentieth article of Mr. Singer's Appendix to the Life by Roper.

Eighth for this fact, saith much of Sir Thomas's praises; at last, speaking of his death, he saith thus to King Henry's counsellors: " What praise or honour could you get by that cruelty, which you exercised against Sir Thomas More? He was a man of known and most laudable humanity, mild behaviour, affability, bounty, eloquence, wisdom, innocency of life, wit, learning, exceedingly beloved and admired of all men; in dignity, besides, highest judge of your country, and next to the king himself; famous from his youth; beneficial to his country for many embassages, and now most venerable for his grey head, drawing towards old age; who having obtained of the king an honourable dismission from his office, lived privately at home with his wife, children, and nephews; having never committed the least offence against any, burdensome to no man, ready to help every body, mild and pleasant of disposition. You have given counsel to have this so good a man drawn out of his own house, out of that sweet academy of learned and devout Christian philosophers, for no other cause but this, that he would not justify your impieties; his guiltless conscience resisting it, the fear of God, and his soul's health withdrawing him from it. Do you believe that this your wicked fact hath ever pleased any one of what nation, sex, or age soever? or ever will please any? It will not surely. You have hurt yourselves more than him, because you have made yourselves murderers, and guilty of shedding most innocent blood. Him have you made most grateful to God, to the citizens of heaven, and to all just men on earth, and a most renowned martyr of Christ; he liveth and reigneth without all doubt with Almighty God. You will never be able to blot out this fault and infamy. It is written of God, ' He knoweth the deceiver, and him that is deceived; he will bring counsellors to a foolish end, judges into amazement. He unlooseth the belt of kings, and girdeth their loins with a rope.'" Thus writeth Cochleus.

Paulus Jovius, Bishop of Nuceria, amongst the praises of divers learned men, writeth thus of Sir Thomas More's unjust death: " Fortune, fickle and unconstant, after her accustomed manner, and always hating virtue, if ever she played the part of a proud and cruel dame, she hath lately behaved herself most cruelly in England, under Henry the Eighth, casting down before her Thomas More, whom the king, whilst he was an excellent admirer of virtue, had raised to the highest places of honour in his realm; that from thence, being by fatal madness changed into a beast, he might suddenly throw him down again with great cruelty, because he would not favour the unsatiable lust of that furious tyrant; and for that he would not flatter him in his wickedness, being a man most eminent for the accomplishment of all parts of justice, and most saintly in all kind of virtues. For when the king would be divorced from his lawful wife, marry a quean, and hasten to disinherit, with shame his lawful daughter, (Marie) More, Lord Chancellor, was forced to appear at the bar, guilty only for his piety and innocence, and there was condemned most wrongfully to a most cruel and shameful death, like a traitor and a murderer, so that it was not lawful for his friends to bury his dismembered members. But Henry for this fact, an imitator of Phalaris, shall never be able to bereave him of perpetual fame by this his unlawful wickedness, but that the name of More shall enjoy constant honour, by his famous Utopia." He speaketh of death, as his sentence did purport.

Now let us join to these, viz. an Englishman, a Low-Country man, a German, and an Italian, a Frenchman also, that we may see how all nations did lament Sir Thomas More's death, and what credit the king and his council thereunto got by it. William Paradine writeth thus: " The troubles and civil dissensions in England, now had lasted a year or two, when in the month of July, John Fisher, Bishop of Rochester, was committed prisoner in London, because he seemed to disallow the king's divorce, and the law newly made against the pope's supremacy. Of that resolution was also Sir Thomas More partaker, being sheriff of London, a man famous for eloquence, and all manner of learning; above the reach of all lawyers most expert and skilful; most faultless in all his deeds. These two, purposing rather to obey God than men, and confirming their minds with constancy, were condemned to death: from which constancy they could be drawn neither by entreaties, hope of rewards, fair promises, nor by any threats whatsoever, which corporal death both of them received most patiently and stoutly." Finally, every writer of that age lamentably deplored the unjust death of Sir Thomas More. Roverus Pontanus, a German, in his Index of memorable matters; Laurence Surius, a Low-Country man, upon the year of 1535; John Fontayne, a Frenchman, in his French history; and most abundantly Onuphrius Patavinus in Paulo, ca. 3. An Italian, Nicolas, Cardinal of Capua, in his French letters; John Secundus of Hague, yea Carion and Sleidan himself speak honourably of Sir Thomas More's death.

But of all Protestants John Rivius speaketh most passionately of King Henry's cruel fact and Sir Thomas's piety, in these words (lib. 2.

De Conscientia): "He that is in a prince's court ought freely, if he be asked his judgment, rather to tell his mind plainly, what is most behoveful for his prince's good, than to speak placentia, tickling his ears with flattery; neither ought he to praise things which are not praiseworthy, nor to dispraise matters that are worthy of high commendations; yea, although he be in danger of getting no favour by persuading to it, but rather punishment and disgrace for gainsaying men's appetites;" then bringing Papinianus, that great lawyer, for a lively example thereof, who chose rather to die than to justify the emperor Caracalla's killing of his own brother, against his own conscience, he addeth, " Such a man was lately in our memory that singular and excellent for learning and piety, yea the only ornament and glory of his country, Thomas More, who, because he would not agree to nor approve by his consent, against his own conscience, the new marriage of the King of England, who would needs be divorced from his first wife and marry another, he was first cast into prison; one that had singularly well deserved of the king himself, and of England; and when he constantly continued in his opinion, which he truly thought to be most just, most lawful, and godly, emboldened to defend it by a sincere conscience, he was put to death by that wicked parricide, that most hateful and cruel tyrant; a cruelty not heard of before in this our age. Oh ingratitude, and singular impiety of the king's! who could endure to consume and macerate with a tedious and loathsome imprisonment, such a sincere and holy good man; one that had been so careful of his glory, so studious of his country's profit. He that had persuaded him always to all justice and honesty, dissuaded him from all contraries, and not convinced of any crime, nor found in any fault, he slew him (oh, miserable wickedness!) not only being innocent, but him that had deserved high rewards, and his most faithful and trusty counsellor. Are these thy rewards, O king? Is this the thanks thou returnest him for all his trusty service and good will unto thee? Doth this man reap this commodity for his most faithful acts and employments? But, Oh More, thou art now happy, and enjoyest eternal felicity, who wouldst lose thy head rather than approve any thing against thine own conscience; who more esteemest righteousness, justice, and piety than life itself; and, whilst thou art deprived of this mortal life, thou passest to the true and immortal happiness of heaven; whilst thou art taken away from men, thou art raised up amongst the numbers of holy saints and angels of bliss."

Last of all, I will recount what the good emperor, Charles the Fifth, said unto Sir Thomas Elliot, then the king's ambassador in his court, after he had heard of Bishop Fisher and Sir Thomas More's martyrdoms, on a time he spoke of it to Sir Thomas Elliot, who seemed to excuse the matter by making some doubt of the report; to whom the emperor replied, "It is too true; but if we had had two such lights in all our kingdoms, as these men were, we could rather have chosen to have lost two of the best and strongest towns in all our empire, than suffer ourselves to be deprived of them, much less to endure to have them wrongfully taken from us."

And although none of these should have written any thing hereof, yet the matter itself speaketh abundantly that the cause was most unjust, the manner thereof most infamous, and Sir Thomas More's patience most admirable; his piety, his learning, his virtues incomparable. Famous was he for his noble martyrdom; infamous King Henry for his most unjust condemnation. These things do aggravate King Henry's fault; first, that he killed him by a law, wherein he never offended, either by word or deed, and by that which concerned not temporal policy, but religion only; not rebellious against the king, but fearful to offend his own conscience; which, though he refused to approve, yet did he never reprove it, or any other man for taking it. Secondly, that he put to death so rare a man, so beloved of all, so virtuous, so wise, so courteous, and witty; which might be motives sufficient even to pardon a guilty offender. Thirdly, for beheading a man that had done him so much service, yea, the whole kingdom, such good offices; his faithful counsellor for twenty years together, his expert ambassador, his just Lord Chancellor, the very flower of his realm. Many things also do amplify and increase Sir Thomas More's immortal glory; first, in that to all the king's demands he had behaved himself so sincerely and impartially, opening his mind ingenuously, innocently, without fear, so that the king seemed still to like him, though his opinion were contrary to his liking. Secondly, that he had suffered already the loss of all his goods, being condemned to perpetual imprisonment, and only for silence. Thirdly, in that he took all crosses for the love of God most patiently. Fourthly, that he died for a controversy of religion, never before called in question, by any precedent example. Finally, that he only of all the council would not flatter the king, nor keep either goods, dignity, or life, with the danger of the loss of his soul. All which prove what a rare man, how admirable and virtuous a Christian, and how glorious a martyr he is.

But because one bald English chronicler, Hall, termeth him a scoffing man, because his writings and doings were full of witty jests, calling him a wise foolish man, or a foolish wise man, let us see by his own writings, the reason why he hath used so many pleasant tales in his books; and it is this: " Even as some sick men," saith he, " will take no medicines, unless some pleasant thing be put among their potions, although perhaps it be somewhat hurtful, yet the physician suffereth them to have it. So because many will not willingly hearken to serious and grave documents, except they be mingled with some fable or jest, therefore reason willeth us to do the like." And in his great volume, page 1048, he saith, that " jests are as it were sauce, whereby we are recreated, that we may eat with more stomach; but as that were an absurd banquet, in which there were few dishes of meat, and much variety of sauces, and that an unpleasant one, where there were no sauce at all; even so that life were spent idly, wherein nothing were but mirth and jollity; and again that tedious and uncomfortable, wherein no pleasure or mirth were to be expected." Which mirth as it may become all men, so most especially did it become such a one as Sir Thomas More was, being a married man, yea a courtier, and a companion to a prince, of whom that may worthily be spoken, which Titus Livius recounteth of Cato, thus: "In this man there was such excellency of wit and wisdom, that he seemeth to have been able to have made his fortune, in what place soever he had been born; he wanted no skill either for the managing of private or public business; he was skilful both in country and city affairs; some are raised to honour, either because they are excellent lawyers, singularly eloquent, or of admirable virtues; but the towardliness of this man's understanding framed him so to all matters, that you would deem him born for one alone. In the practice of virtues, you would judge him rather a monk than a courtier; in learning a most famous writer. If you would ask his counsel in the law, he was most ready to advise you the best; if he were to make an oration, he would show marvellous eloquence. He was admirable in all kind of learning, Latin, Greek, profane, divine. If there were an embassage to be undertook, none more dextrous to finish it. In giving sound counsel in doubtful cases, none more prudent; to tell the truth without fear, none more free; as far from all flattery, as open and pleasant, full of grace in delivering his judgment," and that, which

Cato had not, therein was he most happy; for Livy saith, "That he had a sour carriage, and a tongue immoderate, free, and full of taunting;" but Sir Thomas being Christ's scholar, and not any stoic, was mild, and of humble heart, neither sad nor turbulent, and besides of a pleasant conversation, never stern but for righteousness; a great contemner either of unlawful pleasures, or of inordinate riches and glory. As Cato had much enmity with divers senators, so many of them on the other side did exercise his patience, that one can hardly discern whether the nobility did press him more, or he the nobility; but on the contrary side, Sir Thomas More never had any private or public quarrel with any man; yea, no man can reckon any to have been his enemy, being born wholly to friendship and affability; wherefore being nothing inferior to Cato for gravity, integrity, and innocency, as exact a hater of all vice, and stern to all wicked men as he, yet did he far excel him in mildness, sweetness of behaviour, and pleasantness of wit; yea, I do him injury to compare him to any moral philosopher whatsoever; for he was absolutely well seen in the school of Christ, and endued with all supernatural perfections, a great saint of Christ's church, and a holy martyr of his faith, and high in God's favour; which was well testified in his daughter, my aunt Dauncy, who being sore sick of that disease, of which she after died, fell into a long trance, and afterwards returning to herself, she professed, with abundance of tears, that she had felt in that while most grievous torments, and should have suffered them for ever, had not her father's prayers and intercession begged of God a little longer space to repent her of her former life. It was also credibly reported, that two of John Heywood's sons, Jasper and Ellis, having one of the teeth of Sir Thomas More between them, and either of them being desirous to have it to himself, it suddenly, to the admiration of both, parted in two.

Now, to conclude, let us consider why God culled this man out above all other to preserve the unity of his church, and to be an illustrious witness of the glorious cause for the which he died; for, lest men should think that if only the clergy had died, they might seem partial in their own cause; behold God picked out this worthy layman, such as, I suppose, all Christendom had not the like, who should be as his especial ambassador for the laity, as was the famous Bishop of Rochester for the clergy; such were these two for learning, as they could reach into all matters; such for excellency of wit, that no subtle dealing could entrap them unawares, easily foreseeing any danger; such for virtue and integrity of life, that God of his great mercy would not suffer such men, in so great a point as this, to be deceived. And let no man think this was no martyrdom; yea, rather it was greater than that of those who would not deny the faith of Christ, according as that worthy bishop and confessor Denis of Alexandria saith, that that martyrdom which one suffereth, to preserve the unity of the church, is more than that which one suffereth, because he will not do sacrifice to idols; for in this a man dieth to save his own soul, in the other he dieth for the whole church.

OF SIR THOMAS MORE'S BOOKS.

AMONG his Latin works are his epigrams, partly translated out of Greek, and partly of his own making, so wittily devised and penned, as they may seem nothing inferior, or to yield to any of the like kind written in our days, and perchance not unworthy to be compared with those of like writers of old. These epigrams, as they are learned and pleasant, so are they nothing biting or contumelious.

He also wrote elegantly and eloquently the life of King Richard the Third, not only in English, which book is abroad in print, (though corrupted and vitiated) but in Latin also, not yet printed.* He did not perfect nor finish that

---

* It is observed by the former editor, after Hearne, that this is a mistake; the Latin Life of King Richard III. having been printed at Louvaine in 1566.

book, neither any sithence durst take upon him to set pen to paper to finish it, neither in the one or other tongue, all men being deterred and driven from that enterprise, by reason of the incomparable excellency of that work; as all other painters were afraid to perfect and finish the image of Venus, painted but imperfectly by Apelles, for his excellent workmanship therein.

But the book that carrieth the prize of all his Latin books, of witty invention, is his Utopia; he doth in it most lively and pleasantly paint forth such an exquisite platform, pattern, and example of a singular good common-wealth, as to the same, neither the Lacedæmonians, nor the Athenians, nor yet the best of all other, that of the Romans, is comparable, full prettily and probably devising the said country to be one of the countries of the new-found lands, declared to him in Antwerp, by Hythlodius, a Portingall, and one of the sea-companions of Americus Vesputius, that first sought out and found those lands; such an excellent and absolute estate of a common-wealth, that saving the people were unchristened, might seem to pass any estate and common-wealth, I will not say of the old nations by me before mentioned, but even of any other in our time. Many great learned men, as Budeus, and Joannes Paludanus, upon a fervent zeal wished, that some excellent divines might be sent thither to preach Christ's Gospel; yea there were here amongst us at home, sundry good men and learned divines very desirous to undertake the voyage to bring the people to the faith of Christ, whose manners they did so well like. And this said jolly invention of Sir Thomas More's seemed to bear a good countenance of truth, not only for the credit Sir Thomas was of in the world, but also for that about the same time many strange and unknown nations and countries were discovered, such as our forefathers never knew; especially by the wonderful navigation of the ship called Victoria, that sailed the world round about, whereby it was found that ships sail bottom to bottom, and that there be antipodes, which thing Lactantius and others do flatly deny, laughing them to scorn that so did write. Again it is found, that under the zodiac, where Aristotle and others say, that for the immoderate and excessive heat there is no habitation, is the most temperate and pleasant dwelling, and the most fruitful country in the world. These and other considerations caused many wise and learned men nothing less to mistrust, than that this had been nothing but an inventive drift of Sir Thomas More's own imagination; for they took it for a very true story, wherein they were deceived by Sir Thomas, as wise and as well learned as they were. In this book, amongst other things, he hath a very godly process, how there might be fewer thieves in England, and a marvellous opinionable problem of sheep, that whereas men were wont to eat the sheep, as they do in other countries, now contrarywise sheep in England pitifully do devour men, women and children, houses, yea, and towns withal. Like a most thankful man, he maketh honourable mention of Cardinal Morton, archbishop of Canterbury and lord chancellor of England, in whose house, as we have said, himself was in his tender youth brought up, albeit it be by the dissembled name of the said Hythlodius, whom he imagineth to have been in England, and to have been acquainted with the said cardinal.

And as this book in this kind is singular and excellent, containing and describing a commonwealth far passing the common-wealths devised and used by Lycurgus, Solon, Numa, Plato, and divers others: so wrote he in another kind and sort a book against Luther, no less singular and excellent. King Henry the Eighth had written a notable and learned book against Luther's book De Captivitate Babylonica, most evidently and mightily refuting his vile and shameful heresies against the catholic faith, and Christ's holy sacraments, which did so grieve Luther to the heart, that having no good substantial matter to help himself withal, he fell to scoffing and saucy jesting at the king's book in his answer for the same, using nothing throughout the said answer, but the fourth figure of rhetorick called sauce-malapert, and played the very varlet with the king. To whom Sir Thomas More made reply, and doth so decipher and lay open his wretched vile handling of the sacred Scriptures, his monstrous opinions, and manifold contradictions, that neither he nor any of his generation durst ever after put pen to paper to encounter and rejoin to his reply: in which, besides the deep and profound debating of the matter itself, he so dresseth Luther with his own scoffing and jesting rhetoric, as he worthily deserved. But because this kind of writing (albeit a meet cover for such a cup, and very necessary to repress and beat him with his own folly, according to the Scripture, 'Responde stulto secundum stultitiam ejus,') seemed not agreeable and correspondent to his gravity and dignity: the book was set forth under the name of one Gulielmus Rosseus.

He wrote also and printed another proper and witty treatise against a certain epistle of John Pomerane, one of Luther's standard-bearers, in Germany. And after he was shut up in the Tower, he wrote a certain exposition in Latin, upon the passion of Christ, not yet printed, which was not perfected, and is so plainly and exquisitely translated into English, by his niece Mrs. Bassett,* that it may seem originally to have been penned in English by Sir Thomas More himself. Some other things he wrote also in Latin, which we pretermit; and now we will say somewhat of his English works, which all (besides the Life of John Picus, earl of Mirandula, and the foresaid Life of King Richard the Third, and some other profane things,) concern matters of religion for the most part.

The first book of this sort, was his Dialogues, made by him when he was chancellor of the duchy of Lancaster, which books occasioned him afterwards (as according to the old proverb, ' One business begetteth another,') to write divers other things. For whereas he had amongst many other matters touched and reproved William Tindall's adulterate and vicious translation of the New Testament, Tindall being not able to bear to see his new religion, and his own doings withal to have so foul an overthrow, as Sir Thomas More gave him, after great deli-

* ' Niece' is here used for ' grand-daughter.' Mrs. Bassett was Mary, daughter of Margaret Roper, married first to Stephen Clarke, and secondly to James Bassett. She was one of the maids of honour to Queen Mary, and was celebrated for her learning and virtues. See Ballard, p. 106.

beration and consultation with his evangelical brethren, took in hand to answer some part of his dialogues, especially touching his aforesaid corrupt translation; but what small glory he won thereby, is easy to be seen of every man, that with indifferent affection will vouchsafe to read Sir Thomas More's reply, whereof we shall give you a small taste; but first we will note unto you the integrity, sincerity, and uprightness of the good and gracious nature and disposition of the said Sir Thomas More in his writing, not only against Tindall, but generally against all other protestants. First then it is to be considered in him, that he doth not, (as many other writers do against their adversaries, and all protestants do against him and other catholics,) wreathe and wrest their words to the worst, and make their reasons more feeble and weak, than they are; but rather enforceth them to the uttermost, and oftentimes further than the party himself doth or perhaps could do. And he was of this mind, that he said, he would not let, while he lived, wheresoever he perceived his adversary to say well, or himself to have said otherwise, indifferently for both to say and declare the truth. And therefore himself after the printing, finding the books divulged and commonly read of the Debellation of Salem and Bizance, albeit many had read the place and found no fault therein; yet he finding afterwards that he mistook certain words of the Pacifier, without any man's controlment, merely of himself reformed them. The like he counselled his learned friends, especially Erasmus to do, and to retract many things that he had written; whose counsel (wherein he had a notable precedent in the worthy doctor St. Augustine) if Erasmus had followed, I trow his books would have been better liked of by our posterity, which perchance shall be fain either utterly to abolish some of his works, or at least to redress and reform them. Here is now further to be considered in his writings, that he never hunted after praise and vain glory, nor any vile and filthy gain and commodity; yea, so that envenomed and poisoned books might be once suppressed and abolished, he wished his own on a light and fair fire. Yet did the evangelical brethren, after he had abandoned the office of lord chancellor, as they otherwise spread and writ many vain and false rumours to the advancement of their new gospel, and oppressing of the Catholics, lay to his charge in their books, that he was partial to the clergy, and for his books received a great mass of money of the said clergy. And Tindall and divers others of the good brethren affirmed, that they wist well that Sir Thomas More was not less worth in money, plate and other moveables, than twenty thousand marks; but it was found far otherwise, when his house was searched, after he was committed to the Tower, where a while he had some competent liberty, but after on a sudden he was shut up very close, at which time he feared there would be a new and more narrower search in all his houses, because his mind gave him, that folks thought he was not so poor as it appeared upon the search; but he told his daughter Mrs. Roper that it would be but a sport to them that knew the truth of his poverty, unless they should find out his wife's gay girdle, and her gold beads. The like poverty of any man, that had continued so in high favour with the king, and had borne many great offices, hath, I trow, seldom been found in any layman before, and much less since his time. As for his partiality to the clergy, saving the reverence due to the sacred order of priests, by whom we are made Christian men in baptism, and by whom we receive the other holy sacraments, there was none in him; and that they felt, that were naught of the clergy; they had so little favour at his hands, that there was no man, that any meddling had with them, into whose hands they were more loath to come, than into his; but for fees, annuities or other rewards, or any commodity that should incline him to be ever propense and partial to the clergy, none can be showed. First, touching any fees he had to his living, after that he had left the chancellorship, he had not one groat granted him since he first wrote, or began to write the Dialogues, and that was the first book that ever he wrote in matters of religion. And as for all the lands and fees he had, besides those of the king's gift, was not, nor should be, during his mother-in-law's life, (who lived after he relinquished the office of chancellorship), worth yearly the sum of one hundred pounds, and thereof he had some by his wife, some left by his father, some he purchased, and some fees had he of temporal men; and so may every man soundly guess that he had no great part of his living of the clergy to make him partial to them. Now, touching rewards or lucre, which rose to him by his writing, (for which good Father Tindall said he wrote his books, and not for any affection he bare to the clergy, no more than Judas betrayed Christ for any favour he bare to the scribes and pharisees,) it is a most shameful lie and slander, as may appear by his refusal of the four or five thousand pounds offered him by the clergy.

Concerning Tindall's false translation of the New Testament; first it is to be considered, as these good brethren partly deny the very text itself, and whole books of the sacred Scripture, as the book of the Maccabees, and certain others; and Luther Saint James's Epistle also; and as they adulterate and commaculate and corrupt the whole corps of the same with their wrong and false expositions, far disagreeing from the comment of the ancient fathers and doctors, and from the faith of the whole catholic church; so have they for the advancing and furthering of the said heresies, of a set purpose perverted and mistranslated the said Holy Scriptures. And after such shameful sort, that amongst other their mischievous practices, whereas in the Latin Epistle of Saint Paul is read in the old translation " fornicarii," in the new they have " sacerdotes," that is, priests, for adulterers, for the good devotion they bear to the sacred order of priesthood. And their patriarch Luther, with his translation of the said Holy Scripture into the Dutch tongue, hath wonderfully depraved, corrupted, and defiled it, as we could by divers proofs easily show, whom his good scholar Tindall, in his English translation, doth match, or rather pass; wherein he turneth the word " church" into " congregation;" " priest" into " senior," or " elder;" which word " congregation," absolutely of itself, as Tindall doth use it, doth no more signify the congregation of Christian men, than a fair flock of unchristian geese; neither this word " presbyter," for " elder,' signifieth any whit more a priest, than it doth an elder stick. Many other parts of his translation are suitable to this; as where, in spite of Christ's and his holy saints' images, he turneth " idols" into " images;" and for the like purpose of setting forth his heresy—" charity" into " love," " grace" into " favour," " confession" into " repentance," and such like; for which, as also for divers of his false, faithless, heretical assertions, as well that the apostles left nothing unwritten that is of necessity to be believed; that the church may err in matter of faith; that the church is only of chosen elects; touching the manner and order of our election; touching his wicked and detestable opinion against the free will of man; touching his fond and foolish paradoxes of the elect, though they do abominable heinous acts, yet they do not sin; and that the elect that doth once heartily repent, can sin no more; he doth so substantially and pleasantly confute and overthrow Tindall, that if these men that be envenomed and poisoned with those pestilent heresies, would, with indifferent minds, read the said Sir Thomas More's answer, there were good hope (as it hath, God be thanked, chanced to many already) of their good and speedy recovery. But, alack the while, and woe upon the subtle craft of the cursed devil, that so blindeth them, and the reckless, negligent regard that these men have to their soul's health, that can be content to suck in the deadly poison of their souls, by reading and crediting these mischievous books, and yet will not once vouchsafe to take the wholesome depulsive triacle, not to be fetched from Geneva, but even ready at home at their hands in Sir Thomas More's books against this dreadful deadly infection. But to return now again to the said Tindall: Lord, what open, foul, and shameful shifts doth he make for the defence of his wrong and pestiferous assertions, and with what spiteful shameful lies doth he belie Sir Thomas More, and wretchedly depraveth his writings! Not being ashamed, though his plain and manifest words lie open to the sight of all men to the contrary, to deprave his answers. And amongst other, that he should affirm, that the church of Christ should be before the Gospel was taught or preached; which things he neither writeth nor once thought as a most absurd untruth, but that it was, as it is very true, before the written Gospel. And the said Sir Thomas More seeing that, by Tindall's own confession, the church of God was in the world many hundred years before the written laws of Moses, doth well thereof gather and conclude against Tindall, that there is no cause to be yielded, but that much more it may be so, and is so indeed, that in the gracious time of our redemption, the Holy Ghost that leadeth the church from time to time into all truth, being so plentifully effused upon the same, the church of Christ is, and ever hath been, in many things instructed necessary to be believed, that be not in any Scripture comprized. These and many other strong reasons do prove the common known catholic church, and none other, to be the true church of Christ. And seeing we do not know the very books of Scripture, which thing Luther himself confesseth, but by the known catholic church, we must of necessity take the true and sound understanding of the said Scriptures, and all our faith from the said church; which understanding is confirmed in the said church from the apostles' time by infinite miracles, and with the consent of the old fathers and holy martyrs, with many other substantial reasons that Sir Thomas More so layeth forth, that he have so appalled and amazed Tindall, that he is like a man that were in an inexplicable labyrinth, whereof he can by no means get out; and Tindall being thus brought oftentimes to a bay and utter distress, he scuddeth in and out like a hare that had twenty brace of greyhounds after her, and were afeared at every foot to be snatched up. And as Sir Thomas More merrily yet truly writeth, he did wind himself so wilily this way and that way, and so shifteth him in and out, and with his subtle shifting so bleareth our eyes, that he maketh us as blind as a cat; and so snareth us up in his matters, that we can no more see whereabout he walketh, than if he went visible before us all naked in a net, and in effect playeth the very blind hob about the house; sometimes when there is no other shift, then Tindall is driven to excuse himself and his doings, as he doth for the word "presbyter," which he translated first "senior," then "elder;" wherein for excuse of his fault, at great length he declareth four fair virtues in himself, malice, ignorance, error, and folly. And where that he said he had amended his fault in translating "elder" for "senior," this is a like amending, as if he would, where a man were blind on the one eye, amend his sight by putting out the other.

As Sir Thomas More answered Tindall, touching his unknown church, so did he also Friar Barnes; for in that point both agreed, and would have the church secret and hid in hugger mugger; but in the mean season they handle the matter so handsomely and so artificially, that their own reasons pluck down their unknown church. And albeit they would have us believe the church were unknown, yet do they give us tokens and marks whereby it should be known. And in perusing their unknown church they fall into many foolish and absurd paradoxes, that Sir Thomas More discovereth. And this unknown church would they fain rear up in the air to pluck down the catholic known church on the earth, and so leave us no church at all; which church to overthrow is their final and only hope; for, that standing, they well know their malignant church cannot stand, being by the catholic church both now and many hundred years condemned. These and many other things doth Sir Thomas More more at large full well declare, and setteth the limping and halting good wife of the Bottle, at Bottle's Wharf, at disputation with F. Barnes; in which the indifferent reader shall see, that she did not so much limp and halt, as did the lame and weak reasons that F. Barnes brought against her of his unknown church, which she utterly overthroweth; but yet as they do, both Tindall and Barnes, agree, as we have said, in their secret unknown church, so in other points touching their said church, as in many other articles besides, they do jar and disagree, and not so much the one from the other as from themselves, as Sir Thomas More showeth more at large. "For," saith he, "as they that would have built up the Tower of Babylon had such a stop thrown upon them, that suddenly none knew what another said; surely so God upon these heretics of our time, that go busily about to raise up to the sky their foul filthy dunghill of all old and new false stinking heresies, gathered together against the true faith of Christ, that he himself hath hitherto taught his true Catholic church; God, I say, when the apostles went about to preach the Catholic faith, sent down the holy spirit of unity, concord, and truth unto them, with the gift of speech and understanding, so that they understood every man, and every man understood them, hath sent amongst these heretics the spirit of error and lying, of dissension and division, the damnable devil of hell, which so entangleth their tongues and distempereth their brains, that they neither understand one another, nor any of them well himself." The books of the said Tindall and Barnes are more farced and stuffed with jesting and railing than with any good substantial reasoning; and notwithstanding that a man would think that Tindall were in fond scoffing peerless; yet, as Sir Thomas declareth, Barnes doth far overrun him, and oftentimes fareth as if he were from a friar waxen a fiddler, and would, at a tavern, go get him a penny for a fit of mirth; and yet sometimes will the fool demurely and holily preach, and take so upon him, as if he were Christ's own dear apostle, as do also the residue of the brethren that write, and especially Tindall, who beginneth the preface of his book with " The grace of our Lord, and the light of his Spirit," &c. with such glorious glittering salutations, as if it were Saint Paul himself. But Sir Thomas More doth accordingly dress him, and doth discover to the world Friar Luther's and Tindall's, and such other false, feigned, and hypocritical holiness, in their so high and solemn salutations and preachings; and concludeth not more pleasingly, that when a man well considereth these their salutations and preachings, he may well and truly judge those their counterfeit salutations and sermons to be a great deal worse than Friar Frappie (who first curseth, then blesseth and looketh holily, and preacheth ribaldry,) was wont at Christmas to make.

And thus will we leave Tindall and Barnes, and speak of some other of their fraternity; amongst whom there was one that made The Supplication of Beggars, the which Sir Thomas More answered very notably before he wrote against Tindall and Barnes. This Supplication was made by one Simon Fish, for which he became penitent, returned to the church again, and abjured all the whole hill of those heresies, out of the which the fountain of his great zeal, that moved him to write, sprang.

After this Sir Thomas More wrote a letter impugning the erroneous writings of John Frith; and whereas, after he had given over the office of lord chancellor, the heretics full fast did write against him, and found many faults with him and his writings, he made a goodly and learned Apology of some of his answers; which said Apology we have already touched, especially that which they laid to his charge of the slender recital and misrehearsal of Tindall and Barnes's arguments, and showeth that they were calumnious slanderers; and that himself used Tindall and Barnes after a better manner, than they used him. For Tindall rehearseth Sir Thomas More's arguments in every place faintly and falsely, and leaveth out the pith and strength, and the proof that most maketh for the purpose. And he fareth therein, as if there were one having a day of challenge appointed in which he should wrestle with his adversary, and would find the mean by craft before the day to get his adversary into his own hands, and there keep him, and diet him with such a thin diet, that at the day he bringeth him forth feeble, faint and famished, and almost starved, and so lean that he can scarce stand on his legs; and then is it easy, you wot well, to give him the fall. And yet when Tindall had done all this, he took the fall himself; but every one may see, that Sir Thomas

More useth not that play with Tindall nor with any of those folk, but rehearseth their reasons to the best, that they can make it themselves, and rather enforceth, and strengtheneth it, as we have before declared, rather than taketh any thing therefrom.

Whereas also they found farther fault with the length of his book, he writeth amongst other things that it is less marvel, that it seem to them long and tedious to read within, whom it irketh to do so much as to look it over without, for every way seemeth long to him that is weary before he begin. But I find some men, to whom the reading of the book is so far from being tedious, that they have read the whole book over thrice, and some that make tables thereof for their own remembrance, and are men that have as much wit and learning both, as the best of all this blessed brotherhood, that ever I heard of. And for the shortness of Barnes's book, that the adversaries did commend, he writeth that he wotteth not well, whether he may call them long or short; sometimes they be short indeed, because they would be dark, and have their false follies pass and repass all unperceived; sometimes they use some compendious eloquence, that they convey and couch up together with a wonderful brevity four follies and five lies, in less than as many lines; but yet for all this I see not in effect any men more long than they: for they preach sometimes a very long process to a little purpose, and sith that of their whole purpose they prove never a whit at all, were their writings never so short, yet were their work too long at last by altogether.

Besides many other things, his adversaries laid to his charge, that he handled Tindall, Frith, and Barnes, ungodly and with uncomely words, to which he thus answereth; " now when that against all the catholic church, both that now is and ever hath been before from the apostles' days hitherto, both temporal and spiritual, laymen and religious, and against all that good is, saints, ceremonies, service of God, the very sacrament of the altar, these blasphemous heretics in their ungracious books so villainously wrest and rail: were not a man, ween you, far overseen and worthy to be accounted uncourteous, that would in writing against their heresies presume without great reverence to rehearse their worshipful names? if any of them use their words at their pleasure as evil and as villainous as they list, against myself; I am content to forbear any requiting thereof, and give them no worse words again, than if they spake me fair, nor using themselves towards all other folk, as they do, fairer words will I not give them, than if they spake me foul; for all is one to me, or rather worse than better;

for the pleasant oil of heretics cast upon my head, can do my mind no pleasure, but contrariwise, the worse that folk write of me for hatred they bear to the catholic church and faith, the greater pleasure, as for mine own part, they do me; but surely their railing against all other, I purpose not to bear so patiently, as to forbear to let them hear some part of like language, as they speak, howbeit to match them therein, I cannot, though I would; but I am content, as needs I must, to give them therein the mastery, for to match them, were more rebuke than honesty; for in their railing is all their roast meat sauced, all their pot sethed, and all their pie meat spiced, and all their wafers, and all their pottage made." He addeth further, " if they, saith he, will not be heretics alone themselves, and hold their tongues and be still, but must needs be talking, and corrupt whom they can, let them yet at the leastwise be reasonable heretics and honest, and write reason, and leave railing, and then let all the brethren find fault with me, if I use them not after that in words as fair and as mild as the matter may suffer."

About this time, there was one that had made a book of the Spirituality and the Temporality, of which book the brethren made great store, and blamed Sir Thomas More, that he had not in writing used such a soft and mild manner, and such an indifferent fashion, as the same person did. By which occasion, Sir Thomas More discourseth upon the same book, the author whereof pretendeth to make a pacification of the aforesaid division and discord, and openeth many faults and follies, and false slanders against the clergy, under a holy conclusion and pretence of pacification in the said books. To which discourse of Sir Thomas More's there came an answer afterwards in print, under the title of Salem and Bizance; to the which Sir Thomas More replied, and so dressed this pretty proper politic pacifier, that he had no list, nor any man for him afterwards, to encounter with Sir Thomas. The pretty, pleasant, and witty declaration of the said book of Sir Thomas More's, because the book is seldom and rare to be got, I will now, gentle reader, set before thine eyes. The said title is framed in this sort: " The debellation of Salem and Bizance, sometimes two great towns, which being under the Turk, were between Easter and Michaelmas last 1533, by a marvellous metamorphose and enchantment, turned into Englishmen, by the wonderful inventive wit and witchcraft of Sir John Somesay the pacifier, and so conveyed by him hither in a dialogue to defend his division, against Sir Thomas More knight; but now being thus between Michaelmas and Allhallowntide next ensuing, the debellation vanquished, they be fled hence, and be become two towns again, with those old names changed, Salem into Jerusalem, and Bizance into Constantinople, the one in Greece, the other in Syria, where they may see them that will, and win them that can: and if this pacifier convey them hither again, and ten such towns embattled with them in dialogues, Sir Thomas More hath undertaken to put himself in adventure against them all; but if he let them tarry still there, he will not utterly forswear it, but he is not in the mind, age now coming on, and he waxing unwieldy, to go thither to give the assault to such well-walled towns, without some such lusty company, as shall be likely to leap up a little more lightly." This is the title of the aforesaid book; and that indeed Sir Thomas More hath most valiantly discomfited the pacifier, and overthrown his two great towns, may easily appear to such as will vouchsafe to read Sir Thomas More's answer: the circumstances and particulars whereof to set down, would make our present treatise to grow too big; I will only show you one declaration or two, whereby you may make some aim to judge of the whole doing of the said pacifier. "If it were so, saith Sir Thomas More, that one found two men standing together, and would step in between them, and bear them in hand, that they were about to fight, and would with a word put one party back with his hand, and all to buffet the other about the face, and then go forth and say, he had parted a fray, and pacified the parties, some men would say, as I suppose, he had as lief his enemy were let alone with him, and thereof abide the adventure, as have such a friend step in to part them." Another, of a man that were angry with his wife, and haply not without cause; now saith Sir Thomas More, if the author of this book would take upon him to reconcile them, and help to make them at one, and therein would use this way, that when he had them both together before him, would tell all the faults of the wife, and set among them some of his own imagination, and then would go about to avoid his words under the fair figure of 'Some-say;' (which he commonly useth in his book of Pacifying, either by forgetfulness, or by the figure of plain folly;) and then would tell her husband's part perverse too, and say unto him, that he himself had not dealt discreetly with her, but hath used to make her too homely with him, and hath suffered her to be idle, and hath given way to her being too much conversant amongst her gossips, and hath given her over gay gear, and sometimes given her evil words, and called her, as I suppose, cursed quean and shrew, and some say, that behind your back she calls you knave and cuckold; were not there a proper kind of pacification? And yet is this the lively pattern and image of Mr. Pacifier's doings, with the which, and with the spinning of fine lies with flax, fetching them out of his own body, as the spider doth the cobweb, feigning and finding fault with Sir Thomas More for these matters and words, whereof he saith the plain contrary, he had great cause to be ashamed, howbeit little shame could cleave to his cheeks, but that he would soon shake it away, while his name was not at his book.

We have now one book more written in matter of religion, and that is of the blessed sacrament of the altar, by the said Sir Thomas More. We told you before of a letter of his, wherein he impugneth the heresy of John Frith. Now had the said Frith, albeit he was prisoner in the Tower of London, found the means to make answer to that letter, and to convey it beyond the seas, where it was printed, and it was afterwards brought into this realm, as Sir Thomas More did certainly understand, who minded, when the book came to his hands, to answer it; but in the mean season came there from beyond the seas, an Answer made to the same letter by another, and printed without the author's name, entitled, The

Supper of the Lord. But I beshrew, quoth Sir Thomas More, such a sewer, that serveth in such a supper, and conveyeth away the best dish, and bringeth it not to the board, as this man would, if he could convey from the blessed sacrament Christ's own flesh and blood, and leave us nothing therein but for a memorial only, bare bread and wine. But his hands are too lumpish, and this mess too great for him, especially to convey clean, sith every man hath his heart bent thereto, and therefore his eye set thereon, to see where it becometh. This naughty nameless author, Sir Thomas More doth not only by the authority of the sacred scripture, and holy ancient fathers, but by his own reasons and texts that himself bringeth forth, plainly and evidently convince.

Now have we besides, other excellent and fruitful books which he made, being prisoner in the Tower; as his three books of Comfort against Tribulation, a Treatise to receive the blessed Sacrament sacramentally and virtually both; a Treatise upon the Passion, with notable introductions to the same. He wrote also many other godly and devout instructions and prayers; and surely of all the books that ever he made, I doubt whether I may prefer any of them before the said three Books of Comfort, yea or any other man's, either heathen or Christian that have written, (as many have) either in Greek or Latin of the said matter. And as for heathen, I do this worthy man plain injury, and do much abase him, in matching and comparing him with them, especially in this point: seeing that, were they otherwise never so incomparable, they lacked yet, and knew not the very especial and principal ground of comfort and consolation, that is, the true faith of Christ in whom and for whom, and whose glory we must seek and fetch all our true comfort and consolation: well, let that pass; and let us further say, that as the said Sir Thomas More notably passeth many learned Christians, that have of the same matter written before, so let us add, that it may well be doubted, all matters considered and weighed, if any of the rest may seem much to pass him. There is in these books so witty, pithy, and substantial matter, for the easing, remedying, and patiently suffering of all manner of griefs and sorrows that may possibly encumber any man, by any manner or kind of tribulation, whether their tribulation proceed from any inward temptation or ghostly enemy, the devil, or any outward temptation of the world, threatening to bereave or spoil us of our goods, lands, honour, liberty, and freedom, by grievous and sharp punishment, and finally of our life withal, by any painful, exquisite, and cruel death; against all which he doth so wonderfully and effectually prepare, defend, and arm the reader, that a man cannot desire or wish any thing of any more efficacy or importance thereunto to be added. In the which book his principal drift and scope was to stir and prepare the minds of Englishmen manfully and courageously to withstand, and not to shrink at the imminent and open persecution, which he foresaw, and immediately followed against the unity of the church, and the catholic faith of the same; albeit full wittily and warily, that the books might the safer go abroad, he doth not expressly meddle with these matters, but covereth the matter under the name of an Hungarian, and of the persecution of the Turks in Hungary; and of the book translated out of the Hungarian tongue into Latin, and then into the English tongue. Of these books then there is great account to be made, not only for the excellent matter comprised in them, but also for that they were made when he was most straitly shut up and enclosed from all company in the Tower, in which sort I doubt whether a man shall find any other book of the like worthiness made by any Christian; and yet if any such be found, much surely should I yield to the same. But there is one thing wherein these books of Sir Thomas More, by special prerogative surmount (or else I am deceived) all other of this sort; and that is, that they were for the most part written with no other pen, than a coal, as was his Treatise upon the Passion; which copies, if some men had them, they might and would esteem more than other books written with golden letters, and would no less account of it than Saint Hierome did of certain books of the martyr Lucian, written with his own hand, that by chance he happened on, and esteemed them as a precious jewel. And yet is there one thing more in the valuing and praising of these books: he is not, as many great clerks are, like to a whetstone, that being blunt and dull itself, whetteth other things, and sharpeneth them: it was not so with this man; for, though he wrote these books with a dead black coal, yet was there a most hot burning coal, such a one as purified the lips of the holy prophet Esaias, that directed his heart and so enflamed and incensed the same to heavenward, that the good and wholesome instructions and counsel that he gave to other men in his books, he himself afterward, in most patient suffering the loss of his goods and lands, by his imprisonment, and death, for the defence of justice and of the catholic faith, experimented and worthily practised in himself.

And these be in effect the books he made

either in Latin or English; which his English books, if they had been written by him in the Latin tongue also, or might be with the like grace that they now have, translated into Latin, they would surely much augment and increase the estimation which the world hath conceived, especially in foreign countries, of his incomparable wit, learning, and virtue.

THE END.

No. I.

THE EPISTLE DEDICATORY TO QUEEN HENRIETTA MARIA PREFIXED BY THE ORIGINAL EDITOR TO THE FIRST EDITION.

TO THE HIGH AND MIGHTY PRINCESS, OUR MOST GRACIOUS QUEEN AND SOVEREIGN,

MARIE HENRIETTE,

QUEEN OF GREAT BRITAIN, FRANCE, AND IRELAND, LADY OF THE ISLES OF THE BRITISH OCEAN.

Most gracious and Sovereign Lady,

THE author of this treatise, eldest son by descent, and heir by nature of the family of that worthy martyr, whose life is described in it; had he lived himself to have set it forth to the view of Christian eyes, would not have thought upon any other patron and protector to dedicate it unto than your most excellent Majesty. For he was most constantly affected always to the French nation and crown, next after the dutiful obedience which he ought to his own natural lord and sovereign. And this

his affection did he manifest on all occasions, but especially in the treaty of the happy marriage of your highness with the king our sovereign lord and master; assembling, at his own costs and charges, with unwearied industry, all the English persons of note and esteem that then were in and about Rome, and, with them all, (as the mouth of them all,) supplicating to his holiness for the dispatch of this most hopeful and happy contract, yielding such reasons for the effecting thereof, as highly pleased the chief pastor of the church under Christ our Saviour. The same affection did he testify sufficiently in the last period of his life, leaving his body to be buried in the French church at Rome, where, with great content of the French nobility, it lieth interred.

This being the affection of the author of this treatise, I should much wrong his memory, if these labours of his should be offered to the patronage of any other than of your royal Majesty. The glorious martyr himself demands likewise, that his life should be read under your Majesty's protection, since he lost his life in this world (to gain it in the next) in defence of an innocent stranger Queen (for reasons not to be mentioned by us), debarred from her lawful bed. Although (God be praised and magnified therefore) the heavens have rained such graces upon your Majesty, that there never can happen any such causes of defence; your glorious husband and lord, our sovereign king, so dearly affecting you, and the hopeful issue (the chiefest bond of matrimonial love,) so powerfully knitting your hearts together, and your gracious Majesty's goodness, virtues, and debonnaire discretion, so recommending you to him first, and then to all his true loyal subjects of this great united monarchy, that we may undoubtedly expect from Almighty God a long and prosperous enjoyance of your joint government, and a glorious race of happy successors to this crown from your royal loins; which happiness, and heaven after long prosperity on earth, upon my knees I wish unto your royal grace, remaining for ever,

Your Majesty's loyal and obedient
subject and servant,

M. C. M. E.

No. II.

THE PREFACE TO THE SECOND EDITION, 1726.

THE PREFACE.

The following sheets were drawn up by Thomas More, the great grandson of Sir Thomas More, whose history they contain, and are supposed to have been first published in London in quarto, about two years after the author's decease, who is reported to have died at Rome on the 11th of April, 1625, according to the Gregorian computation, and to have left this work behind him there. He is said to have been a person of consideration and character, the agent of the English clergy in Spain, and at the court of Rome, and a zealous asserter of the pope's supremacy. And indeed he managed with such application and integrity in the business of his employment, that upon his leaving the world, the English Roman Catholic clergy erected a monument over his ashes at their own expense, as a testimony of the respect they bore him, and the sense they had of his services. He lies buried in the church of Saint Lewis at Rome, and the inscription over him, as it is given us by Anthony Wood, runs in the form following: " D. O. M. S. Thomæ Moro dioc. Ebor. Anglo, magni illius Thomæ Mori Angliæ Cancellarii et Martyris pronepoti atq; hæredi, viro probitate et pietate insigni, qui, raro admodum apud Britannos exemplo, in fratrem natu minorem amplum transcripsit patrimonium, et presbyter Romæ factus, inde fuisse sedis Apostolicæ in patriam profectus, plusculos annos strenuam fidei propagandæ navavit operam; postea cleri Anglicani negotia septem annos Romæ, et quinque in Hispaniâ, P. P. Paulo V. et Gregorio XV. summâ cum integritate et industriâ, suisq; sumptibus, procuravit. Tandem de subrogando Anglis Episcopo ad Urbanum VIII. missus, negotio feliciter confecto mercedem recepturus, ex hâc vitâ migravit, xi. Apr. An. 1625, æt. suæ 59. Clerus Anglicanus mœstus P." The near relation he bore to Sir Thomas More must necessarily have made him well acquainted with the principal circumstances of his life, and accordingly his performance is said by the learned Oxford antiquary to have been incomparably well written. It was so greedily sought after upon its first publication, that in Mr. Wood's time, it was scarce to be had; and it appears from the few sheets of Sir Thomas More's Life, which Dr. Fiddes has left behind him, that notwithstanding all his enquiries after proper materials for the compiling his history, he had never seen it. It is the scarcity of this work, and the value that has been set upon it, which have given occasion to this new edition, that the world might not be deprived of any information relating to the story of this great man, whose learning and sufferings have so justly recommended him to the esteem of mankind.

His execution is, without exception, one of the greatest blemishes in King Henry the Eighth's reign. As he had been some time in favour with the king, and stood distinguished by his faithfulness and zeal in the administration of justice, by an unexampled generosity and disinterestedness, it might have reasonably been expected, that his present supposed offence would have been overlooked upon the score of his former services, and the rigour of his sentence abated. But his great endowments were turned to his disadvantage, and made use of as so many arguments for hastening his ruin. He was invidiously charged with ingratitude in the preamble to an act of parliament, " for the great favours he had received from the king, and for studying to sow and make sedition among the king's subjects, and refusing to take the oath of succession." And it was further urged, that if no notice was taken of him in so great a change, and he was suffered to escape with impunity, his authority might make an ill impression upon the people; and his example encourage others to fall off from their affection to the king.

Archbishop Cranmer is said to have solicited in his behalf; and there is still extant a letter from him to Secretary Cromwell, dated the 17th of April, wherein he presses, that Sir Thomas More and the Bishop of Rochester might be dispensed with in the present case, and allowed to take the oath to the succession only, without swearing to the preamble, as they had both of them freely offered to do. His wisdom foresaw, that if they once swore to the succession, all others would readily acquiesce in their judgment, and peace be restored to the nation. But the king was too passionately fond of his new queen, and his new power, to admit of any advice, which might seem to reflect upon either. And thus it was resolved to proceed against them with all imaginable severity.

In November following an act was passed in parliament for the farther establishment of the king's supremacy. The tenor of it was very extraordinary, and as it is only referred to in the ensuing discourse, I shall here lay it before the reader.

"Albeit the king's majesty justly and rightfully is, and ought to be supreme head of the church of England, and is so recognized by the clergy of this realm in their convocations, yet nevertheless for corroboration and confirmation thereof, and for increase of virtue in Christ's religion within this realm of England, and to repress and extirp all errors, heresies, and other enormities and abuses heretofore used in the same; Be it enacted by the authority of this present parliament, that the king our sovereign lord, his heirs and successors, kings of this realm, shall be taken, accepted, and reputed, the only supreme head in earth of the church of England, called Anglicana Ecclesia, and shall have and enjoy annexed and united to the imperial crown of this realm, as well the title and style thereof, as all honours, dignities, immunities, profits, and commodities to the said dignity of supreme head of the said church belonging and appertaining. And that our said sovereign lord, his heirs and successors, kings of this realm, shall have full power and authority from time to time to visit, repress, redress, reform, order, correct, restrain, and amend all such errors, heresies, abuses, contempts, and enormities, whatsoever they be, which by any manner of spiritual authority or jurisdiction ought or may lawfully be reformed, repressed, ordered, redressed, corrected, restrained, or amended, most to the pleasure of Almighty God, the increase of virtue in Christ's religion, and for the conservation of the peace, unity, and tranquillity of this realm, any usage, custom, foreign laws, foreign authority, prescription, or any thing or things to the contrary hereof notwithstanding."

Thus, we see the king's majesty, and such as were commissioned by him, were made sole judges in matters of faith, and all ecclesiastical discipline was put into their hand. The commission, which our Saviour had granted to his apostles and their successors, was set aside by an human law, and the authority they derived from heaven transferred upon the state. The care of souls was made to devolve upon the civil power, and the being of Christianity to depend upon the will of the magistrate.

The king began the exercise of his supremacy with naming Cromwell his vicar-general, and general visitor of all the monasteries and other privileged places. He next made him his lord vicegerent in ecclesiastical matters, gave him an authority over the bishops, and precedence next the royal family. And in both these commissions, all jurisdiction as well ecclesiastical as civil, is said to flow from his majesty as supreme head.

Not long after the parliament had dispatched

this business, a Latin Bible was ordered to be set forth, and in his majesty's general preface he addresses the pious reader, in the following strain. " Nos itaque considerantes id erga Deum officii, quo suscepisse cognoscimur, ut in regno simus sicut anima in corpore, et sol in mundo, utque loco Dei judicium exerceamus in regno nostro, et omnia in potestate habentes, quoad jurisdictionem, ipsam etiam ecclesiam vice Dei sedulo regamus, ac tueamur, et disciplinæ ejus, sive augeatur, aut solvatur, nos ei rationem reddituri simus, qui nobis eam credidit, et in eo Dei vicem agentes, Deique habentes imaginem, quid aliud vel cogitare vel in animum inducere potuimus, quàm ut eodem confugeremus, ubi certo discendum esset, ne quid aliud vel ipsi faceremus, vel faciendum aliis præscriberemus, quàm quod ab hâc ipsâ Dei lege ne vel transversum quidem digitum aberrare convinci queat."

And farther, to show how much he triumphed in this new style and title, he some time after caused a medal to be struck, where on one side is to be seen his effigies half faced, in his usual bonnet, fur gown, and collar of rubies, with the following inscription engraved in a double circle:

" HENRICUS. OCTA. ANGLIÆ. FRANC. ET HIB. REX. IN TERR. ECCLE. ANGL. ET HIB. SUB. CHRIST. CAPUT. SUPREMUM." And on the reverse,

H. R.

חנריכוש
שמיני .ג. מלך .באמוח
סגן .ובעדה .אנגליאי
והיברניאי מתחת [משיח
ראש עליון

ΕΝΡΙΚΟΣ. Ο. ΟΓΔΟΟΣ. ΤΡΙΣ
ΒΑΣΙΛΕΥΣ. ΠΙΣΤΕΩΣ ΠΡΟ-
ΣΤΑΤΗΣ ΕΝ. ΤΗ. ΕΚΚΛΗΣΙΑ
ΤΗΣ. ΑΓΓΛΙΑΣ. ΚΑΙ ΙΒΕΡΝΙ-
ΑΣ. ΤΠΟ. ΧΡΙΣΤΩ. ΑΚΡΗ
Η. ΚΕΦΑΛΗ.

Londini 1545.

The late-mentioned statute however had no penalty annexed, and was therefore insufficient to affect the life of Sir Thomas More. For this reason another act was passed in the same session, by which it was made high treason for any person "maliciously to wish, will, or desire by words or writing, to deprive the king's most royal person, the queen, or her heirs apparent, or any of them, of their dignity, title, and name," &c. And thus upon Mr. Rich's evidence, that Sir Thomas More should say, the parliament could not make the king supreme head of the church, he was declared to be within the statute, and was pronounced guilty of high-treason.

But to return to the subject of the following

book. To make it as useful as might be, I have been at the pains to compare it with the several Lives of Sir Thomas More, which have been given us by others, and have made references in the margin to the several places where the like fact is related. The most considerable of these is Mr. Roper's Life of Sir Thomas More, published by Mr. Hearne, at Oxford, in 1716, and Dr. Stapleton's Vita Tho. Mori, &c., which is part of his book entitled, De tribus Thomis, edit. Duac. 1588, and Col. Agripp. 1599. And I may safely affirm, there is no circumstance of any moment taken notice of by either of these, that is not to be met with in the book before us. Mr. Hoddesdon's History is less to be accounted of; it is a bare abstract taken from our author, and the two writers we have mentioned above. But that the reader might be deprived of no satisfaction, it is also referred to amongst the rest.

No. III.

VERSES

ON A PORTRAIT OF SIR THOMAS MORE.

[These lines are found in the printed copy of the Life, and also in Mr. Singer's manuscript.]

Who with as curious care should view
    Each virtue of thy breast,
As was thy face perused by him,
    Whose pencil it exprest;
With ease might see, much to admire,
    But hard to put in shapes;
As Zeuxis could express to life
    The fruitful bunch of grapes;
He sooner should his own life end,
    Than he should finish thine,
Such store of matter would arise
    And gems of virtue shine.
There must he draw a brow,
    Of shamefastness and grace,
Then two bright eyes, of learning and
    Religion, therewith place:

And then a nose of honour must
    Be reared, breathing sweet fame;
Two rosy cheeks of martyrdom,
    With lilies of good name;
A golden mouth for all men pleads,
    But only for himself;
A chin of temperance, closely shaved
    From care of worldly pelf.
The more that he shall look into,
    The more he leaves unviewed,
And still more shows of noble worth,
    Wherewith he was endued.
But lo! the fatal axe upreared,
    And at his very chin,
By envy hath a severance made,
    That More might not be seen.

More like a saint lived he, most worthy martyr ended:
More, fit for heaven, which now he hath, whereto his whole life tended.

No. IV.

COPY OF INSCRIPTIONS ON THE PAINTING OF THE MORE FAMILY, NOW AT BURFORD-PRIORY, THE SEAT OF ―― LENTHALL, ESQ. AS FAR AS THEY CAN BE RECOVERED.

Johannes Morus Dominus Manerii de More in libertate Ducatûs Lancastriæ, Anglicè vocati More Place, in parochia de North Mimms, prope Sanctum Albanium *Eques* auratus; apud Westmonasterium regii concessus Judex, obiit ætatis suæ 77 anno regni 22 H. 8, anno Domini 1530.

Thomas Morus Johannis Mori unicus filius et hæres ætatis suæ 26, Janam ætatis 21, maximam natu filiarum Johannis Colte de Newe Hall in *comitatu* Essex duxit uxorem anno 20 H. 7, 1505. Postea Eques auratus, Dominus Cancellarius Angliæ 1530: decollatus ætatis suæ 55 anno 27 H. 8. 1535.

Johannes Morus Londinensis armiger Thomæ Mori et Janæ unicus filius ætatis 19 *duxit* uxorem Annam Cresacrem Eboracensem ætatis 18 anno 21 H. 8, 1529. Ille decessit ætatis suæ 37 anno primo Edwardi 6. *Illa* obiit ætatis suæ 66 anno 20 Elizabethæ 1577.

Anna Cresacris fuit filia et hæres Edwardi Cresacris ar. hæredis manerii de Baronburgh in libertate Ducatûs *Lancastriæ* vocati Baronburgh Halle prope Doncastrum in Comitatu *Ebor. Edwardus obiit* ætatis suæ 27 anno 4 H. 8, 1512. Quæ Anna nata *fuit apud* Baronburgh *Hall* anno 3 H. 8, et *mortua* est ibidem ætatis suæ 66 anno 20 *Elizabethæ*, 1577.

Margarita filia Thomæ Mori Equitis aurati *et* Janæ predictorum anno Domini 1530 *uxor Gulielmi* Roperi de Eltham in Com. Cant. Ar.

Elizabétha filia Thomæ Mori Equitis aurati et Janæ predictorum uxor Johannis Dancæi ar. filii et hæredis apparentis Johannis Dancæi equitis aurati.

Cecilia filia Thomæ Mori Equitis aurati et Janæ predictorum ætatis 21 *uxor Egidii* Heronis Ar.

Anna unica filia *Johannis* Mori ar. et Annæ predictorum quam *Johannes West duxit in uxorem.*

Thomas Morus ætatis 16 Edwardus Morus ætatis 11. Et Thomas Morus junior ætatis 9: Ac etiam Anna ætatis 6, anno primo regni Edw. 6, anno Domini 1547.

Thomas Morus ar. primogenitus *filius* et heres Johannis Mori ar. et Annæ, natus est in Chelseth in Com. Midd. prope Londinum anno 23 H. 8, 1531, uxorem duxit Mariam Scrope ætatis 19 anno 6 Edv. 6, 1553.

Maria Scrope predicta fuit tertia et *minima* natu filiarum Johannis Scrope ar. defuncti ætatis suæ .... anno primo Edv. 6, 1547, unici fratris Henrici Domini Scrope de Boltonia in libertate Richmundiæ in Com. *Ebor*. Maria nata est in *Hambletonia* in Com. Buck. anno 25 H. 8, 1534.

Johannes et Christophorus Cresacrus maximus et minimus natu quatuor filiorum Thomæ Mori ar. et Mariæ nati in Baronburgh predicto. *Johannes* Morus ætatis 36, 1593. Christophorus Cresacrus ætatis 21, 1593.

Thomas Morus ar. predictus ætatis 62; et Maria uxor ejus predicta ætatis 59 habentes superstites filios quatuor viz. Johannem ætatis 36; Thomam ætatis 27; *Henricum* ætatis 26 et Christophorum Cresacrum Morum ætatis 21; et filias sex viz. Annam ætatis 39; Margaritam ætatis 37; Mariam ætatis 34; *Janam* ætatis 31; Catherinam ætatis 29; et Gratiam ætatis 25, anno regni Elizabethæ 35, anno Domini 1593, anno mundi 5597.

Johannes Morus Eques auratus unus ex judicibus Angliæ ætatis 77, 1530.

Thomas Morus Eques auratus Dominus Cancellarius Angliæ ætatis 50, 1530.

Johannes Morus armiger ætatis 20, 1530.

Anna uxor Johannis Mori ar. ætatis 19, 1530.

Tres filiæ predicti Thomæ Mori equitis aurati: *Margarita* Ropera ætatis 23, 1530. Elizabetha Dancæa ætatis 22, 1530: *Cecilia* Heron ætatis 21, 1530.

Thomas Morus armiger ætatis 62, 1593.

Maria Scrope uxor Thomæ Mori ar. ætatis 59, 1593.

Johannes Morus ætatis 36, 1593.

No. V.

DEDICATION TO CRESACRE MORE OF THE EDITION OF ROBINSON'S TRANSLATION OF THE UTOPIA, PUBLISHED BY BERNARD ALSOP, QUARTO, 1624.

TO THE HONOURABLY DESCENDED GENTLEMAN

CRESACRE MORE,

OF MORE-PLACE, IN NORTH MIMMS, IN THE COUNTY OF HERTFORD, ESQUIRE:

NEXT IN BLOOD TO SIR THOMAS MORE, LORD CHANCELLOR OF ENGLAND, AND HEIR TO THE ANCIENT FAMILY OF THE CRESACRES, SOMETIME LORDS OF THE MANOR OF BAMBROUGH, IN THE COUNTY OF YORK, IN THE TIME OF EDWARD THE FIRST.

Howsoever (in these wretched days) the dedication of books is grown into a wretched respect; because the inducements look awry sometimes from virtue, pointing at ostentation (which is gross), or at flattery (which is more base), or else at gain, which is the most sordid of all other: yet (worthy Sir,) I beseech you be pleased better to conceive of this present; for the inducements which have drawn me to this boldness, carry (I might say a noble, but I dare be bold to say) an honest countenance: to omit the excellency of the work (yet unparalleled in that nature) or the noble parts of the more excellent author (whose remembrance is a mirror to all succeeding nobility), both which might challenge Cæsar for a patron: yet when I look into your honourable pedigree, and find you the undoubted heir of his blood, methought it was a theft of the worst nature, to give to another the inheritance of his virtue, and I might as well take from you the lands of the honourable and ancient family of Cresacre (with which God and your right hath endowed you), as bestow upon a stranger this glorious commonwealth, to which your own blood, your ancestors' virtue, and my duty must necessarily entail you. This consideration, when you please to take to your memory, I doubt not but it will much lessen my presumption, and you will out of the goodness of your own virtue think, since it is my fortune to bestow upon him the new edition, I could not with good manners, but bring him to kiss the hand of his true owner, wishing that as this book is eternal for the virtue, and shall live whilst any book hath being; so your name and goodness may continue amongst us, ever-flourishing and unwithered, so long as the sun and moon endureth.

        Your Worship's
            ever to be commanded,
                BERNARD ALSOP.

No. VI.

EXTRACT FROM ATHENÆ OXONIENSES, VOL. I. COL. 35, CONTAINING THE ACCOUNT WHICH WOOD GIVES OF THE DESCENDANTS OF SIR THOMAS MORE.

Sir Thomas had issue by his first wife, Jane the daughter of *John Cowlt* of *Cowlt-Hall* in *Essex*, three daughters, and one son named *John*, who, being little better than an idiot, (as 'tis said) took to wife in his father's life-time, *Anne*, daughter and sole heir of *Edward Cresacre* of *Baronburgh* in *Yorkshire*, by whom he had issue (1.) *Thomas*, (right heir of his father and grandfather) who had thirteen children, of which five were sons. The four elder lived in voluntary contempt and loathed the world before the world fawned on them. The first was *Thomas*, born anew and baptized on that day of the year (6 *July*) on which Sir *Thomas* suffered death, &c.*
The second son of this said *John More* (son of Sir *Thomas*) was *Augustine*, who died unmarried.

* The account of this Thomas has been given in the Preface.

The third was *Thomas the second,* or *Thomas junior,* born at *Chelsey,* 8 Aug. 23 *Hen.* 8, who, when he came to man's estate *degenerated from the Catholic religion and lived and died a professed minister,* leaving issue several children, of whom the eldest *Cresacre More* (who was born at *Baronburgh* in *Yorkshire,* 3 July, 1572,) *lived afterwards in no commendable fashion.* The fourth son *Edward, born after Sir Thomas his death and having not his blessing as Thomas* (the first,) *and Augustine had, degenerated from the Catholic religion.* The fifth was *Bartholomew* who died young of the plague in *London.*

No. VII.

EXTRACT FROM " RICHARDI PACEI, INVICTISSIMI REGIS ANGLIÆ PRIMARII SECRETARII, EJUSQUE APUD ELVETIOS ORATORIS, DE FRUCTU QUI EX DOCTRINA PERCIPITUR, LIBER. IN INCLYTA BASILEA." 4to. 1517.

[This remarkable passage, which occurs at p. 82, appears to have been overlooked by the writers on the Life of More.]

DE MORO.

" Sed hoc in loco, ut omni respondeatur objectioni, illud vos monebo, neminem unquam extitisse, qui non ex verbis collegerit omnes sententias, excepto uno Thoma Moro nostro Nam is e contrario, ex sententiis colligit verba et præcipue in Græcis intelligendis et transferendis. Ceterum hoc non est a grammatica usquequaque alienum, sed paulo plus quam grammaticum, id est, ingeniosum. Est enim Moro ingenium plusquam humanum. Doctrina vero non excellens modo, sed et varia, adeo ut quocunque te vertas, nihil nescire videatur. Quantum autem Græce sciat, testis sit Incredulus, quem Paulus Bombasius valde laudat.

Porro facundia non incomparabilis tantum, sed et duplex, cum in sua, tum in aliena lingua, id est, Latina. Jam adeo non vulgariter facetus est, et urbanus, ut leporem ipsum ei patrem, et facetiam matrem fuisse judices. Et interdum, hoc est, quando res postulat, bonos imitatur cocos, et omnia acri perfundit aceto. Habet et nasum, quum vult, etiam inter nasutissimos, quem tam artificiose etiam detrahit, ut eo detracto, nullum faciei desit lineamentum. In philosophia nulla secta est, quam non aliqua ex parte probat, et ut quæque maxime excellit, ita eam maxime admiratur. Sed uni præcipue (quod faciunt fere omnes) se addixit, id est, Democriticæ. De illo autem Democrito loquor, qui omnes res humanas risit, quem non modo diligentissime est imitatus, verum etiam una syllaba superavit. Nam ut ille humana omnia ridenda censuit, ita hic deridenda. Unde Richardus Paceus, Morum amicissimum suum, Democriti filium, vel successorem, per jocum appellare solet. Is denique magnum bellum istis indixit, qui nec vera, nec verisimilia, atque a personis suis alienissima loquuntur. Quale contigit, quum audiret duos Theologos Scotistas. ex his qui graviores habentur, et pulpita conterunt, (quique in te, O Colete, satis non indocte modo, sed etiam impie insurrexerunt, quum diceres salutarem pacem, pernicioso bello longe esse præferendam.) Quum audiret, inquam, serio affirmantes inter se, Arcturum regem (quem aliqui natum negant, aliqui nunquam obiisse, sed nescio quo disparuisse contendunt) togam sibi ex gigantum barbis, quos in prælio occiderat, confecisse. Et quum Morus interrogasset illos, qua ratione hoc posset fieri, tum senior, composito in gravitate vultu, Ratio, inquit, O puer, est aperta, et causa evidens, quod scilicet cutis hominis mortui mirifice extenditur. Alter hanc rationem auditam, non solum approbavit, sed etiam ut subtilem et Scoticam, admiratus est. Tum Morus adhuc puer, Hoc, inquit, semper antea æque mihi incognitum fuit, atque illud est notissimum, alterum ex vobis hircum mulgere, alterum cribrum subjicere. Quod dictum quum perciperet illos non intellexisse, ridens sibi, et eos deridens, abivit. Hoc unum (quod dolenter refero) Morum meum persequitur infortunium, quod quoties peritissime et acutissime loquitur inter vestros leucomitratos patres, in sua ipsorum, quam ipse quoque callet scientia, toties illi eum damnant, et puerilia omnia quæ dicit, nominant, non quod revera eum damnandum censeant, aut aliquid puerile audiant, sed quod mirabile ingenium ei invideant, et alias, quarum ipsi ignari sunt, scientias, quod denique puer (ut ipsi vocant) sapientia senibus longe antecellit. Sed hæc hactenus de Moro, ad rem meam jam revertar.

No. VIII.

LETTER OF LADY MORE TO SECRETARY CROMWELL, 1534-5.

[From " A Collection of Letters," by L. Howard, D.D. 4to. 1753.]

RIGHT honorable, and my especyall gud Maister Secretarye: In my most humble wyse I recommend me unto your gud mastershypp, knowlegyng myself to be most deply boundyn to your gud maistershypp, for your monyfold gudnesse, and lovyng favor, both before the tyme, and yet dayly, now also shewyd towards my poure husband and me. I pray Almyghtye God continew your gudness so styll, for thereupon hangith the greatest part of my poure husbands comfort and myne.

The cause of my wrytyng at this tyme, is to certyfye your especiall gud maistershypp of my great and extreme necessytè, which ov' and besydes the charge of myn owne house, doe pay weekly 15 shillings for the bord-wages of my poure husband and his servant; for the mayntaining whereof, I have been compellyd, of verey necessytè, to sell part of myn apparell, for lack of other substance to make money of. Wherefore my most humble petition and sewte to your maistershipp, at this tyme, is to desyre your maistershypp's favorable advyse and counsell, whether I may be so bold to attende uppon the King's most gracyouse Highnes. I trust theyr is no dowte in the cause of my impediment; for the yonge man, being a ploughman, had ben dyseased with the aggue by the space of 3 years before that he departed. And besides this, it is now fyve weeks syth he departed, and no other person dyseased in the house sith that tyme; wherefore I most humblye beseche your especyal gud maistershypp (as my only trust is, and ells knowe not what to doe, but utterly in this world to be undone) for the love of God to consyder the premisses; and thereuppon, of your most subundant gudnes, to shewe your most favorable helpe to the comfortyng of my poure husband and me, in this our great hevynes, extreme age, and necessytè. And thus we, and all ours, shall dayly, duryng our lyves, pray to God for the prosperous successe of your ryght honorable dygnytè.

By your poure contynuall oratryx,

DAME ALIS MORE.

To the Ryght honorable, and her especyall gud maister, Maister Secretarye.

No. IX.

CHRONOLOGICAL ABSTRACT OF THE LIFE OF SIR THOMAS MORE.

1480 Birth at his father's house in Milk-street.

1487-1494 At school at St. Anthony's and living in the family of Cardinal Morton.

1495-1497 These probably the two years spent at Oxford.

1498 Probable date of his admission at New Inn.

1499 Probable date of his removal to Lincoln's Inn.

1500 October. Death of Cardinal Morton.

1502 In parliament. He opposes a grant of money to the king.

1505 Having lived some years among the Carthusians, he marries Elizabeth Colt, his first wife, and practises the law.

1509 April 22. Death of Henry VII., and accession of Henry VIII.

1510 Birth of his only son, and youngest child, John More.

1511 About this time appointed to an office in the city of London.

1512 Reader at Lincoln's Inn.

1514 Probable year of his second marriage.

1515 Reader a second time at Lincoln's Inn.
1516 Diplomatic mission to Flanders, with Tunstall.—In this year he is supposed to have written his Utopia, of which there were two impressions before 1518.
1517 Retained in the great prize question.—Made Master of the Requests, a Privy Counsellor, and knighted.—Luther published against the Indulgence.
1518 Treasurer of the Exchequer.
1523 April 5. Chosen Speaker of the House of Commons.—Publishes against Luther, under the name of Ross.
1525 Concludes a treaty with the Commissioners of the Regent of France.—Made Chancellor of the Dutchy of Lancaster.
1527 Again Embassador in Flanders and France.
1529 Embassador with Tunstall at Cambray.—In Michaelmas Term made Lord High Chancellor, on the disgrace of Wolsey.—Marriage of his son with Anne Cresacre.
1530 November. Death of Cardinal Wolsey.—Death of Sir John More.
1532 May 16. Surrenders up his office of Chancellor.

1534 April. In this month Anne Bullen proclaimed queen, Elizabeth Barton executed, and Sir Thomas More committed to the Tower.

1535 May 7. Arraigned.

July 1, Thursday. Tried, convicted, and sentenced.

July 6, Tuesday. Executed on Tower-Hill.

FINIS.

Thomas White, Printer,
Crane Court.